T0262978

—— Byzantine Coins ——
Influenced by the Shroud of Christ

Jenny Stanford Series on Christian Relics and Phenomena

Series Editor
Giulio Fanti

Titles in the Series

Jenny Stanford Series on Christian Relics and Phenomena — Volume 3

Byzantine Coins
Influenced by the Shroud of Christ

Giulio Fanti

JENNY STANFORD
PUBLISHING

Published by

Jenny Stanford Publishing Pte. Ltd.
Level 34, Centennial Tower
3 Temasek Avenue
Singapore 039190

Email: editorial@jennystanford.com
Web: www.jennystanford.com

British Library Cataloguing-in-Publication Data
A catalogue record for this book is available from the British Library.

Byzantine Coins Influenced by the Shroud of Christ

Copyright © 2022 Jenny Stanford Publishing Pte. Ltd.

All rights reserved. This book, or parts thereof, may not be reproduced in any form or by any means, electronic or mechanical, including photocopying, recording or any information storage and retrieval system now known or to be invented, without written permission from the publisher.

ISBN 978-981-4877-88-6 (Hardcover)
ISBN 978-1-003-21992-7 (eBook)

We are often happy for a discovery made,
without realizing that often
the Holy Spirit blows in us.

Contents

Foreword

We all know that there are three characteristics that distinguish man from all other animal creatures, at least mammals, present on the planet: the upright position, language and clothing. The human sciences have always investigated them, both those interested in the biological order regarding the first characteristic, and the intellectual ones that explore the notes of freedom and intelligence linked to the expressions of language, to the real culture, to which it is undoubtedly to ascribe also the third prerogative: man is an animal that dresses himself. Over the centuries, fashions and customs illustrate the variety and the material and spiritual richness of human clothing studied in the sphere of its most peculiar aspect, the aesthetic and ideological significance of each piece of clothing.

Wanting to know and understand the origin and importance of this anthropological aspect starting from Divine Revelation, we discover that dressing is not a pure physical necessity for man linked to meteorological variations of time and space, but rather it is a consequence of the original fault, *"and the eyes of them both were opened and they knew that they were naked; and they sewed fig leaves together, and made themselves loincloths"* (Gn 3,7). Why then *"the Lord God make for Adam and for his wife tunics of skins"* (χιτώνας δερμάτινους, leather tunic), *"and clothed them"* (v.21) before driving them out of the garden of Eden? This divine intervention means that the rebels had passed into the service of the only animal that sheds "the skin." Now men are covered with this "skin" because they have become subjects no longer of the Lord God, but servants of the ancient Serpent.

Well, towards the end of the Holy Scriptures, we find another significant mention of the term tunic, *"when they crucified Jesus they took his clothes"* (ἱμάτια, himatia plural of himation) *"and the tunic ... but the tunic was seamless,"* (χιτών αραφος ... chiton arafos) (Jn 19:23). It is the famous uncut tunic, the symbol of the one, holy, Catholic Church. The cultural value, the meaning attributed to the garment allows for further theological observation. It allows us to establish a link between original sin and its reparation which took place with the death on the cross of Jesus, the Man-God, the Son of God, who takes away from man the sign of the slavery of Satan, the *tunic of skin*, and gives him the gift of his own *tunic*, that of the Holy Spirit, the tunic of supernatural Grace.

What then will the tunic of Jesus the Risen be? Once again the apostle John, witness of the tunic cast by lot under the cross, helps us when he reveals his experience on the *"island of Patmos ... on the day of the Lord,"* that is on the day in which the Resurrection is celebrated, on Sunday, when he heard: *"That you see, write it in a book and send it to the seven Churches ..."* (Rev 1,11). And what did he see? *"... one similar to t(he) Son of (the) man dressed in a tunic (χιτώνα, chitona) long to the feet (ποδήρη, foot) and girded on the chest with a belt (ζώνην) of gold"* (v.13). The Risen appeared dressed in the typical priestly robe prescribed by Jhwh (Jahvè) to Moses: *"you will put on Aaron the tunic (χιτώνα ποδήρη, tunic to the foot) ..., of the ephod ..."* (Ex 29.5).

The liturgical meaning of this *linen tunic* allows for further study if we read its use in the vision of the prophet Ezekiel on the destruction of Jerusalem, the city profaned by the idolatry of priests in the Temple, in the House of Jhwh (Jahvè). The man *dressed in linen-ποδήρη,* (to the foot) is given the order to mark with a Tau the faithful, preserved from the slaughter of all the inhabitants, starting from the sanctuary (Ez 9,2.3.11) and to pour out hot coals over the city destined for destruction (10,2.6.7). In the Hebrew text the term used to define the garment of the mysterious messenger, the exterminator, is always the same, it allows to identify the man *dressed in linen* with the archangel Gabriel as he appears dressed in the terrifying vision of Daniel (10–12) in which the two major Greek versions propose the following. The first is a slavish literal translation of the Hebrew word *βαδδίν (baddin, dress of linen)*, and the second is the Greek equivalent of *βύσσινα (byssus)* (see 10.5; 12.6.7). But there is also something more in the Greek version; in Ez 9,2.3.11 the *man* who saves with the Tau and who is a figure of Christ wears a tunic-*ποδήρη* (to the foot) while the destroyer of the rebellious Jerusalem, who is still the same person, wears a *στολή (stole)* as a *holy garment*. It follows that for the Greek translator the two different terms used for the same holy garment are synonymous, that is πoδήρη=στoλή *(foot=stole)*, and this datum is very important to understand the logic of the final suggestion which will be discussed later.

With these Greek terms, the reader will become familiar by scrolling through the pages of this new book by the illustrious Shroud expert, Prof. Giulio Fanti, a tireless researcher in a field of scientific analysis in which he has already set a milestone. He established with irrefutable and definitive exactness the age of the most dear and precious Relic of Christianity: first century after Christ. The eminent scholar questioned the radioactive carbon dating following a methodological technique, showing for various reasons that this method was unsuitable for the investigation because the Holy Shroud was subjected to multiple historical vicissitudes and manipulations. In his first numismatic research on the representations of the face of Christ, the author had already indicated and subsequently increasingly ascertained the hypothesis that now becomes the fascinating thesis of this book: Only the empirical knowledge of the image of the Sacred Linen would have allowed the various artists a coinage strictly linked to fixed parameters. The face that Jesus crucified left imprinted on the Shroud, as the author demonstrates, precedes in logic and science any subsequent numismatic representation.

The establishment of this relationship in an unambiguous and incontrovertible way allowed the man of science and faith to proceed in the research whose results are illustrated in this book with all the rigor and seriousness that is recognized to him. The absolute novelty, never before discovered and that the author reveals and illustrates copiously, is the frequent attestation in the clothing of the Risen One of some unmistakable traits to be considered by logic of things as a representation of the Shroud, worn over the garments, like one carries a trophy, the trophy of the Risen One which attests the victory of the Man-God over death.

This scientific fact is even more fascinating than the previous study on the face. Faith in the Resurrection broadens the author's rational basis even further. Science had already gone beyond the limiting and inaccurate theological criterion of the empty tomb, investigating the Relic seen and witnessed by the apostles Peter and John as present in the empty tomb. The mystery of this Relic still challenges human reason committed to solving at least some of the innumerable enigmas contained in the Divine Imprint. Evoking the historical foundation of his faith, the astonishing passage of the sea of rushes which marked the end of the slavery of Egypt and the entry into the world of freedom, the psalmist sang: *"Your way was in the sea, Your path in the great waters, And Your footsteps remained invisible/were not known."* (Psalm 77.20). What was said about the *Mirabilia Dei* in the ancient exodus, invisible footprints, is far exceeded and extraordinarily changed in the new exodus. There is reported that Jesus, the Son of God, who died on the cross for us, left an indelible mark on His funeral Sheet, a mysterious but clearly visible and recognizable imprint in which science still finds traces of that precious Blood in which *"they have washed their robes (στολάς, stoles).... those who come from the great tribulation."* (Rev 7,14).

The scientist's audacity, spurred on by faith, is revealed in the amazing results that emerged from the rigorous investigation of an intellect made expert by the great love of truth. In the book that the reader is holding, the famous expert on the Holy Shroud offers a painstaking analysis of the countless numismatic images that he shows dependent on the visible imprint of Christ as witnessed in the Sacred Linen. How else to explain the mensural cross that the Byzantine emperors had minted on their coins starting at least from the beginning of the fifth century AD, a cross that shows the exact physical dimensions of Jesus Christ? Can an image so eloquent in its rational logic be attributed to chance? Moreover, the author asks his skeptical contemporary reader flattened in an agnosticism considered to be the fruit of scientific seriousness, what about the image of the risen Christ *arising from the empty tomb*? Could a strange confusion be admissible between the depiction of the empty tomb and the image of a *stool*, which is found under the feet of a Judge Christ, *seated* on the throne of His glory? Reason clarifies and illuminates the error that faith unmasks in the nebulosity of its inconsistent logic.

What fascinates even more in this extraordinary research by Prof. Giulio Fanti is the discovery of the detail of the robe exhibited by the risen Christ in the attitude of the blessing. What is, the author asks consciously and asks whoever listens to his question, the value of a garment that replaces and gives visible blessing, prolonged over the centuries, to a humanity that forgets the Mercy of its Redeemer, an effective blessing for who venerates and adores the visible imprint of God made Man in the image of the precious Relic? The acute observation does not deceive.

The Holy Shroud, he argues with strength and rigor of logic, wraps the body of Christ both in the form of the *himation-pallium* and in that of the simplified *loros*. They are both signs of the victory trophy of the High and Eternal Priest, who appeared to John on the day of his triumph over death, wrapped in the priestly linen tunic (*ποδήρη, to the foot*). It is the linen, which the artist minted on the coin in its original form, known and seen by him and still visible to the reader, that is the Linen of the Holy Shroud.

Deep gratitude is due to the author for his precious final suggestion on the value and meaning of the characteristic and typical liturgical clothing of the Christian priest, the stole: The logical meaning that he attributes to this garment is a visible sign of the mystery celebrated in the liturgy, the death and Resurrection of Christ. Isn't the stole the Holy Shroud, the linen robe that wrapped the body of the crucified Man and on which the imprint of the extraordinary supernatural event of the Resurrection remained?

What science seeks with great love for the truth and what it finds and suggests is a source of great joy and deep gratitude for every man of good will and especially for every Catholic Christian. To the linen of the Shroud is approached that of the corporal, the linen on which the Bread of eternal life is placed in every Holy Mass, the true Food, the Flesh of Jesus who died and rose. The flesh that He drew from the Virgin Mary to redeem all human flesh, that same Flesh which left His visible imprint on the Shroud.

May this book offer all its readers that spiritual, cultural and faith richness of which its author makes them partakers with a further gift in which so many treasures of humanity and grace are contained. To him, my esteem, my gratitude and by virtue of the priesthood my personal blessing.

Don Lieto Massignani

Professor of Sacred Scripture and Doctor of Medicine and Surgery
Retired from Facoltà Teologica dell'Italia Settentrionale-Padova, Italy

Background to This Study

In Turin, Italy, there is a linen burial cloth that according to ancient tradition is the cloth that wrapped Jesus Christ in the sepulcher. Its size is about 4.4 m by 1.1 m (14 ft 5 in by 3 ft 7 in). The Relic is unique in that it contains full-size front and back images of a man who was crucified exactly like Jesus was crucified, as recorded in the Gospels of the New Testament. The cause of the image is not explained. Scientific examination of the image during the Shroud of Turin Research Project (STuRP) in 1978 indicated that the image is not due to pigment, any liquid, a scorch from a hot object, or common photography. Subsequent studies have confirmed these conclusions. To solve its many mysteries, including the image, the date, and the blood on the Shroud, more scientific research has been conducted on the Shroud than on any other ancient artifact.

It might seem incredible that the burial cloth of Jesus could still be in existence, but what are the options? When Peter and John found Jesus' burial cloths in the tomb [John 20:3-9], they probably would not have left them to be taken by the Romans or religious leaders. The collapsed body cloth was probably the key evidence that brought John to believe in Jesus' Resurrection [John 20:8-9]. The earliest believers emphasized the importance of Jesus' blood in their salvation, and thus His burial Shroud containing His blood would have been protected from moisture, insects, and intentional destruction. Under these conditions, linen would only decay due to dehydration and oxidation, which are very slow processes. This explains why museums contain many examples of linen that are more than 5000 years old.

Clues suggest the Shroud was well known and revered in Constantinople at least from 944 AD up to 1204 AD. It is likely that it was previously in Edessa, Turkey, and prior to that in Jerusalem. These clues include the following:

- The report (1203–1204) of French crusader Robert de Clary that Jesus' burial cloth was exhibited weekly at the Church of St. Mary in the Blachernae district of Constantinople.

- The Hungarian Pray Codex or Manuscript, dated on historical grounds to 1192–1195, contains peculiar details of images of Jesus Christ similar in many respects to those on the Shroud.
- Byzantine coins back to about 692 AD contain images of Christ very similar to the image on the Shroud.
- Christian art back to the sixth century contains images similar to the image on the Shroud.
- Paul may have used the Shroud for evangelism and apologetics in Galatia (Gal. 3:1).

The third clue mentioned above, the image of Jesus on Byzantine coins and its resemblance to the Shroud image, is the main subject of this book. Giulio Fanti should be commended for his detailed research in this area which argues that surely the coins were copied from the Shroud image and not vice-versa.

It is hoped that the evidence in this book will aid in the realization that the Shroud of Turin was highly respected for several centuries during the Byzantine empire prior to 1204. During this period, the emperor's image on many coins was removed, or moved to the back of the coins, and replaced by the image of Jesus Christ. Our current culture needs to take this to heart, to learn the same lesson, that Jesus Christ should be exulted in our estimation and respect.

Giulio Fanti's work helps to expand the Shroud's history which aids in validating its authenticity as the true burial cloth of Christ. The image on the Shroud is not only a visual display of the Gospel (Jesus' death, burial, and Resurrection) but also, as concluded by Russ Breault [www.shroudencounter.com], it is God's receipt for the finished transaction that offers us a right relationship to Him.

Robert A. Rucker

Retired from Pacific Northwest National Laboratory, USA
Independent researcher with the Shroud Research Network, USA
www.shroudresearch.net

Acknowledgements

The author thanks **Jesus Christ** for having brought him closer to the Holy Shroud and for having given him the opportunity to study the Relic so closely that it can be understood as a *"direct way of communication"* between man and God; he also thanks the **Holy Spirit** for having enlightened him during his research.

The author thanks Dr. Giuseppe **Baldacchini** of ENEA of Frascati, Italy, for his gift, the interesting book on the *Mensural Cross* of Frascati that inspired the numismatic research on the theme.

Thanks to Dr. Anna **Gannon,** historian of St Edmund's College, Cambridge, Great Britain, and expert in numismatics of the Anglo-Saxon *sceattas* for her precious comments.

The author is very grateful to Dr. Don Lieto **Massignani**, professor of Sacred Scripture and physician, for the continuing moral support and biblical advice.

The author is grateful to Professor Veronica **Piraccini** for her artistic advice and for having followed his directions in having her students paint the images of interest for this research.

Thanks to Father Filippo, born Tommaso **Resta**, Benedictine monk and Prior of the Abbey of Santa Giustina in Padua, Italy, for the important information furnished about the origin of the stole.

Thanks to Engineer Robert A. **Rucker** of www.shroudresearch. net/, who deeply revised the English language of this book.

Initial Note

To make easier the reading of a book suitable for everyone, some simplifications are adopted here; therefore, some notes useful for the reader follow:

- As almost all the many dates reported in the various chapters refer to the period after the birth of Jesus Christ, the letters AD (Anno Domini) are implied.
- To make the discussion clearer to the reader, the book contains some repetitions of important concepts with the relative references to the sections in which the topic is dealt.
- Like many texts of numismatics, the ordinal numbers are frequently indicated by using the Roman numbers; the following table shows the correspondence between Roman and Arabic numbers.
- Figure numbers refer to the chapter; for example, Fig. 33 of Chapter 3 will be Fig. 3.33. References are reported in square brackets in the text.
- The use of plots and tables summarizes and clarifies some data resulting from the analysis; equations, when necessary, are reported in the Appendix. Clarifications are reported in footnotes.
- To show the size of the coins, bars corresponding to millimeters are shown on the left and at the bottom of some figures.

Correspondence between Roman and Arabic numbers

Roman	Arabic	Roman	Arabic	Roman	Arabic	Roman	Arabic
I	1	XI	11	XXX	30	CL	150
II	2	XII	12	XL	40	CLIX	159
III	3	XIII	13	XLIX	49	CXC	190
IV	4	XIV	14	L	50	CC	200
V	5	XV	15	LX	60	CCC	300
VI	6	XVI	16	LXX	70	CD	400
VII	7	XVII	17	LXXX	80	D	500
VIII	8	XVIII	18	XC	90	DC	600
IX	9	XIX	19	XCIX	99	CM	900
X	10	XX	20	C	100	M	1000

Introduction

The title of this book *Byzantine Coins influenced by the Shroud of Christ* can seem quite strange. Why should a book be written about the face of Christ depicted on Byzantine coins? Moreover, why should this book analyze the influence of the Shroud on Byzantine coins? These are important questions because many people are convinced that the Shroud of Turin, also known as the Shroud of Christ, the Holy Shroud or simply the Shroud, is a medieval artifact of the 1300s and is therefore subsequent to the Byzantine Empire that flourished until to 1204, the year of the fall of its capital, Constantinople.

In answer to the first question, for the past twenty years, the author has been intrigued by the fact that in ancient times, there were several coins that depicted the face of Christ. Nevertheless, when he tried to deepen his understanding, he found various difficulties. He could not find a book that dealt in detail with this topic and one of the few numismatic articles [Moroni, 1986] dealt with the topic relatively briefly by presenting only some of the coins minted by different countries in the world up to the dawn of the second millennium.

Most of the coins depicting the effigy of Jesus Christ were minted by the Byzantine Empire, but the various numismatic books [Sear et al., 1987; Grierson, 1973, 1982, 1999; Grierson and Mays 1992; Grierson and Hendy, 1993–99] generally present the different coins minted under the various emperors without extensive discussion of the details of the face of Christ, except perhaps Breckenridge [1959], who, however, deals only with the coins of Justinian II.

Byzantine Coins Influenced by the Shroud of Christ
Giulio Fanti
Copyright © 2022 Jenny Stanford Publishing Pte. Ltd.
ISBN 978-981-4877-88-6 (Hardcover), 978-1-003-21992-7 (eBook)
www.jennystanford.com

It is also curious to note that among the Byzantine coins, as well as coins from other locations, those depicting the face of Christ take on a much higher numismatic value than those without Christ's face. This indicates the great interest from collectors for this type of coin, which however does not seem to find an appropriate consideration in the books published on the subject. Therefore, the author, noting this shortcoming, has sought to reduce, even if only minimally, the existing gaps.

The second question concerns the influence of the Shroud on Byzantine and other coins. The author recognized the importance of this topic when he discussed it with numismatic experts from the United Kingdom. These experts claimed that the image of the face on the Byzantine coins of the first millennium is remarkably similar to the face on the Shroud probably because the fourteenth-century artist who produced the Shroud had copied it from the image on the coins!

This is absurd because of what we now know about the image. Chapter 2 will better explain why, but, for example, experimental tests showed that the image: (1) is not due to pigment so could not have been made by paint, dye, or stain, (2) does not fluoresce under ultraviolet light so could not be a scorch from a hot object, and (3) contains 3D information so could not be a common photograph. In addition, attempts by scientists and artists over many decades have been unable to reproduce all together the very peculiar characteristics of the Shroud's body image [Jumper et al., 1984; Fanti, 2011, 2018].

This indicates there is no known method for an artist or forger to have made the image on the Shroud, so that the image could not have been copied from the effigy on a coin. This is a very important fact because it indicates that the effigies of Jesus Christ on the coins must have been copied from the Shroud rather than the reverse. The author affirms this not only from a subjective point of view, but he proves it in a later chapter by means of experimental tests performed with the help of an expert in the field.

This book, which should be understandable to everyone, focuses on the face of Christ on coins especially during the Byzantine period. This is because a careful analysis shows the coins minted from the seventh century onwards are not only a clear proof of the existence of the Shroud in the Byzantine period but also they add new interesting information on the topic.

To allow many Shroud scholars not experts on the subject, to understand the numismatic theme addressed in the book, at the beginning of the book the author synthetically mentions the Byzantine numismatic history. At the same time, the author makes a mention of historical-scientific analysis on the Shroud, not known to all, to allow numismatists and art historians to better perceive the close correlations detected between the Byzantine coinage and the most important Relic of Christianity.

Dr. Anna Gannon, Emeritus Fellow of St Edmund's College, Cambridge (Great Britain), an early medieval art historian commented on this book saying, "*Yours is a more than ambitious project and in my opinion you would need specialist collaborators for the areas you touch.*" The author answers that this "*more than ambitious project*" is only the initial part of a study that will require various insights and comparisons with various experts in the various areas touched upon such as numismatics, history of art and Christian religion, Byzantine history, theology, scientific studies of the Shroud, painting, image processing, dimensional analysis, statistics and probability calculation.

In agreement with A. Gannon, while the work "*as an engineer on the reconstructed images and models*" is "*convincing and very interesting,*" the numismatic and art history analyses will have to be completed and reviewed by experts in the sector. In fact, "*There are innovative declarations that will have to be investigated and verified also by numismatic and art history experts.*" To this note, the author underlines that his book absolutely does not claim to be a text on the history of art or numismatics, but aims to be a book, the first of its kind, which lays the foundations for an attempt at joining numismatics, history of art and study of the Shroud.

After a brief presentation of the Byzantine coinage of Chapter 1, which provides an overview of the sequence in which the topics are treated in the book, the scientific aspects of the Shroud are discussed in Chapter 2. This provides evidence for the Resurrection of Jesus Christ.

In Chapter 3 concerning the images of Christ in the Byzantine era, after a brief description of the clothes used at the time, the different images of Christ are presented on the coins with His dresses. The next Chapter 4 lists a series of details of Christ's face that have a close correlation with the face of the Shroud. For completeness, Chapter 5 presents other early medieval coins minted outside the Byzantine Empire.

Chapters 6 and 7, respectively, include a probabilistic calculation applied to a coin depicting the face of Christ and a quantitative analysis based on image processing which shows that these faces were copied from the Shroud. In order not to burden the discussion, the rigorous mathematical formulation is reported in appendix.

Finally, with the help of an expert, an aesthetic analysis of the faces depicted on the coins is made in Chapter 8 and, based on experiments, it is shown that the Shroud was the reference model for Christ's image on the coins.

In conclusion, this book presents a new argument that demonstrates the strong influence that had the Shroud in the Byzantine period from 692 AD up to the fall of Constantinople in 1204. It is therefore clearly evidenced that a hypothetical medieval artist did not copy the Shroud from the images of Christ on Byzantine coins. The Shroud must have already existed in 692, when the emperor Justinian II coined the first face of Christ, in agreement with the fact that the Shroud is Jesus' burial sheet showing His image formed during the Resurrection.

Chapter 1

Byzantine Coinage

While the history of Byzantine coins lasted about one millennium, this book focuses on the period from 692 to 1204 with some mention up to 1254 AD and later as it relates to the Shroud. The entire millennium will first be summarized to frame the numismatic period of interest in a more general context. The detailed development will begin with the monetization of the first appearance of the face of Christ in 692 AD during the reign of Justinian II.

Our main interest for the Byzantine coins will end with the sack of Constantinople in 1204 AD when the Shroud disappeared for more than a century before being seen again in Europe at Lirey in France. However, coins minted in the Empire of Nicea under John III Ducas-Vatatzes up to 1254 AD and during the Venetian Republic will also be discussed because some of these coins were greatly influenced by the Shroud.

1.1 Byzantine Coinage Overview

The official period of the Byzantine Empire starts in 395 AD and ends in 1453 AD, it is, however, not easy to define a fixed date for

Byzantine Coins Influenced by the Shroud of Christ
Giulio Fanti
Copyright © 2022 Jenny Stanford Publishing Pte. Ltd.
ISBN 978-981-4877-88-6 (Hardcover), 978-1-003-21992-7 (eBook)
www.jennystanford.com

the beginning of the Byzantine coinage [Grierson, 1982], because there was a gradual development out of a Roman predecessor. Grierson & Mays [1992] describes the coins of the transition period from the Roman Empire starting with Arcadius (395–408 AD), while both Bellinger [1966] and Sear [1987] start the Byzantine coinage with emperor Anastasius (491–518 AD).

Following the death of Theodosius I in 395, the Roman Empire was divided between his two sons, Arcadius and Honorius, and in the fifth century the eastern provinces were ruled by Arcadius.

An important and lasting monetary reform that remained unchanged for centuries during the Byzantine Empire was that of 309–310 introduced by the Roman emperor Constantine the Great. This was necessary due to the scarcity of gold coins.

Many scholars identify the beginning of Byzantine coinage with the monetary reform of Anastasius (491–518) in 498. It seems appropriate to divide Byzantine coinage into the five periods in Tables 1.1a and 1.1b [Grierson, 1999], though some expand it into seven periods [Wroth, 1908].

First period. This period begins in 498 with emperor Anastasius I (491–518) and is characterized by the gold *solidus* (or *histamenon nomisma*) with its fractions, *semissis* and *tremissis*, the silver *hexagram* and the copper *follis*, *half-follis*, *decanummium*, *pentanummium* and *nummus*. This wide range of coins made of three different metals was similar to modern coinage. This period was one of relatively flourishing public finances and monetary economy.

Second period. This begins with emperor Justinian I (527–565) who simplified the coinage by using only three kinds of coins, one for each metal: the gold *solidus* (or *histamenon nomisma*), the silver *hexagram* (or the thinner *miliaresion*) and the copper *follis*. During this period, there was a general contraction of monetary public resources. Other kinds of coins like the *tetarteron* were minted later.

Third period. This starts with the monetary reform of 1092 made by emperor Alexius I Comnenus (1081–1118) when he was forced to use several denominations of debased metal because of the economic crisis in the Byzantine Empire. The coins produced in this period were different from the common coins because they were concave instead of flat.

Table 1.1a Simplified Byzantine coinage of the First and Second period [Sear, 1987; Grierson, 1999; Sommer, 2010; Fanti and Furlan, 2019]

Period	Denomination	Metal	Weight [g]	Purity	Exchange ratio
I 498– Approx. 550	*Solidus-Nomisma*	Gold	4.55	≈100%	1
	Semissis	Gold	2.27	≈100%	2
	Tremissis	Gold	1.52	≈100%	3
	Hexagram	Silver	6.7		12
	Follis	Copper			288
	Half-Follis	Copper			576
	Decanummium	Copper			1152
	Pentanummium	Copper			2304
	Nummus	Copper			11520
II Approx. 550–1092	*Solidus or Hista-menon Nomisma*	Gold or Electrum	4.55	11% (*Electrum*) up to ≈100%	1
	Semissis	Gold	2.27	≈100%	2
	Tremissis	Gold	1.52	100%	3
	Tetarteron	Gold	≈4	90%	1
	Hexagram	Silver	6–6.7		12
	Miliaresion	Silver	2.3–3.0		12
	2/3 or 1/3 of Miliaresion	Silver			18 or 36
	Follis	Copper			288
	Fraction of Follis	Copper			

Therefore, the old *solidus* (or *histamenon nomisma*) was replaced with coins called a *hyperpyron*, which contained a lower percentage of gold; coins called a *trachea*[a] were minted with a lower percentage of silver and eventually were made of copper; some coins that previously were copper were made of lead. Many baser gold coins, i.e. those with a reduced gold content, were made of the famous alloy of silver-gold with copper

---

[a]The term trachy from Greek, plural trachea, means rough or uneven, is used to describe the cup-shaped or scyphate coins.

impurities called *electrum*[b]. This period initially saw an expansion in the resources of the empire, despite a phase of serious debasement in the mid-eleventh century. This period ends with the fall of Constantinople in 1204.

Table 1.1b Simplified Byzantine coinage from the Third to the Fifth Period [Sear, 1987; Grierson, 1999; Sommer, 2010; Fanti and Furlan, 2019]

Period	Denomination	Metal	Weight [g]	Purity	Exchange ratio
III 1092–1204	*Hyperpyron-Nomisma*	Gold	4.55	98–60%	1
	Nomisma Trachy	Electrum	4.55	10–30% gold	3–12
	Aspron Trachy	Billon*	4.55	copper–silver	48–384
	Tetarteron	Copper	4		≈864
	Half-Tetarteron	Copper	2		≈1728
IV 1204–1367	*Hyperpyron-Nomisma*	Gold	≈4.5	50–60%	1
	Basilikon	Silver	≈2		12
	Tournesion	Billon			96
	Aspron Trachy	Billon	0.75		384
	Assarion	Copper	3–4		768
V 1367–1453	*Hyperpyron*	Gold	≈4		1
	Stavraton	Silver	7–9		2
	Half-Stavraton	Silver	3–5		4
	Ducat	Silver	1.1		16
	Tournesion	Copper	≈2.4		192
	Follaro	Copper	≈0.8		≈576

*The *billon* is an alloy used for coinage, containing silver (or gold) with a predominating amount of copper or other base metal.

Fourth period. This begins in the thirteenth century after the fall of Constantinople in 1204 and its recovery in 1261, when both the silver *basilikon*, modeled on the silver *ducat* of Venice,

---

[b]The *electrum* is a natural or artificial alloy of gold with at least 10 percent of silver, used as early as the third millennium BC in Lydia and East Greece. The first coins of *electrum* and date back to VII BC, but were very common in the Byzantine Empire especially after the XI century AD. *Electrum* was better for coinage than gold, because harder and more durable.

and a small copper coin named *assarion* are introduced. The *basilikon* reflected the influence of Western powers in this area.

Fifth period. This begins in 1367 and ends with the fall of the Byzantine Empire in 1453. During this period, gold coins disappeared and the *stavraton* with the *half-stavraton*, both of pure silver were used in substitution. The disappearance of gold-derived coins is a sign of the return to debasement caused by weakened finances in the Empire.

1.2   Types of Coins, Metals and Alloys

The Byzantine currency at the beginning consisted of many different coins from the gold *solidus* to the bronze *nummi*. The *nummus* was a very small bronze coin, less than 10 mm in diameter, with a weight of 0.5 g.

1.2.1   Gold Coinage

The gold *solidus* [Vasilita, 2020] (either *nomisma*, from Greek, or *bezant*, from "*Latin bizantius aureus*") was used in the Middle Ages in Western Europe (Fig. 1.1). It had a weight of 4.55 g (0.160 oz), and was equal to 1/72 of a Roman pound.

Fractions of *solidus* were also produced, called *semissis* (half-solidus) and *tremissis* (a third of solidus). The word "soldier" is ultimately derived from solidus, referring to the *solidi* with which soldiers were paid. The *solidus* replaced the aureus as the main gold coin of the Roman Empire and has a diameter of about 20 mm. On the one side, the emperor is depicted with a three quarter or fully frontal bust. The reverse shows the Victory supporting a Mensural Cross (see Section 1.3) that became the seated Victory with the reign of Justin II (565–578) and a cross in steps from Maurice Tiberius II (578–582). Starting from Heraclius (610–642), the *solidus* had the portrait of the emperor and his son. Justinian II (692–695), substituted his portrait on the obverse with the portrait of Jesus Christ and depicted his portrait holding a cross on the reverse. However, a few years later the so-called "iconoclast emperors" removed the face of Christ on these coins up to the return of the same emperor Justinian II in

705–711 (II reign) who replaced the face of Christ on the obverse. Nevertheless, this replacement lasted only for few years because, starting from 712, the emperors substituted again their effigies to that of Christ. In 852 with Michael III, again the Jesus portrait was restored and lasted for centuries, sometimes also seated on a throne or standing on the sepulcher. The face of Christ became the symbol of the *solidus* (or of the *nomisma*, as it was named in Greek).

Figure 1.1 Gold *solidus* of Justinian II reproduces the bust of Christ on the one side with the legend "IHS CRISTOS REX REGNANTIUM" (Latin: Ihesus Cristus Rex Regnantium; and English "Jesus Christ King of the Rulers") and the Emperor Justinian II on the reverse side with the legend: AUGST IUS SERU CHRISTI—CONOB (Latin: "Augustus Justinianus Servus Christi—Constantinople"; and English "Emperor Justinian servant of Christ—Constantinople").

Nichephoros II (963–968), persuaded by financial problems, introduced a new gold coin called the *tetarteron* (or quarter), a 3/4 weight *solidus,* which was smaller and thicker than the full weight gold coin, also named *histamenon*. Nichephoros hoped to force the market to accept the underweight coins at the value of the full weight coins, but this failed.

Emperor Michael IV in 1034, pushed by economic problems, began the process of debasing both the *tetarteron nomisma* and the *histamenon nomisma* that continued for more than a century. In 1071, after the defeat of the empire at Manzikert, the gold percentage in the coins was lowered to about 33% and sometimes even gold plated coins were minted, see Table 1.2.

Table 1.2 Example of alloys in Byzantine coinage representing Jesus Christ [Fanti and Furlan, 2019]

Age [AD]	Emperor	Au [%]	Ag [%]	Cu [%]	Alloy	Coin ref.
692	Giustinian II	100	0	0	Pure gold	1
692–695	Giustinian II	100	0	0	Pure gold	315
976–1025	Basilius II	100	0	0	Pure gold	364
1028–1034	Romanus III	98	2	0	Gold with impurities	124
1028–1034	Romanus III	97	3	0	Gold with impurities	Cfr. 124
1028–1034	Romanus III	94	6	0	Gold with impurities	47
1059–1067	Costantine X	96	4	0	Gold with impurities	17A
1059–1067	Costantine X	89	9	2	Gold with impurities	28
1068–1071	Romanus IV	88	10	2	*Electrum*	49
1068–1071	Romanus IV	88	12	0	*Electrum*	293
1071–1078	Michael VII	95	4	1	Gold with impurities	295
1071–1078	Michael VII	92	7	1	Gold with impurities	199
1071–1078	Michael VII	83	15	2	*Electrum*	51
1071–1078	Michael VII	72	26	2	*Electrum*	50
1071–1078	Michael VII	71	25	4	*Electrum*	17B
1071–1078	Michael VII	67	30	3	*Electrum*	199A
1071–1078	Michael VII	66	30	4	*Electrum*	151
1071–1078	Michael VII	60	30	10	*Electrum*	296
1078–1081	Niceforus III	46	49	5	*Electrum*	134
1181–1118	Alexius I	98	1	1	Gold with impurities	128
1181–1118	Alexius I	95	3	2	Gold with impurities	129
1181–1118	Alexuis I	28	55	17	*Electrum*	56
1122–1143	John II	38	62	0	*Electrum*	58
1143–1180	Manuel I	89	9	2	*Electrum*	222
1143–1180	Manuel I	87	10	3	*Electrum*	28B
1143–1180	Manuel I	85	12	3	*Electrum*	407
1143–1180	Manuel I	38	41	21	*Electrum*	52
1143–1180	Manuel I	87	11	2	*Electrum*	405
1143–1180	Manuel I	35	51	14	*Electrum*	224
1143–1180	Manuel I	33	62	5	*Electrum*	127
1195–1197	Alexius III	94	6	0	Gold with impurities	320
1195–1197	Alexius III	0	92	8	Silver with impurities	332

Note: Au, gold; Ag, silver; Cu, copper.

The debasement came down to 0–33% of gold during the first years of the reign of Alexius I (1081–1118). In 1092, he introduced a new gold coin named *hyperpyron* that was "super refined b fire" with a weight of about 4.55 g, a diameter of about 26 mm, a concave shape, and a gold content greater than 90%, but the gold content was again reduced during the reign of Andronicus II (1282–1328).

The scyphate or cup-shaped coins known as *trachy*[c] were issued in both *electrum* (debased gold) and *billon* (debased silver) tending to get thinner and wider up to becoming thin wafers that could be bent by hand.

The gold *solidus* or *nomisma* remained a standard of international commerce until the eleventh century, when it was debased. This debasement of the *solidus* continued up to John VI (1347–1352).

Very frequently, the mintage of new gold coins was authorized by the emperor himself and the coins with the face of Christ were considered a relic [d].

1.2.2   Silver Coinage

As silver was not a common metal in the Byzantine Empire, we find few coins minted with this metal. Heraclius introduced the *hexagram* (meaning six grams) in 615. It was minted up to the end of that century by Justinian II, though he preferred a currency system only based on gold and copper.

In 720, Leo III introduced a silver coin known as the *miliaresion*, which was thinner and broader than the *hexagram* and the weight was reduced to about 2 g. It was quite rare up to the reign of Theophilus (829–842) when it was fully introduced in the currency system. For example, Fig. 1.2 depicts[e] the Mother of God with Her Son.

In 1091–1092, the *miliaresion* was replaced by a *billon* (meaning *white*) coin, the *aspron trachy*, showing either Christ

---

[c]The reason for the shape of such coins is not known, but many think that they were shaped for easier stacking.

[d]Section 7.3 will describe in the details the various kinds of relics.

[e]The depiction corresponds to the icon of the Mother of God of the Sign.

on a throne or His Mother. It only contained 10% or less silver and was 1/48th part gold probably corresponding to one quarter of the obsolete *miliaresion*.

Figure 1.2 Silver *miliaresion*, depicts the Mother of God of the Sign holding before Her the Infant Christ, minted under Emperor Basil II (976–1025). The three stars that appear on the head and shoulders of the Virgin are an ancient Syriac symbol of virginity. They have two meanings. The first is symbolic of Mary's chastity and Her perpetual virginity before, during and after Childbirth; the second is the symbol of the Holy Trinity.

Under Alexius I (1081–1118) the *billon aspron trachy* initially corresponding to 1/48 the value of a *hyperpyron* up to 1/384 was introduced with a 7% silver plated. The *electrum aspron trachy* was about 75% silver and corresponded to a third of a *hyperpyron*.

With the reign of Andronicus II (1320–1325), a new coin was introduced: the silver *basilikon* or "the coin of the emperor," which was a copy of the Venetian *ducat* or *grosso* with it worth 1/12 of the *hyperpyron*. Unlike the *trachy*, it was small and flat and made of pure silver, but it was dropped soon after 1350 because of the silver shortage. Emperor John V in about 1367 issued the *stavraton* (from the name of the cross in Greek, *stavra*) and the *half-stavraton*, both of pure silver. The disappearance of coins containing gold was a sign of the return to debasement caused by weakened finances in the empire.

1.2.3 Bronze Coinage

Silver coins were rare in ancient Byzantine Empire. However, bronze coinage was very common in their currency system.

In 498, emperor Anastasius introduced some heavier coins, marked with numerals, as multiples of the low-weight *nummus*[f]. The largest coin was the *follis* worth 40 *nummi*, which was marked with the letter M and weighed from 9 to 18 g. Fractions of the *follis* were coins worth 20 *nummi* marked with the letter K, coins worth 10 *nummi* (*decanummium*) marked with an I, and coins worth 5 *nummi* (*pentanummium*) marked with an E.

The reign of Justinian I (528–564) saw the weight of the follis increase to 25 g with it worth 1/288 of the gold *solidus*. In the tenth century, many types of *folles* coins were "anonymous" (Fig. 1.3) because they did not include an image of the emperor. They showed only the image of Christ on one side and frequently the inscription "*XRISTUS/bASILEU/bASILE*" ("Christ, Emperor of Emperors") on the other side. Sear [1987] subdivided these types of *folles* coins into in various classes from A to N.

Figure 1.3 Bronze *follis* of the tenth century is called "anonymous" because it shows the portrait of Christ but not the emperor.

If we don't consider the arrival of the Mandylion-Shroud in Constantinople (see Section 2.4.2), it is strange that, starting from

---

[f]Nummus is a Latin term meaning coin, used technically for a range of low-value copper coins issued by the Roman and Byzantine empires.

the reign of John I (969–976) up to the reign of Alexius I (1081–1118), the bronze coins of the Byzantine Empire suddenly replaced the head of the emperor with the image of Christ.

Alexius I minted additional anonymous bronze coins but in 1091 he introduced a new bronze coin named the *tetarteron*. It was small and flat and probably was one-fourth of one *follis*. These coins depicted the bust or standing figures of the emperors and representations of Christ, the Virgin and saints (Fig. 1.4).

Figure 1.4 Bronze *tetarteron* representing the resurrected Christ from the sepulcher (box on the bottom, see Sections 1.3.14 and 1.3.21) on one side and the emperor John II (1118–1143) on the reverse side.

A half *tetarteron* is also known, sometimes made from lead.

It was during the reign of Andronicus II and Andronicus III (1328–1341) that a new coin named the *assarion* appeared in the Byzantine coinage. The *assarion* was replaced in 1367 by the copper coins named the *tournesion* and *follaro* which lasted until the fall of the empire.

1.3   Jesus Christ in the Byzantine Coinage

The purpose of this book is to discuss the many examples of Christ's image on Byzantine coins, as summarized in Table 1.3. Other periods are briefly mentioned as well to better frame the Byzantine coinage in its historical period.

Table 1.3 Byzantine coins that include the image of Jesus Christ [Sear, 1987; Grierson, 1999; Sommer, 2010; Fanti and Furlan, 2019]

Period	Denomination	Metal	Weight [g]	Purity	Exchange Ratio
Byzantine I period 437–450	Roman Ceremonial solidus	Gold	4.55	≈100%	1
Byzantine II period Justinian II 692–695 and 705–711	Solidus or Histamenon	Gold	4.55	≈100%	1
	Semissis	Gold	2.27	≈100%	2
	Tremissis	Gold	1.52	≈100%	3
	Hexagram	Silver	6–6.7	≈100%	12
Byzantine II period 711–841	Iconoclasm	—	—	—	—
Byzantine II p. 842–1028	Solidus or Histamenon	Gold	4.55	≈100%	1
	Tetarteron Nomisma	Gold	4.05	≈100%	1
	Follis	Copper	4–11	≈100%	≈288
Byzantine II period 1028–1092 Debasement	Histamenon Nomisma	Gold	4.55	Up to 98%	1
	Tetarteron Nomisma	Gold	≈4	Up to 98%	1
	Histamenon or Aspron Trachy Nomisma	Electrum	≈4	10%–30% Au 80%–60% Ag ≈10% Cu	3
	1 or 2/3 Miliaresion	Silver	2.3–3	≈100%	12 or 18
	Follis	Copper	4–11	≈100%	≈288
Byzantine III period 1092–1204 Monetary reform	Solidus or Histamenon	Gold	4.55	60% to 95%	1
	Tetarteron	Gold	≈4	≈100%	1
	Hyperpyron	Electrum	≈3	≈60% Au	≈1
	Histamenon or Aspron Trachy Nomisma	Electrum	≈4	10%–30% Au 80%–60% Ag ≈10% Cu	3 up to 12
	1 or 2/3 Miliaresion	Silver	2.2 –3	≈100%	12 or 18
	Billon Aspron Trachy	Billon	4.55	0% to 6% Ag up ≈100% Cu	48 up to 384
	1 or 1/2 Tetarteron	Copper	1–4	up to 100%	≈864 or ≈1728
Byzantine IV-V period After 1204	Hyperpyron-Nomisma	Gold	≈4.5	50%–60% gold	1
	Hyperpyron	Electrum	≈3	40–60% Au	1
	Basilikon	Silver	≈2	≈100%	12
	1 or 1/2 Stavraton	Silver	≈8 or ≈4	≈95% Ag	2 or 4
	Aspron Trachy	Billon	4.55	up to 100% Cu	48 to 384
	Trachy	Copper	≈0.7	≈100%	384

There are not many in-depth numismatic studies [Breckenridge, 1959; Moroni, 2000; Whanger and Whanger, 1998; Fanti and Malfi, 2020] of Jesus Christ's image on coins that were minted during the Byzantine Empire. The lack of detailed information caused some controversies [Nicoletti, 2011] about some Shroud scholars' assertions [Whanger and Whanger, 1985, 1998, 2007] that observed a remarkable similarity between the face of Christ depicted in the first millennium icons and the face of Christ on the Shroud (see Chapter 2).

Therefore, it is appropriate to explore when and how the numismatic representation of the face of Christ developed throughout history in order to understand how the Shroud face influenced this representation. Christianity became the official religion of the Roman Empire in AD 313. The Western Roman Empire fell in 476, whereas the Eastern Roman Empire, also known as the Byzantine Empire, survived for another 10 centuries with Constantinople as its capital.

In agreement with Mario Moroni [1986], the Byzantine period coins celebrated an event, thus making it official, so they have an irreplaceable value as a historical source. Furthermore, according to the Byzantine liturgical regulation, great care was taken to assure that the image on their coins represented reality as closely as possible. The images had to portray the real features, avoiding any kind of alteration by the engraver from reality. Thus, the details of the numismatic depictions should be considered as historical evidence of events that truly happened and not a result of the artist's fantasies.

Many centuries passed from the death of Jesus Christ until there was an indication of Him on any coin. The Ethiopian Axumite Empire was the first one that minted a coin with a cross remembering Jesus' death, see Fig. 1.5. This was during the reign of Exana (either Aezana or Aizan, 320–360 AD). After his conversion to Christianity, he began to feature the Cross on his coins for the first time in numismatic history.

The first indirect numismatic reference to the Shroud appears around 420 when the Byzantine emperors minted in Constantinople gold *solidi* showing the Victory standing holding a jeweled Mensural Cross[g], see Figs. 1.6 and 1.6a. While experts

---

[g]The term "Mensural Cross" means a cross as tall as Jesus Christ's stature and as wide as His shoulders; it is therefore a cross with a shorter horizontal arm than normal.

simply define these crosses as "high" [Sear, 1987; Grierson and Mays, 1992], their human height and reduced width of the horizontal arm clearly suggest a Mensural Cross.

Figure 1.5 Coin of Axum, Ethiopia (circa 370 AD). This empire was the first in numismatic history to feature the cross on coins.

The depiction of this kind of cross on coins continued for a century and a half up to the emperor Justinian I (527–565) included. However, no other historic references have been found regarding the Mensural Cross, studded with gems, reproduced in the gold *solidi* from about 420.

Later, according to historical sources [Baldacchini and Baldacchini, 2020; Suarez, 2010] the Emperor Justinian I sent trusted men to Jerusalem to take the measurements of Jesus Christ. He then made in Constantinople around 560 a Mensural Cross in gilded silver and studded with precious gems, the so-called "Crux Mensuralis Aurea" (Golden Mensural Cross). Unfortunately, traces of this Mensural Cross were lost after the fall of Constantinople in 1204, but a marble copy, erected in 1627 and restored in 1890, is still on display in the Exarchic Monastery[h] of Grottaferrata, Italy. The Grottaferrata's Cross is 178.4 cm (70.2 in.) tall and 48.7 cm (19.2 in.) wide with a height/width ratio of 3.7. The monks of the monastery report that according to an unwritten tradition, this Mensural Cross shows the dimensions of the body of Jesus Christ as they result from the Shroud.

---

[h]The Monastery was built in 1004 under the Byzantine Empire.

Figure 1.6 From the top, gold *solidus* of Theodosius II (420–423), gold *solidus* of Leo I (462–466) and gold *solidus* of Justinian I (527-565). The obverse shows the bust of the Emperor while the reverse shows the Victory's Angel supporting a *"long cross"* according to Sear [1987] and other experts or better a jeweled Mensural Cross, according to the author. The height/width ratios of the Mensural Crosses are respectively $R = 2.4$; 4.4; 6.8 (mean $R = 4.6$), similar to that of Grottaferrata's Mensural Cross ($R = 3.7$) and very different to that of a typical Byzantine Cross ($R = 1.4$), see Fig. 1.6a.

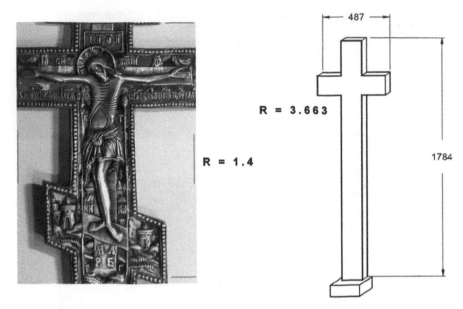

Figure 1.6a On the left typical Byzantine Cross having a height/width ratio $R = 1.4$, very different to $R = 3.7$ of the Grottaferrata's Mensural Cross, on the right.

The height/width ratio of about 3.7 of the Grottaferrata's Mensural Cross is very different from that of about 1.4 of a traditional Byzantine Cross, see Fig. 1.6a.. It is instead more similar to the ratios of 2.5, 4.4 and 6.8 (mean 4.6) of the gold *solidi* shown in Fig. 1.6, thus confirming that the crosses depicted on the three coins really represents a Mensural Cross.

Obviously, starting from the first coins of the early 400s, to build a Mensural Cross it was necessary to have at least the measurement of the height of Jesus Christ, and what was the way to catch this information if not to measure the length of Christ on the Shroud directly from the Relic? The author does not know any alternative method to catch this information and therefore the Mensural Cross reported on the coins seems an interesting confirmation about the presence of the Shroud in that period.

The first images attributed to Christ [Breckenridge, 1959] have been discovered on Roman coins dating back to the first half of the fifth century and are ceremonial gold *solidi*. Two of them are the following: one related to the Licinia Eudoxia and

Valentinian III wedding celebrated on October 29, 437, see Fig. 1.7, and the other commemorating the marriage between Saint Pulcheria and Marcian on July 28, 450. This last solidus is unique and is located at the Hunteriam Museum & Art Gallery of the Glasgow University (Scotland).

Figure 1.7 Golden wedding solidus minted at Thessalonica of Licinia Eudossia & Valentinian III, 437 AD (courtesy of Classical Numismatic Group, Inc. http://www.cngcoins.com).

The reverse side of both coins show the standing figures of the emperor and the empress united by the figure between them identified as Christ. His hand is on their shoulders with the words *"FELICITER NUBTIIS"* (happy marriage) on either side.

These coins show Christ's face with short curly hair and beardless. This was typical of the first pictorial and iconographical images of that age and is very similar to the Savior's representations in the Roman catacombs of the early centuries (see Section 3.3). The absence of elements similar to the image on the Shroud suggests that the image of Christ on the Shroud was not known at that time in the Roman Empire.

The Byzantine Empire was the first in the world that officially minted coins containing the image of Jesus Christ. This was done during its first period (Table 1.3) by emperor Justinian II, though some have suggested that Christ's image was on earlier coins. Professor L. Travaini[i] supposes that the Merovingian Reign minted a face of Christ around 625. According to the author,

---

[i]Prof. Lucia Travaini [2003] of Milan University found a Merovingian coin dated about at 625 showing a face similar to those of Christ minted under the later reign of Justinian II, but engraved in a rougher way.

other Merovingian coins could have represented the face of Christ copied from the Shroud, for example, the silver coins of Fig. 1.8; in fact, the elongated face and the swollen cheeks are typical of the face on the Relic.

Figure 1.8 Merovingian coins from Rouen (Rotomo Civitas of seventh century) showing on the obverse an elongated face vaguely similar to the Shroud image, with swollen cheeks, with the legend "O/N-E/O" on the lower coin. On the reverse, there is a six-petals-flower. The upper coin shows the legend "ERMOBERTO M," while the lower one the legend "+TOD[]ΛOY" and a cross demonstrating a connection with Christian religion.

It seems that around 680–710 also the Visigoths (for example, in Mérida and Mentesa in Spain[j]) minted coins with the face of

---

[j]Gold *tremissis* from Sixbid Coin Collector's Archive (https://www.sixbid-coin-archive.com/#/de), Roma Numismatics, Auctions XIII-2017 and XVII-2019.

Christ, recognizable by a rough cross behind it, but the engraving is so coarse (not even beard and hair are portrayed on the circular face) that it is not easy to recognize a face similar to that of Christ and even less to that of the Shroud, see also Section 9.1.

In 692, canon number 82 of the Council in Trullo (or Quinisextum) decreed that Christ had to be exhibited in images in human form instead of the ancient lamb, as the custom was in that time. Simultaneously, Emperor Justinian II Rinotmetus (685–695) minted the first official coins with the face of Christ in the gold *solidus*, *semissis*, and *tremissis* and the silver *hexagram* [Fanti and Malfi, 2020].

A list of images of Jesus Christ on Byzantine coins follows in order of date.

1.3.1   Justinian II Rhinotmetos—First Period: 692–695

The first official images depicting Jesus Christ [Breckenridge, 1959] on coins are those minted in 692 by Emperor Justinian II (685–695), including the gold *solidus* (Fig. 1.9), *semissis* (Fig. 1.10), and *tremissis* (Fig. 1.11) and the silver *hexagram* (Fig. 1.12) [Bellinger, 1966; Fanti and Malfi, 2020]. This followed canon 82 of the Council in Trullo (or Quinisextum), also in 692, that decreed that Christ had to be exhibited in images in human form instead of as a lamb, as was the custom at that time, see also Section 4.2.1.

Figure 1.9 Gold *solidus* of Justinian II, First Period (692–695), reproducing the bust of the blessing Christ on the obverse side.

Figure 1.10 Gold *semissis* of Justinian II, First Period (692–695), reproducing the bust of the blessing Christ on the obverse side.

Figure 1.11 Gold *tremissis* of Justinian II, First Period (692–695), reproducing the bust of the blessing Christ on the obverse side.

Figure 1.12 Silver *hexagram* of Justinian II, First Period (692–695), reproducing the bust of the blessing Christ on the obverse side.

Breckenridge [1959, pp. 10-11, Fanti and Malfi, 2020] observes that the Acts of the Quinisextum Council were never signed by the pope and he refused to permit their publication within his domain. It is interesting to notice, confirming this historical record, the absence of any coins in this period with the face of Christ minted by the Italian mints that were under papal domain.

The coin of Fig. 1.9 showing the bust of Christ in frontal position with a cross behind His head, can be observed. He has long, wavy hair, a beard, and a mustache, wears a *pallium*[k] over a *colobium*[l], bestowing a blessing with His right hand, and holding the book of the Gospels in His left hand. As we will discuss in Chapter 3, the so-called *pallium* recognized by various experts [Sear, 1987; Bellinger, 1966; Grierson, 1982] could instead, according to the author, be the representation of the Shroud. Written around His head is *"Jesus Christ King of the Rulers"* (see Fig. 1.1). On the reverse side, there is the emperor effigy with the writing *"Emperor Justinian, the servant of Christ."*

There was a remarkable series of coins minted depicting Christ, attributed to several coin laboratories located in the Byzantine Empire [Sear, 1987]. Observing the images of Christ depicted on these coins, we find ourselves in front of a Shroud-like face of Christ. Shroud resemblances of this face will be analyzed in Chapter 4, but it is interesting to note that likely not all the engravers had the chance to directly copy the face of Christ from the Shroud, and this is the reason why there is a considerable variety of interpretations of some details caused by the reproduction of previous copies.

The first engravers who could directly observe the Relic did the most faithful depictions, whereas others just copied the previously minted coins or some then-available images painted from the Shroud, making the human features more similar to a perfect man but decreasing the peculiar features that made the face unique. Like the clear marks of His Passion, such as the swelling on the cheeks caused by blows to the face, the asymmetrical shortage of the right side of the beard, and the asymmetrical hair shape are some examples.

---

[k]A *pallium* is a liturgical vestment consisting of a band of white wool worn on the shoulder. It symbolizes the lost sheep that is found and carried on the Good Shepherd's shoulders. It signifies the bishop's pastoral role as the icon of Christ (see Section 3.1.5).

[l]A *colobium* is a tunic without sleeves or with short, close-fitting sleeves worn by the early monks (see Section 3.1.2).

Regarding the direct observation of the Shroud by the engravers, it is hypothesized that they were sent to Edessa, a friendly city of the Byzantine Empire, to copy the image that was preserved there. The Arabs, who had occupied Edessa since 639, did not prevent the veneration of the Holy Face on a cloth called the Mandylion[m] that was well known throughout the East.

Furthermore, during the period of Emperor Justinian II, Byzantines were allowed to keep control on the Melkite community, which was established by iconophile Christians who collected many relics. Byzantine artists had therefore access to those places, and among those relics, the Shroud could also have been preserved.

In addition to the decisions of the Council in Trullo, according to the scholar Alan Whanger [2000], there were two reasons for Christ's appearance on Justinian II coins.

The first reason is that the empire was threatened by Muslims who had become militarily aggressive, so the emperor needed a powerful symbol that God would protect the Byzantine population, which could be used and recognized everywhere. What symbol could better represent the power of God than the image of Christ minted on the highest-valued coins like the gold *solidus*?

The second reason is that Egypt was the source of paper (papyrus) for the Byzantine Empire and Egypt was controlled by Muslims. The emperor was irritated that Muslims had written a verse from the Koran on each of the papyrus sheets sold to him. Therefore, as a reaction, the emperor decided to pay for those paper sheets with gold coins portraying the image of the face of Christ. This reply was considered by Muslims to be offensive, so they melted the gold coins and used the metal for minting others with verses from the Koran.

1.3.2 Justinian II Rhinotmetos—Second Period: 705–711

Justinian II Rhinotmetos was overthrown following a coup d'etat led by Leontios II (695–698), and his iconoclast collaborators (Monophysites) who took power. During the reign of the usurper

---

[m]According to several historians [Wilson and Schwortz, 2000], as will be explained in Chapter 2, the Shroud is the same piece of cloth as the Mandylion, so will be called the Mandylion-Shroud.

and of his successor Tiberius III (698–705) coin mintages got back into tradition, without the face of Christ.

Figure 1.13 Gold *solidus* of Justinian II, II Period (705–711), reproducing the bust of the blessing Christ on the obverse and the bust of Justinian II on the reverse.

Figure 1.14 Gold *semissis* of Justinian II, II Period (705–711), reproducing the bust of the blessing Christ on the obverse and the bust of Justinian II on the reverse.

As soon as Justinian II regained the throne in the period between 705 and 711, he minted coins with Christ's face again but this time using an image different from the Shroud. The gold *solidus* (Fig. 1.13), *semissis* (Fig. 1.14), and *tremissis* (Fig. 1.15) [Bellinger, 1966; Fanti and Malfi, 2020] were introduced by the emperor. The Syrian model of Christ's face depicted on these coins refers to a man with bushy curly hair and a short beard, see Fig. 1.16 and 3.1. Many hypotheses have been proposed to explain this change in the image. One hypothesis is that the emperor wanted to take the Camuliana Image[n] as an example, which also should have been located in Constantinople at that time.

Figure 1.15 Gold *tremissis* of Justinian II, II Period (705–711), reproducing the bust of the blessing Christ on the obverse and the bust of Justinian II on the reverse.

Figure 1.16 On the left is a "Syrian" face of Christ, dated as post-sixth-century, fresco in a burial crypt at Abu-Girgeh near Alexandria (from Breckenridge [1959]). On the right is one of the best known representations of Olympian Zeus of Phidias found at Otricoli, Italy, now at the Vatican Museum.

---

[n]According to Breckenridge [1959], the Camuliana Icon (or Kamoulia) was present from 574 in Constantinople, and a Syriac version of Christ's face was also found in the miniatures on Syriac manuscripts dated 585 and 634.

We must remember that in the sixth century, there was some controversy about the favored images of Christ, see also Section 3.3.2.

- The first one or "Semitic" form showed Jesus with short and "frizzy" hair.
- The second one showed a bearded Jesus with hair parted in the middle, very similar to the Shroud image (see Chapter 2). Breckenridge [1959] instead, who probably did not know the face of Jesus represented on this Relic, thought of associating this face of Christ with the depictions of Zeus (Fig. 1.16).

Until the Shroud was widely known, the Church Fathers[o] insisted that Jesus had short curly hair [Belting 1994]. This can be an explanation as to why on the gold coins Justinian II preferred the face of Christ to be similar to the Shroud during his first reign, while during his second reign he changed it to a face with curly hair.

During his second reign (705–711), Emperor Justinian II minted two kind of coins with Christ's face. While at the beginning he coined only his bust on the reverse, he later added his son Tiberius, see Figs. 1.17–1.19.

Figure 1.17 Gold *solidus* of Justinian II, II Period (705–711), reproducing the bust of the blessing Christ on the obverse and the bust of Justinian II with his son Tiberius on the reverse.

[o]The Church Fathers include St John of Damascus, Theophanes the Confessor, Theodore Lector and Gennadius.

Figure 1.18 Gold *semissis* of Justinian II, II Period (705–711), reproducing the bust of the blessing Christ on the obverse and the bust of Justinian II with his son Tiberius on the reverse.

Figure 1.19 Gold *tremissis* of Justinian II, II Period (705–711), reproducing the bust of the blessing Christ on the obverse and the bust of Justinian II with his son Tiberius on the reverse.

1.3.3 Michael III Drunkhard—842–867

After Justinian II, because of the continuing iconoclastic controversy, the practice of depicting the face of Christ on coins disappeared for more than a century. Faces of emperors replaced it.

This iconoclastic struggle officially began with Leo III (717–741), erupting in 725. Depictions of holy images were forbidden because they were considered to be idols. Consequently, for about 150 years, the representation of Christ's face on Byzantine coins ceased.

According to Moroni [1986], the Shroud disappeared from Constantinople so that it could be protected during these struggles. It was carried to Edessa in 754, where it was kept until 944, and then it was brought back to the Byzantine capital.

In 787, the Council of Nicaea established the clear difference between image veneration, which was allowed, and adoration, which was prohibited because only God can be adored. However, a second wave of iconoclastic controversies started and lasted until 843, when the March Synod of Constantinople finally revoked the iconoclastic decrees.

At the end of those struggles, the young Emperor Michael III the Drunkard (842–867) encouraged by his mother Theodora, an iconophile, and by two other church rulings, started again to mint gold coins with the Shroud-like face of Christ (Fig. 1.20) quite similar to that minted by Justinian II during his first period. It seems likely that in this period some engravers would have had the chance to directly observe the Shroud before minting the coins. The image of Christ on these coins is similar to the image on coins of the first period of Justinian II. Like the coins of Justinian II, the bust of Christ is in a frontal position and a cross could be seen behind His head. He has long, wavy hair, a beard, and a mustache, wears either a *pallium* or a sheet representing the Shroud over a *colobium* bestowing a blessing with His right hand, and holding the book of the Gospels in His left hand.

It is interesting to make a comparison of Christ's faces between the coin in Fig. 1.20 where the young Emperor Michael III is represented on the reverse with his mother Theodora (842–856) with the similar face of Christ in Fig. 1.21 (857–867) where the Emperor alone is depicted. The face of Christ on the earlier coin (Fig. 1.20) appears more Shroud-like, for example, the hair is more asymmetric, perhaps because only the engraver of this coin saw the Relic directly, while the engraver of the later coin (Fig. 1.21) copied the face from the previous one.

Figure 1.20 Gold *solidus* of Emperor Michael III (842–856) depicting a Shroud-like bust of the blessing Christ on the obverse and Michael III with his mother Theodora on the reverse.

Figure 1.21 Gold *solidus* of Emperor Michael III (857–867) depicting a Shroud-like bust of the blessing Christ on the obverse and Michael III alone on the reverse.

1.3.4 Basil I the Macedonian–867–886

During the years from 867 to 944 when the Shroud was triumphantly brought to Constantinople there was a numismatic innovation. Instead of minting just the face of Christ, Byzantine emperors minted coins with the image of *"Christ on the throne,"* consistent with the Third Canon of the Fourth Council of Constantinople that imposed image veneration[p]. The first emperor in this period was Basil I the Macedonian (867–886), who introduced the Savior as a full figure with this writing: "IHS-XPSREX REGNANTIUM" (Jesus Christ, King of those who rule). The image appeared on the gold *solidus* (Fig. 1.22) showing Christ Pantocrator sitting on the throne wearing a nimbus with a pallium and colobium, raising His right hand in benediction and holding the book of the Gospels in His left hand. In addition, Basil I also minted a very rare *four-solidi* gold coin [Wroth, 1908] showing the bust of the blessing Christ similar to that in Fig. 1.21.

Figure 1.22 Gold *solidus* of Basil I (867–886) reproducing the blessing Christ on the throne on the obverse.

It must be observed that, in agreement with Breckenridge [1959], the attributes of the Christ figure are of the greatest importance in the imperial symbolism; therefore no details, even if at first sight it seems insignificant, can be ignored.

The detail of the enthroned Christ's right foot, smaller and almost right-angle rotated, is therefore noteworthy. This is consistent with the tradition of the *"lame Christ,"* mentioned in Section 3.4.8, which probably was derived from the interpretation of the particular position of the feet of the Man on the Shroud.

In agreement with Shroud expert Moroni [1983, p. 3], the bare feet are not to be ignored. They are also depicted on later coins of Leo VI and Constantine VII, contrary to normal practice for

[p]From the third Canon: "We decree that the sacred image of our Lord Jesus Christ must be venerated with the same honor as is given the book of the Holy Gospels ... for what speech conveys in words, the picture announces and brings out in colors."

high-ranking people, but is in good agreement with what can be observed on the dorsal body image on the Shroud, on which the image of bloody bare feet is clear (see Chapter 2).

1.3.5   Leo VI the Wise—886–912

After Basil I, other emperors followed his example to depict Jesus Christ on a throne on the obverse of the gold *solidi*; among them his son Leo VI the Wise (886–912).

The image of Christ on the throne on these coins (Fig. 1.23) is very similar to that of Fig. 1.22, but it is interesting to observe the right-handed blessing. While it was extended in the previous coins, it now is bent behind either the *pallium*—as suggested by the expert numismatist [Sear, 1987]—or the Shroud as supposed by the author of this book (see Section 3.2.2). This configuration of the hand agrees with the depiction of Christ made by Justinian II and Michael III. The author suggests that the *pallium*-Shroud was likely an important item of clothing by which the blessing hand of Christ was partially covered.

Figure 1.23 Gold *solidus* of Leo VI (886–912) reproducing the blessing Christ on a throne on the obverse.

1.3.6   Constantine VII Porhyrogenitus and Romanus I Lekapenos with Associate Rulers—913–959

Other emperors depicted the image of Jesus Christ on a throne on the obverse of the gold *solidi* like Alexander (912–913), Leo's brother, and Constantine VII Porphyrogenitus (913–944) with Romanus I Lekapenos (949–959), see Fig. 1.24. These coins show the blessing right arm again extended.

Figure 1.24 Gold *solidus* of Romanus I (921–931) reproducing the blessing Christ on a throne on the obverse.

Figure 1.25 Gold *solidus* of Romanus I (921–931) standing with Christ who stands facing and crowning the emperor with His right hand on the obverse. In this very rare case in the Byzantine coinage, Christ appears with the left foot rotated instead of the right as it is almost always consistent with what is seen on the Shroud.

During this period another depiction of Jesus Christ appeared. Romanus I (924–931) minted a rare coin showing himself on the obverse (Fig. 1.25) standing with His left hand extended toward Christ who stands facing outward with a cross behind His head wearing a colobium and pallium, crowning the emperor with His right hand, and holding in His left hand the book of the Gospels.

In addition to this new image, the bust of Christ reappears on the obverse of the gold *solidus* of Constantine VII (949–959), see Fig. 1.26.

Figure 1.26 Gold *solidus* of Constantine VII (949–959) showing the bust of the blessing Christ on the obverse.

As will be mentioned in Section 2.4.3, in 944 the Shroud was brought to Constantinople and since then, images of the face of Christ reappeared on coins, some of which were very similar to the Shroud face and richer in details typical of the Relic, but with more softened features compared to the first coins minted by Justinian II. For example, Fig. 1.26 clearly shows the swelling of the right cheek and the hair longer on His left side.

1.3.7 Nicephorus III Phocas—963–969

Following Romanus II (959–963) who coined the bust of Christ on a rare gold *solidus*, Emperor Nicephorus III Phocas (963–969) reigned throughout this period with co-emperors Basil II and Constantine VIII (but this did not appear on the coinage). He continued the classical depiction of the bust of Christ initiated with Justinian II and recovered by Constantine VII (Fig. 1.27).

During this reign a new lightweight gold coin, the *tetarteron*, was introduced and it was distinguishable from the *solidus* or *histamenon nomisma* only by its weight [Sear, 1987].

Figure 1.27 Gold *solidus* of Nicephorus II (963–969) showing the bust of the blessing Christ on the obverse.

1.3.8 John I Tzimisces—969–976

Emperor John I Tzimisces (969–976) reigned throughout this period with co-emperors Basil II and Constantine VIII, though this did not appear on the coinage. He continued the classical depiction of the bust of Christ on the gold *solidus* (Fig. 1.28).

Figure 1.28 Gold *solidus* of John I Tzimisces (969–976) showing the bust of the blessing Christ on the obverse.

On the reverse, the bust of John on the left is touched by the Virgin's hand on the right. Above the Emperor is depicted the *Manus Dei* (Hand of God) [Grierson and Mays, 1992].

This reign saw the commencement of the Anonymous Copper Coinage[q] [Sear, 1987] with the bust of Christ similar to that of the solidus on the obverse.

1.3.9 Basil II Bulgaroktonos—976–1025

Basil I Bulgaroktonos became emperor when he was eighteen years old and he reigned for half a century just when the Byzantine Empire reached the zenith of its power [Sear, 1987].

During this period, different coins of Christ were minted. The gold *histamenon* showing the bust of the blessing Christ on the obverse is interesting because the face of Jesus is very similar to the Shroud face (Fig. 1.29). This is consistent with the Shroud being venerated in Constantinople during this period and therefore was easier to copy directly. A gold *tetarteron*, very similar to the *histamenon*, was also minted (Fig. 1.30).

Figure 1.29 Gold *histamenon nomisma* of Basil II Bulgaroktonos (976–1025) showing the bust of the blessing Christ on the obverse.

The reign of Basil II saw the distribution of the Anonymous Copper Coinage with the bust of Christ similar to that shown in Fig. 1.31 on the obverse. Many of these include on Christ's

[q]Starting from Emperor John I Tzimisces (969–976) up to the Reform of Emperor Alexius (1092) various anonymous bronze *folles*, with purely religious legends and motifs monopolized the output of the Byzantine mint; they are classified chronologically in alphabetical sequence from A1 to N [Sear, 1987].

face the initials IC XC, indicating Jesus Christ, which in Greek is "*Ιησούς Χριστός*" (*Iēsous Christos*). The first and the last letter of each word written in capital letters is "Ις Χς."

Figure 1.30 Gold *tetarteron* of Basil II Bulgaroktonos (976–1025) showing the bust of the blessing Christ on the obverse.

Figure 1.31 Class A1 [Sear, 1987] copper *follis* attributed to Basil II Bulgaroktonos (976–1025) showing the bust of the blessing Christ on the obverse. The reverse shows the inscription "+RIhSUS XRISTUS/ bASILEU/bASILE" ("Jesus Christ, Emperor of Emperors").

These copper coins classified by letters from A to N [Sear, 1987] have purely religious motifs and were minted for almost a century, see Figs. 1.3, 1.31 and 1.32. The copper coins with imperial effigies returned under the reign of Constantine X (1059–1067), see Fig. 1.45. It is interesting that this kind of religious coin was produced just when the Byzantine Empire reached its maximum power.

Figure 1.32 Class A2 [Sear, 1987] copper *follis* attributed to Basil II Bulgaroktonos (976–1025) showing the bust of the blessing Christ on the obverse. The reverse shows the inscription "+RIhSUS XRISTUS/bASILEU/ bASILE" ("Jesus Christ, Emperor of Emperors").

The silver *miliaresion* showed on the obverse another depiction of Jesus Christ, the Infant with the Mother of God (Fig. 1.2). The three stars that appear on the head and shoulders of the Mother are an ancient Syriac symbol of Her perpetual virginity before, during and after Childbirth, and sometimes were interpreted as the symbol of the Holy Trinity too.

1.3.10   Constantine VIII—1025–1028

Constantine VIII (1025–1028) became Emperor at the death of his brother Basil II but reigned for only three years. He continued to mint the same gold *histamenon* showing the bust of the blessing Christ on the obverse with only his image on the reverse (Fig. 1.33).

Figure 1.33 Gold *histamenon* of Constantine VIII (1025–1028) showing the bust of the blessing Christ on the obverse.

1.3.11   Romanus III Agyrus—1028–1034

With Emperor Romanus III Agyrus (1028–1034) the image of Christ seated on the throne was resumed after about 90 years of absence and this lasted longer than the empire's fall during the reign of Alexius III (1195–1204) due to the siege of the Fourth Crusade in 1204 (Fig. 1.34).

Figure 1.34 Gold *histamenon* of Romanus III (1028–1034) showing the blessing Christ enthroned on the obverse.

The anonymous copper *follis* of Fig. 1.35 is attributed to this Emperor too.

Figure 1.35 Copper anonymous *follis* attributed to Romanus III (1028–1034), Class B [Sear, 1987] showing the bust of Christ blessing on the obverse.

1.3.12 Michael IV the Paphlagonian—1034–1041

Following the reign of Romanus III, Emperor Michael IV the Paphlagonian (1034–1041) preferred the depiction of the bust of the blessing Christ to that of Christ on a throne of his predecessor (Fig. 1.36). This coin has the famous cup-shape (or scyphate) that was very common in various coins minted in the Byzantine Empire from that time on. Under this Emperor, the *debasement* of the Byzantine gold coinage was initiated, and the purity of this metal was lowered up to 20 carats (83.3%).

A new depiction of Jesus Christ appears in this period on the copper *follis*. The image of Christ Antiphonetes[r] is a three-quarter length figure of the blessing Jesus Christ wearing a pallium (or

---

[r]The image of Christ Antiphonetes (άντιφωνητής, "the one who responds," also "the guarantor") depicted on the coin derived from the icon of Christ Antiphonetes. Many miracles were attributed to this famous icon, which was located in the Church of Theotokos Chalkoprateia at Constantinople dedicated to the Virgin Mary. Justin II (565–578) and his wife Sophia repaired this church, adorning it with gilded coffered ceiling and doors made of silver, *electrum* and gold. Three chapels were also added including a chapel dedicated to Christ, which housed the miraculous icon of Christ Antiphonetes. Unfortunately, the icon has not survived to the present day.

Shroud according to the author) and a colobium holding the book of the Gospels in His left hand (Fig. 1.37). On the reverse we read the letters as "*IC-XC NI-KA,*" meaning "Jesus Christ Conquers." This kind of depiction of Christ Antiphonetes also appeared in the very rare copper *histamenon nomisma* minted by Empress Zoe (December 10–13, 1041).

Figure 1.36 Gold scyphate *histamenon nomisma* of Michael IV the Paphlagonian (1034–1041) showing the bust of the blessing Christ on the obverse.

Figure 1.37 Copper *follis* Class C [Sear, 1987] attributed to Michael IV the Paphlagonian (1034–1041) showing a three-quarter length of the blessing Christ Antiphonetes on the obverse. According to the author, the left arm of Christ holds the Shroud.

1.3.13   Constantine IX Monomachus—1042–1055

Emperor Constantine IX Monomachus (1042–1055) did not take his responsibility seriously and squandered the public treasury, which had been greatly increased by his predecessor, Basil II. Instead, he focused on art and culture with the establishment of a university in 1045 [Sear, 1987].

Figure 1.38 Gold scyphate *histamenon nomisma* of Constantine IX Monomachus (1042–1055) showing the blessing Christ on a throne on the obverse.

Figure 1.39 Gold *tetarteron* of Constantine IX Monomachus (1042–1055) showing the bust of the blessing Christ on the obverse.

He continued with the images of Jesus Christ established by his predecessors minting Christ on a throne on the gold *histamenon nomisma* (Fig. 1.38) and the bust of the blessing Christ both on the gold *histamenon nomisma* and the gold *tetarteron* (Fig. 1.39). The copper follis attributed to this Emperor is of an anonymous type of Class D [Sear, 1987] (Fig. 1.40), depicting Christ on a throne. In this period, the production of the famous scyphate or cup shaped coins continued with the *histamenon nomisma* (Fig. 1.38). This kind of coin remained for centuries in the Byzantine Empire.

Figure 1.40 Copper anonimus *follis* attributed to Constantine IX Monomachus (1042–1055), Class D [Sear, 1987], showing the bust of Christ blessing on the obverse.

1.3.14   Theodora Porphyrogenita—1055–1056

The last surviving descendant of Basil the Macedonian was Theodora who reigned for only one and a half years (1055–1056), but this reign seems significant from a numismatic point of view.

She was an avid coin collector [Suarez, 2010], and introduced two new interesting images of Christ on the gold *tetarteron* (Fig. 1.40a) and on the gold *histamenon* (Fig. 1.41). The face of Christ on the rare gold *tetarteron* of Fig. 1.40a, evidences a beard lengthened downwards, probably reproducing the *"wet beard"* of the Orthodox icons referring to the legend of King Abgar (see Section 1.3.18). This image remained forgotten for more than a dozen years until Emperor Michael VII Ducas (1071–1078) largely reproduced this depiction on the *electrum* scyphate *histamenon nomisma*.

Figure 1.40a Gold *tetarteron nomisma* of Theodora (1055–1056), showing the bust of Christ blessing on the obverse; the beard lengthened downwards is evident (see Section 1.3.18, courtesy of Ira & Larry Goldberg Coins & Collectibles Inc. U.S.A. www.goldbergcoins.com).

The image of Christ on the gold *histamenon* according to some experts it can be the image of Christ Chalkites[s] [Engberg, 2004]. Goodacre [1967 p. 233] describes the image of Christ on this coin in the following way. *"The standing figure of the Savior on the reverse of the nomisma is believed to represent the image of the Savior of Chalce which stood above the gate of that part of the palace known by his name."*

This image, see Section 3.4.3, appears to the author very important regarding the Shroud, even if it seems, up to now, not well understood at the iconographic-numismatic level. According to the experts, the obverse of the gold histamenon nomisma shows *"Christ standing facing out on a footstool, wearing a nimbus cruciger (halo with a cross), pallium and colobium, and holding a book of the Gospels with both hands ...."* [Sear, 1987] or *"Christ standing on square souppedion[t] .... facing out, bearded, with a cross*

---

[s]The image of Christ Chalkites (Ξαλκίτης), or Christ of the Chalke Gate is a famous image of Christ posed on the Chalke gate of Constantinople. According to Jelena Bogdanovic [2008], *"Chalke (Bronze) Gate, rendered from Greek "Brazen House," was the main vestibule of the Great Palace, so named either for bronze tiles of its roof or for its bronze doors. A famous icon of Christ was placed over the doors. Now lost, this imperial Gate originally facing the Augustaion, south of Hagia Sophia, was one of the most important architectural symbols of Constantinople."*

[t]The *"suppedion"* was a carpet with a raised shape, the probable meaning of which was to underline the difference between the Emperor and the rest of the world; its function of Christ's vicar, in fact, placed him in an intermediary situation between Heaven and Earth.

nimbus, wearing tunic and himation; right hand raised in blessing in sling of cloak and left hand holding a book ...." [Grierson, 1999].

Figure 1.41 Two gold *histamena nomisma* of Theodora (1055–1056), one with hole[u], showing a new depiction of Jesus: "*Christ standing facing out on a footstool*" according to numismatic experts or Christ resurrected from the sepulcher according to the author. The slight differences between the two coins are evident. Noteworthy is the fact that while the partially blessing right hand on the coin above holds the dress interpreted by the author as the Shroud, the dress/Shroud is so important that both hands of Christ on the image below hold it.

Differently from the description of Sear [1987], Grierson [1999] and other experts, the author proposes another interpretation of the "*footstool*" (or the "*square souppedion*") under Christ's feet: it seems just the Byzantine representation of the sepulcher thought as a box[v]. More important, the depiction seems not of

[u]We often find Byzantine coins with holes, especially if in gold and depicting Jesus Christ, because used as medals to wear with necklaces, see also Fig. 1.43.

[v]A. Gannon [2020] observes that the lozenge-shaped "*footstool*" could just be the stone of the Jesus' sepulcher that at least in the Anglo-Saxon context is considered as short-hand for signifying the Resurrection. She adds [2013a] that in the seventh century Adomnán of Iona reported that the stone functioning as the door to Christ's tomb was split in two pieces. The smaller one was still in front

Figure 1.42 Russian icon of the eighteenth century representing the resurrected Christ. It is interesting to observe the shape of the sepulcher (box under the feet of Christ) which is similar to the image in Fig. 1.41.

---

of the entrance of the sepulcher and used as a quadrangular altar, whilst the other, of similar shape, but larger and covered by linen cloths, was used as an altar in the East part of the church. The Monza's Ampulla #5 shows a lozenge corresponding to this stone of the sepulcher.

A. Gannon notes that the *"footstool"* is shown elsewhere. In some contemporary representations reference is made to Psalm 110: *"Donec ponam inimicos tuos scabellum pedum tuorum (While I will set your enemies as the stool of your feet)"* (or you will reign on my right hand, even when you subjugate your enemies). It is also similar to a depiction of Roman Emperor Constantinus II (317–361) (https://en.wikipedia.org/wiki/Chronograph_of_354#/media/File:07_onstantius2Chrono354.png) who, nevertheless, is seated as in Fig. 3.22 and not standing as Jesus Christ on the coin in question.

a simple *"Christ standing"* but of the resurrected Christ. In fact, this image is very similar to the Orthodox icon of the resurrected Christ shown in Fig. 1.42. As it will be discussed in Chapter 3, this depiction of the resurrected Christ is important because it probably shows the Shroud wrapped around the glorious body of Christ coming out from the sepulcher.

1.3.15 Isaac I Comnenus—1057–1059

After the brief reign of Michael VI Stratioticus (August 1056–August 1057) who minted a gold *histamenon nomisma* with the bust of Christ very similar to that of Michael IV shown in Fig. 1.36, Isaac I Comnenus (1057–1059) went to the throne. He confiscated a certain amount of the Church property for his purpose and he was soon forced by the Byzantine people to abdicate. He coined a gold *histamenon nomisma* showing Christ on a throne (Fig. 1.43) and a gold *tetarteron* showing the bust of Christ similar to that of Fig. 1.36.

Figure 1.43 Gold scyphate *histamenon nomisma* with hole (See note of Fig. 1.41) of Isaac I Comnenus (1057–1059) showing Christ on a throne.

1.3.16 Constantine X Ducas and Eudocia—1059–1067

Emperor Constantine X Ducas (1059–1067) was represented in his coinage with his wife Eudocia Makrembolitissa. He continued with the images of Jesus Christ established by his predecessors by minting Christ on a throne on the gold *histamenon nomisma* (Fig. 1.44). One type of copper *follis* copied the image of the resurrected Christ introduced by Empress Theodora (1055–1056), see Fig. 1.45, while a second type of copper *follis* reproduced the bust of Christ.

Figure 1.44 Gold scyphate *histamenon nomisma* of Constantine X (1059–1067) shows a blessing Christ on a throne.

Figure 1.45 Copper *follis* of Constantine with Eudocia (1059–1067) shows Theodora's depiction of Jesus (see Fig. 1.41): "*Christ standing facing out on footstool*" according to numismatic experts or Christ resurrected from the sepulcher according to the author, also similar to the image of Christ Antiphonetes of Fig. 1.37.

1.3.17 Romanus IV Diogenes—1068–1071

After the reign of Eudocia in the second half of 1067 (May 31–December 31), during which she coined a gold *histamenon nomisma* again showing Christ on a throne, Emperor Romanus IV Diogenes (1068–1071) reigned with associate rulers (Michael VII, Constantius, Andronicus and Eudocia). During this reign, the gold *histamenon nomisma* minted by Romanus IV depicts Christ (Fig. 1.46) in a new way. Taking a cue both from the wedding *solidus* of Licinia Eudossia & Valentinian III dated 437 (Fig. 1.7) and the Gold *histamenon nomisma* of Theodora dated 1055–1056 (Fig. 1.41), this coin seems (according to the author) to show Christ resurrected from the sepulcher. The reverse of this new gold *histamenon nomisma* reproduces the image of Christ crowning both Romanus IV on the left and Eudocia on the right in a display similar to that of Fig. 1.7, but, while in this depiction the three persons are standing on a common footstool, only Christ is depicted on the sepulcher in Fig. 1.46. Another interesting difference between Christ's face in Fig. 1.7 and Christ's face on the coin of Romanus IV is that the first represents a beardless man with short hair, instead of a face similar to the Shroud with a beard and long wavy hair, showing that the Shroud image was the predominant model in that age.

Figure 1.46 Scyphate gold *histamenon nomisma* of Romanus IV (1068–1071) showing Christ resurrected from the sepulcher standing among Romanus IV and Eudocia.

The silver *2/3 miliaresion* (Fig. 1.47) showing the bust of the blessing Christ on the obverse was also added to the Byzantine coinage along with two copper *folles*: the first shown in Fig. 1.48, the other, an anonymous one of Class G (Fig. 1.49) shows the bust of the Virgin praying on the reverse. It is interesting to observe that this last *follis* shows a folded cloth under the blessing hand of Christ that could possibly be a depiction of the Shroud.

Figure 1.47 Silver *2/3 miliaresion* of Romanus IV (1068–1071) showing the bust of the blessing Christ on the obverse.

Figure 1.48 Copper *follis* of Romanus IV (1068–1071) showing the bust of the blessing Christ on the obverse.

Figure 1.49 Copper *follis* of Romanus IV (1068–1071) showing the bust of the blessing Christ on the obverse and the bust of the Virgin praying on the reverse.

1.3.18 Michael VII Ducas—1071–1078

During the reign of Michael VII Ducas (1071–1078) the Byzantine Empire was close to collapse. Nevertheless, the coinage was enriched with new types of depictions.

The gold scyphate *histamenon nomisma* showing the blessing Christ on a throne on the obverse (Fig. 1.50) and the *electrum* scyphate *histamenon nomisma* showing the bust of the blessing Christ on the obverse, similar to that of Michael IV, were added but with a somewhat different appearance for the face of Christ (Fig. 1.51). Taking care from the image of Christ minted by Empress Theodora (Fig. 1.40a), his beard is lengthened downwards probably reproducing the *"wet beard"* of the Orthodox icons referring to the legend of King Abgar. According to this, Jesus once pressed a cloth to his wet face, and his image was miraculously transferred to it, thus creating the supposed first Christian icon, see also Section 3.3.1.

In addition to these coins, there is an *electrum tetarteron nomisma* reproducing the bust of the Virgin holding before Her the Infant Christ very similar to the Orthodox icon of the Mother of God of the Sign (Fig. 1.52), a silver *2/3 miliaresion* showing Christ enthroned (Fig. 1.53), a silver *1/3 miliaresion* showing the bust of Christ (Fig. 1.54) and a copper *follis* and *half follis* (Fig. 1.55) with the bust of Christ.

Figure 1.50 Gold scyphate *histamenon nomisma* of Michael VII (1071–1078) showing the blessing Christ on a throne.

Figure 1.51 *Electrum* scyphate *histamenon nomisma* of Michael VII (1071–1078) showing the bust of the blessing Christ having a beard lengthened downwards in reference to the "*wet beard*" of Agbar's legend.

Figure 1.52 *Electrum tetarteron nomisma* of Michael VII (1071–1078) showing the bust of the Virgin holding before Her the Infant Christ.

Figure 1.53 Silver *2/3 miliaresion* of Michael VII (1071–1078) showing the blessing Christ enthroned.

Figure 1.54 Silver *1/3 miliaresion* of Michael VII (1071–1078) showing the bust of Christ.

Figure 1.55 Copper *half follis* of Michael VII (1071–1078) showing the bust Christ.

1.3.19   Nicephorus III Botaniates—1078–1081

The reign of Nicephorus III Botaniates was not long (1078–1081) because he abdicated in favor of Alexius I in 1081 due to the disruptions present in the declining Byzantine Empire.

Figure 1.56 *Electrum* scyphate *histamenon nomisma* of Nicephorus III (1078–1081) showing the blessing Christ on a throne.

Figure 1.57 Anonymous copper *follis* of Nicephorus III (1078–1081) of Class I, showing the bust of the blessing Christ on the obverse.

Following the coinage of his predecessors, he minted two kinds of *electrum*, including the scyphate *histamena nomisma* showing the blessing Christ enthroned, but without the back (Fig. 1.56) and the bust of the blessing Christ. Moreover, he minted an *electrum tetarterum* showing the bust of Christ, *folles* with a three-quarter length image of Christ and anonymous ones with the bust of the blessing Christ of Class I (Fig. 1.57).

Nicephorus Basilacius, who was a general under Michael VII, in 1078 minted a copper follis showing the bust of the blessing Christ.

1.3.20 Alexius I Comnenus—1081–1118

The dynasty of Comnenus, that reigned for about a century, gave the Byzantine Empire new life and delayed its inevitable disintegration. Alexius I (1081–1118) worked busily for the reconstruction of the Empire and secured the help of the Venetian Republic in exchange for trading privileges. In 1092, he performed the coinage reform mentioned in Section 1.1 so we find a great variety of coins during his reign.

Among them, we find the Pre-Reform (1092) *electrum* or silver *histamenon nomisma* (Fig. 1.58) and the *electrum* or silver *tetarteron nomisma* with the bust of Christ, or Christ enthroned; a silver *2/3* and *1/3 miliaresion* with the Virgin holding the Infant Christ on Her breast; an anonymous *folles* (Class J in Fig. 1.59, also Class K, L, M and N) showing the bust of Christ or Christ enthroned.

Figure 1.58 Pre-Reform *electrum* scyphate *histamenon nomisma* (Thessalonica mint) of Alexius I (1081–1092) showing the bust of the blessing Christ.

Figure 1.59 Pre-Reform copper *follis*, Class J of Alexius I (1081–1092) showing the bust of the blessing Christ.

After the Reform of 1092, Alexius I coined a gold scyphate *hyperpyron* showing the blessing Christ enthroned on the obverse (Fig. 1.60); an *electrum* scyphate *aspron trachy* showing either the Virgin enthroned holding before Her a haloed head of the Infant Christ facing Her (Fig. 1.61) or Christ enthroned; various copper *tetartera* showing the bust of Christ and Christ enthroned, and *billon aspron trachea* showing Christ enthroned or the bust of Christ.

Figure 1.60 Post-Reform gold scyphate *hyperpyron* of Alexius I (1092–1118) showing the blessing Christ enthroned.

Figure 1.61 Post-Reform *electrum* scyphate *apron trachy* of Alexius I (1092–1118) showing the Virgin enthroned holding before Her a haloed head of the Infant Christ facing Her.

1.3.21   John II Comnenus—1118–1143

The Byzantine Empire increased its power under Emperor John II Comnenus (1118–1143) who however prematurely died during a hunting accident. He coined a gold *hyperpyron* (Fig. 1.62) and an *electrum aspron trachy* with the blessing Christ enthroned; a *billon aspron trachy* showing a blessing bust of Christ, a copper *tetarteron* with the bust of Christ and another one with *"Christ standing facing out on a footstool"* according to Sear [1987] or better with the resurrected Christ standing on the sepulcher according to the author (Fig. 1.4). A copper *half tetarteron* of the same type as the last (Fig. 1.63) was coined as well.

Figure 1.62 Gold *hyperpyron* of John II (1118–1143) showing the blessing Christ enthroned on the obverse.

Figure 1.63 Copper *half tetarteron* of John II (1118–1143) showing *"Christ standing facing out on a footstool"* according to Sear [1987] or better with the resurrected Christ standing on the sepulcher according to the author.

1.3.22 Manuel I Comnenus—1143–1180

Before the catastrophe of 1204, the Byzantine Empire blossomed during the long reign of Manuel I Comnenus. This period is associated with a great variety of coins produced under this Emperor. Among them, we find a new image of Christ's face showing a younger and beardless Christ, the Christ Emmanuel (Fig. 1.64). This perhaps was coined as an analogy to the name Manuel of the Emperor.

Figure 1.64 Gold scyphate *hyperpyron* of Manuel I (1143–1180) showing the bust of Christ Emmanuel on the obverse.

We therefore have two relatively rare exceptions, the Syriac face of Christ of Emperor Justinian II in his second period of reign and the Christ Emmanuel, compared with the countless images that are more similar to the Shroud, confirming the real importance that the Shroud should have had in those centuries.

Manuel I coined a gold scyphate *hyperpyron* showing the bust of Christ Emmanuel (Fig. 1.64), an *electrum* scyphate *apron trachy* again with the bust of Christ Emmanuel (Fig. 1.65), a bearded enthroned Christ (Fig. 1.66), a bearded resurrected Christ on the sepulcher (Fig. 1.67), *billon aspron trachea* showing the bust of Christ Emmanuel and the enthroned Christ (Fig. 1.68) and a copper *tetarteron* showing the bust of Christ Emmanuel (Fig. 1.69).

Figure 1.65 *Electrum* scyphate *aspron trachy* of Manuel I (1143–1180) showing the bust of Christ Emmanuel on the obverse.

Figure 1.66 *Electrum* scyphate *aspron trachy* of Manuel I (1143–1180) showing a bearded enthroned Christ on the obverse.

Figure 1.67 *Electrum* scyphate *aspron trachy* of Manuel I (1143–1180) showing a bearded resurrected Christ on the sepulcher on the obverse.

Figure 1.68 *Billon* scyphate *aspron trachy* of Manuel I (1143–1180) showing an enthroned Christ on the obverse. Some coins like this show two stars probably referring to comets, which appeared in that period.

Figure 1.69 Copper *tetarteron* of Manuel I (1143–1180) showing Christ Emmanuel on the obverse.

1.3.23   Andronicus I Comnenus—1183–1185

Following Manuel I, reigned Alexius II Comnenus (1180–1183) who probably never struck coins [Sear, 1987] and Andronicus I Comnenus (1183–1185) who had various political problems like that with the Normans who sacked Thessalonica in 1185, the second city of the Byzantine Empire.

He minted a gold *hyperpyron*, an *electrum aspron trachy*, a *billon aspron trachy* (Fig. 1.70), a copper *tetarteron* and a *half tetarteron*, all with the Virgin praying or holding the head of the Infant Christ on one side and Christ bearded with Andronicus I on the reverse.

Figure 1.70 *Billon* scyphate *aspron trachy* of Andronicus I (1183–1185) showing the Virgin praying on one side and Christ with Andronicus I on the reverse. In agreement with Sear [1987], differently from the coins of the resurrected Christ, the Virgin seems here *"Standing on a dais"* because of the irregular and rounded shape of the support. The curvature of the cup coin is shown on the right.

1.3.24   Alexius III Angelus-Comnenus—1195–1203

After Isaac I Comnenus of Cyprus (1184–1191) and Isaac II Angelus (1185–1195) who minted a gold *hyperpyron,* an *electrum aspron trachea,* and a *billon aspron trachy* with the Virgin praying or holding the head of the Infant Christ or, more rarely a bust of Christ beardless, reigned Alexius III Angelus-Comnenus (1195–1203) up to the fall of Constantinople caused by the Fourth Crusade in 1203.

He minted a gold *hyperpyron* with the blessing *"Christ standing facing out on a dais"* according to Sear [1987] or better with the blessing resurrected Christ standing on the sepulcher according to the author (Fig. 1.71).

Figure 1.71 Scyphate *Electrum hyperpyron* of Alexius III (1195–1203) showing the blessing resurrected Christ on the sepulcher on the obverse.

He also minted an *electrum aspron trachy* showing the blessing Christ enthroned (Fig. 1.72) and a *billon aspron trachy* with the beardless bust of Christ Emmanuel (Fig. 1.73).

Figure 1.72 Scyphate *Electrum aspron trachy* of Alexius III (1195–1203) showing the blessing Christ enthroned on the obverse.

Figure 1.73 Scyphate *billon aspron trachy* of Alexius III (1195–1203) showing the bust of the beardless Christ Emmanuel on the obverse.

1.4 Byzantine Coinage after the Fall of Constantinople of 1204

The principal aim of this book is to address the relationship between the Shroud of Christ and the Byzantine coinage. As we will see in Chapter 2, there is no indication of the Shroud's presence in Constantinople after the sack of the city in 1204, though it reappeared later in Europe. It might therefore be argued that the Byzantine engravers of coins would not have been directly influenced by the Shroud after 1204. In fact, all the depictions of Christ on coins minted after 1204 should be thought of in reference to either copies of the Shroud still present in the Byzantine Empire or copies of images present in previous coins.

The Byzantine coinage showing Jesus Christ continued for centuries after the sack of Constantinople. We continue by presenting the most important images of Christ reproduced in that period.

Following the fall of Constantinople and the establishment of the Latin Empire, various reigns formed, and at Nicea the restored Byzantine Empire formed under Theodore I Comnenus-Lascaris (1208–1222) and John III Ducas-Vatatzes (1222–1254) who coined a gold scyphate *hyperpyron* showing the blessing Christ enthroned on the obverse (Fig. 1.74).

Figure 1.74 Gold scyphate *hyperpyron* of John III (1208–1222) showing the blessing Christ on a throne on the obverse.

Andronicus II and Michael IX of Constantinople (1295–1320) coined a gold scyphate *hyperpyron* showing the bust of the Virgin praying within the city walls on the obverse. The reverse shows Andronicus and Michael kneeling on either side of the standing Christ, crowning both emperors on the reverse (Fig. 1.75).

Figure 1.75 Gold scyphate *hyperpyron* showing the bust of the Virgin praying on the obverse and Christ standing, crowning both Andronicus and Michael (1295–1320) on the reverse.

They also coined a silver *basilikon* copying on the obverse the image of the blessing Christ enthroned depicted in the famous Venetian *grosso*. On the reverse, appears Andronicus and Michael standing holding the patriarchal cross between them (Fig. 1.76), or the Virgin enthroned holding a seated Christ Child on Her left arm [Grierson and Mays, 1992] (Fig. 1.77).

Figure 1.76 Silver *basilikon* of Andronicus and Michael (1295–1320) showing the blessing Christ enthroned depicted in the famous Venetian *grosso* on the obverse and Andronicus and Michael standing on the reverse.

Figure 1.77 Religious silver *basilikon* of Andronicus and Michael (1295–1320) showing the blessing Christ enthroned depicted in the famous Venetian grosso on the obverse and the Virgin Mary enthroned holding a seated Christ Child on Her left arm on the reverse.

John V, during his fourth phase (1354–1376) [Grierson and Mays, 1992], recovered the depiction of the bust of the blessing Christ first minted by Justinian II in 692 on the silver *stavraton* (Fig. 1.78).

Figure 1.78 Silver *stavraton* of John V (1354–1376) reproducing the blessing bust of Christ first produced by Justinian II in 692.

It has been partially shown, and will be better clarified in the next chapters, that the predominant guide for the depiction of Christ on Byzantine coins was the image on the Shroud. The next chapter will therefore give a detailed description of the Shroud for the reader to better understand the close connection that is evident between the image on the Relic and the image of Jesus Christ on Byzantine coins.

Chapter 2

The Shroud of Christ

The so-called Shroud of Christ, Holy Shroud, Shroud of Turin, Mandylion-Shroud or more simply the Shroud, is the most studied object in the world, in the scientific, archaeological and obviously in the religious field. On this subject, hundreds of books in many different languages and dozens of scientific papers have been written, and articles are published every day both in newspapers and on the web.

The great scientific interest is not only due to the failure of science to explain the image but also due to the failure of anyone to reproduce it. The great religious interest is because, according to Christian tradition, it was Jesus' burial sheet and that the image represents Jesus Christ in his Resurrection after his death by crucifixion. This tradition has not been disproven by scientific analysis. Even though the Shroud is the most important Relic in the world, the Catholic Church does not impose our devotion of it. Nevertheless, having the author recognized for sure as Jesus Christ Jesus of the Shroud, hereinafter this Man will be named with his name.

Byzantine Coins Influenced by the Shroud of Christ
Giulio Fanti
Copyright © 2022 Jenny Stanford Publishing Pte. Ltd.
ISBN 978-981-4877-88-6 (Hardcover), 978-1-003-21992-7 (eBook)
www.jennystanford.com

In this chapter, the reader will be synthetically[a] led to consider the mysteries of the Shroud.

2.1   The Most Important Christian Relic in the World

There are many shrouds in the world, many are in Italy and Spain, but these are all believed to be copies of the Shroud in Turin. These copies were made because of the great interest in this Relic, especially during the seventeenth century. Since photography had not yet been discovered, many painters realized copies of the Relic to allow people to look at the peculiar image of Christ. Some examples are the shroud of Arquata and of Palma di Montechiaro in Italy.

The Italian term *Sindone* (Shroud), from the Ancient Greek *sindon* (σινδων), means a sheet or piece of cloth for a specific use. This Greek word probably derives from *sindia* or *sindien*, which refer to cloth in India.

It is believed that the Shroud is the burial cloth of Jesus Christ and the double body image on it was probably produced when He resurrected from death. The Shroud is therefore the tangible proof of His Resurrection.

From a scientific point of view, the Shroud is an ancient linen cloth, 4.4 m long and 1.1 m wide, which wrapped the corpse of a tortured man, scourged, crowned with thorns, crucified and pierced by a spear in the chest. The corpse was in rigor mortis and was wrapped in the Shroud for not more than forty hours. The double (front and back) body image is not reproducible and cannot be explained scientifically. Among the many hypotheses of body image formation, that related to a phenomenon acting at a distance such as a form of electromagnetic energy, appears the most acceptable currently.

On the Shroud we can observe stained various areas of importance that may not be easily distinguishable at first glance

---

[a]The most important notes about the Shroud are reported here, but they are obviously not complete; for additional information, the reader can refer to a recently book published by the same Editor [Fanti and Malfi, 2020].

because their partial superposition can make identification difficult. The most important items are the double body image, front and back, of a corpse (Fig. 2.1) and the blood stains corresponding to the Man's wounds (Fig. 2.2).

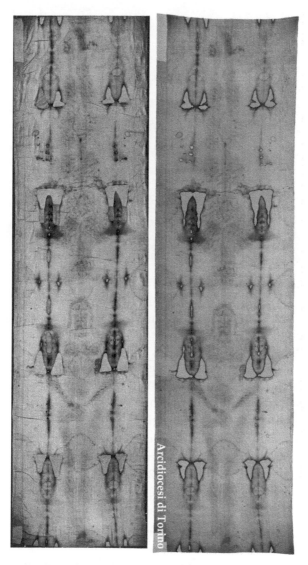

Figure 2.1 The Shroud before it was refurbished in 2002 (on the left, A. Guerreschi) and after (on the right, Archdiocese of Turin).

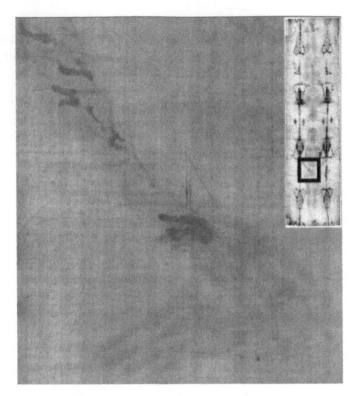

Figure 2.2 Blood stains on the wrist and the left arm. In the frame on the top-right corner, the position of the detail on the cloth is shown.

Other marks like water stains, areas of scorching and burn holes are of minor importance but cannot be neglected because they can overlay or interfere with other items.

The larger water stains like those in Fig. 2.3 were produced by an ancient poorly understood-accident when the Shroud was probably in a jar [Guerreschi and Salcito, 2002, 2005]. Instead, the smaller water stains visible (Fig. 2.4) along the scorch lines were produced with these lines during the AD 1532 Chambéry fire when the Shroud was kept in that city in France.

The larger burn holes were also produced by the Chambéry fire while the smaller ones called "poker holes" were produced by an unknown older accident. As shown in Fig. 2.4, these poker holes are present in four sets of four holes.

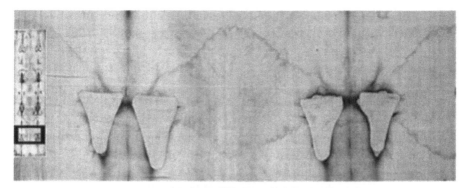

Figure 2.3 Example of three larger water stains. In the picture are also evident four patches sewn onto the cloth by Poor Clare nuns to repair the damage caused by the Chambéry fire.

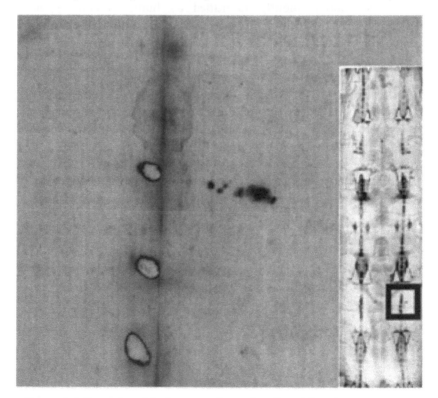

Figure 2.4 Example of holes preceding the Chambéry fire and some little stains probably caused by the water used for extinguishing the fire.

Before the Shroud was refurbished in June 2002, it was possible to observe the patches sewn by the Poor Clare nuns in 1534 to repair the damage produced by the Chambéry fire. Now these patches have been removed and holes due to fire are evident [Ghiberti, 2002].

The faint yellow linen sheet is still in good condition because it has been kept in a relatively dry environment for the past two millennia. The body image is darker but has a lower contrast than it was originally, compared to the background, because of the yellowing of the sheet due to aging.

Since the body that was wrapped in the Shroud formed the image, the image is right/left reversed. For example, the right arm in Fig. 2.2 is actually the left arm of Jesus. The red stains have been independently identified as human blood by A. Adler [1996] and P. Baima Bollone [1982]. The author discovered blood particles among the dust vacuumed from the Shroud [Fanti and Zagotto, 2017].

Indirect weight measurements on the Relic carried out also by the author on small parts of the cloth lead to a total weight of 1.05 kg (2.31 lb), and thus a mass per unit area of 0.22 kg/m^2 (0.045 lb/ft.^{2}). The cloth is about 0.34 mm (0.013 in.) in thickness and the average diameter of linen yarns is 0.25 mm (0.0098 in.). The traditional dimensions of 436 cm (14.30 ft.) long by 110 cm (3.61 ft.) wide [Baima Bollone, 1998] were increased by centimeters when the Shroud was refurbished in 2002 because the patches and some of the folds were removed and the Sheet stretched [Ghiberti, 2002].

Every yarn is composed of about 200 fibers. The diameters of linen fibers vary from 0.007 mm (0.00027 in.) to 0.020 mm (0.00079 in.) [Baima Bollone, 1982; Raes, 1976, 1995; Vial, 1995; Fanti and Malfi, 2020].

2.2 The Body Image

The most interesting feature of the Shroud consists of the front and back head-to-head images of a full-size human body separated by an image free space (Fig. 2.5). This image reveals such peculiar characteristics that science cannot reproduce all these characteristics on a single cloth.

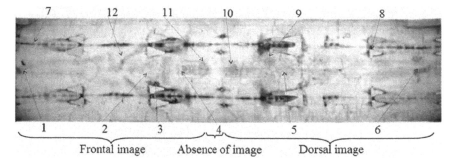

7   12   11   10   9   8

1   2   3   4   5   6

Frontal image   Absence of image   Dorsal image

Figure 2.5 Negative body image and visible signs on the Shroud. (1) Scourge wounds on the legs. (2) Water stains caused by an accident prior to 1532. (3) Chest wound. (4) Fabric creases. (5) Scourge marks on the back. (6) Nail injury to right foot. (7) Charred lines due to the Chambéry fire in 1532. (8) Patches sewn by the Poor Clare nuns after the Chambéry fire. (9) Bruises perhaps derived from body rubbing on the Cross. (10) Head wounds caused by the crown of thorns. (11) "ε" or reversed "3"-shaped forehead wound. (12) Nail injury to the left wrist.

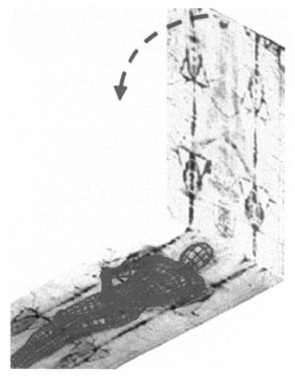

Figure 2.6 Computer representation of the position of Jesus of the Shroud.

The image is more visible in the negative than in its natural sepia color. Since the image lacks a sharp outline, observers must be at least one meter away from the cloth to see the image.

The image shows a man that was about 30 years old with a beard and long hair that was wrapped in the Shroud (Fig. 2.6) after his death. That He was dead is indicated by rigor mortis [Fanti and Marinelli, 2001].

The rigid corpse was laid out on half of the Shroud, the other half was then drawn over the head to cover the body. Two images were left, one dorsal and one frontal (Fig. 2.5 and 2.6). By means of a computer analysis, it has been verified that the frontal and dorsal imprints of Jesus of the Shroud are anatomically superimposable on a manikin and the Man's racial features could be attributable to the Semitic race [Fanti et al., 2010].

2.2.1 Typical Features

In 2005, 24 scientists of the Shroud Science Group[b] described 187 peculiar characteristics [Fanti et al., 2005] of the Shroud image; some of the most important features, from the chemical, physical, and optical points of view are here reported.

Chemical point of view. The image is due to a molecular modification of the surface of the linen fiber that is made up of polysaccharides (chains of glucose). These polysaccharides underwent an alteration because of a phenomenon acting-at-a-distance that produced dehydration with oxidation. The image is therefore not composed of painting or pigments.

Physical point of view. The body image has two levels of superficiality. The first is that the coloration that makes the image resides on the outermost layer of the linen fibers. Only the polysaccharide outer layer in a fiber is colored. This outer layer is approximately 0.2 thousandth of a millimeter (about 0.000008 in.) thick. The inside of the fiber is not colored. The second level of superficiality is that this coloration that forms the image is only in the top two or three fibers in a thread (Fig. 2.7). In the image, where one thread passes over another one in the weave, the bottom thread is not colored where the top one passes over it.

---

[b]Established in 2002 and coordinated by the author, the Shroud Science Group is formed by about 100 scientists, mostly American (www.shroud.com/pdfs/doclist.pdf).

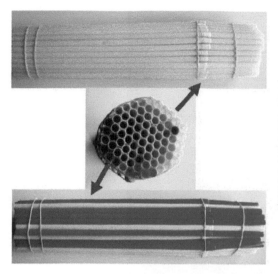

Figure 2.7 Macro model of the linen thread using drinking straws. This is equivalent to a magnification of about 300 times. Left: Only the top two or three fibers in a thread are colored. Right: A fiber is only colored in the outer layer. The inside of the fiber is not colored.

In addition to this double level of superficiality of the Shroud image, there is another surprising aspect. There are, it seems, also very dim images of the face and the hands on the backside of the cloth. This means that the images on the side of the cloth that faced the body are more faintly reproduced on the back side. Between the two sides, in the Shroud thickness, there is no coloration of the fibers and thus no image [Fanti and Maggiolo, 2004].

To make an analogy, you can imagine a book with the face of Jesus of the Shroud on the cover; on the back, another, even fainter, image of the face, and in the middle, only blank pages, without any sign of the image.

Another peculiarity of the image is that the image fibers are equally colored in the circumferential direction, but they can have some color variation longitudinally [Fanti, 2011].

Optical point of view. The body image has three-dimensional features (Fig. 2.8), in the sense that a mathematical relationship can be defined between the body–cloth distance and the degree of coloration in the image. It looks like a photographic negative (Fig. 2.9) and it is not fluorescent.

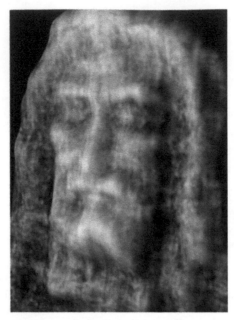

Figure 2.8 Three-dimensional processing of the face of Jesus of the Shroud based on the degree of coloration in the image (Mario Azevedo).

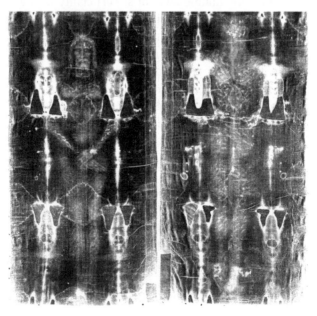

Figure 2.9 Front and back images of Jesus of the Shroud in the photographic negative (Giuseppe Enrie).

From a more general point of view, the following evidence can be highlighted.

The image corresponds to a body wrapped in a sheet, in which there are noncontact areas, such as those between the nose and cheeks. The blood stain formation process has different characteristics compared to that of the body image; blood stains went onto the fabric first imbibing it and then the body image formed on it.

The image does not show any sign of decomposition, implying that Jesus was wrapped in the sheet for a short time, according to specialists for no longer than about 40 hours. This fact is supported also by the signs of rigor mortis, which usually disappear after this lapse of time.

Detailed studies of a human body [Fanti et al., 2010] show that, apart from the arms that were moved during transportation to the sepulcher, the physical configuration of Jesus of the Shroud is consistent with someone that has had rigor mortis set in while hanging on a cross after his death.

2.2.2 How Was the Image Formed?

Because of the above-mentioned peculiar characteristics of the Shroud body image and many others not listed here for brevity, it is impossible to reproduce a copy of the Shroud. Several researchers proposed different hypotheses of body image formation that are interesting but capable of only partially reproducing these characteristics. Hypotheses can be grouped in artistic production, gas diffusion, direct contact and radiation mechanisms.

Some researchers proposed the intervention of an artist who could have used painting, bas-relief, or more elaborate techniques using acids, as claimed by L. Garlaschelli [2010].

To understand the huge difficulties that a hypothetical artist would have run into in order to obtain results similar to the Shroud, especially at the microscopic level, let us see the model in Fig. 2.7. If ideally we extract a thread of the body image of the Shroud, whose diameter is 0.25 mm (0.0098 in.), and if we magnify it by about 300 times, we can think it as analogous to a bundle of drinking straws. Each straw is, in this case, a linen fiber with a diameter of 0.015 mm (0.00059 in.). From one side of the bundle we can see a dozen colored straws side-by-side with uncolored straws. If we remove the colored film of the linen fiber, we can observe that the cellulose in the inner side is uncolored.

Now, let us think of a hypothetical artist who tries to reproduce these characteristics on a linen cloth using a simple painting technique: difficulties seem insurmountable. First, the artist should dip the brush, not in the color, because there are not pigments on the threads, but in an acid capable of shading the linen chemically. However, the artist has to see what he or she is painting, so the acid (usually transparent) must first be colored. And when the work is completed, he or she would have to eliminate any evidence of pigment, because on the Shroud there is no pigment.

Since colored fibers are side-by-side uncolored ones, the brush must have only one bristle with a diameter not greater than 0.01 mm (0.00039 in.). Since the color is uniformly distributed around the circumference of the fiber, the artist must be able to color the part of the straw on the inner side of the bundle without coloring the adjacent straws.

Then, the acid must be placed on the fiber just for a split second because it must have no time to color the cellulose on the inside of the fiber. Also, the acid must to be uniformly spread along all the circumference of the straw.

Finally the artist would have to paint in the same way all the million straw-fibers that constitute the image using a microscope (not existing in the Middle Ages). He would have to do this work while observing his artwork from at least a meter away. This distance corresponds to about 300 m (984 ft.) from the straws in the analogous model. This is because, when we get closer to the Shroud, the body image cannot be seen. If these difficulties seem unsolvable using today's technology, for a hypothetical, though brilliant, medieval artist they are far more problematic!

P. Vignon [1938] first and others later proposed the diffusion mechanism in order to explain the formation of the body image. Specifically, they proposed that gases developed between the corpse and the sheet which could have reacted with the cloth, triggering the typical chemical reaction of the linen. R. Rogers [Rogers and Arnoldi, 2002] proposed a mechanism based on the Maillard reaction[c], but did not take into consideration that there were no signs of decomposition on the Shroud.

Other scholars, among whom was J. Volckringer [1991], proposed the body–cloth direct contact mechanism as an explanation of the image formation. This hypothesis is based on the verification that after leaves are kept in a herbarium for several years, they leave a footprint on the paper they are in touch with. What is more, this footprint is negative.

However, this fails to consider that the Shroud image exists even where the cloth would not have been in contact with the body, like, for example, the space between the nose and cheeks. This evidence indicates that the correct image formation hypotheses must be based on a mechanism that acts at a distance, which suggests some type of radiation mechanism.

Several scholars such as G. B. Judica Cordiglia [1986], F. Lattarulo [1998] and G. De Liso [2000] proposed a natural radiation mechanism derived from strong electromagnetic fields[d]. They think that the body image could have been caused by an electrostatic field, perhaps related to an earthquake that could have generated a peculiar phenomenon called a corona discharge[e] that caused the production of the image. Other researchers like O. Scheuermann [2003], G. B. Judica Cordiglia [1986], J. B. Rinaudo [1998], and E. Lindner [2002] supposed the presence of a radiation source coming from the internals of the body as it was wrapped in the Shroud, but with no success in explaining the cause physically.

---

[c]Maillard reaction occurs, for example, by heating sugar until a brownish caramel is obtained.

[d]A field refers to a force that varies from one point to another in space, for example, according to the gravitational field a man has a certain weight on Earth's surface that progressively decreases as the distance from Earth increases.

[e]Corona discharge is an electric discharge brought on by a high electrical charge difference in a neutral fluid, usually air. It takes place when the potential is large enough to trigger the ionization of the insulating fluid but not sufficient to generate an electric arch (lightning). If ionized, the fluid becomes plasma and passes charge completing the circuit once the electric charge carried by the ions slowly reaches the ground. Corona discharge produces light, UV rays, local heating, ozone, and noise.

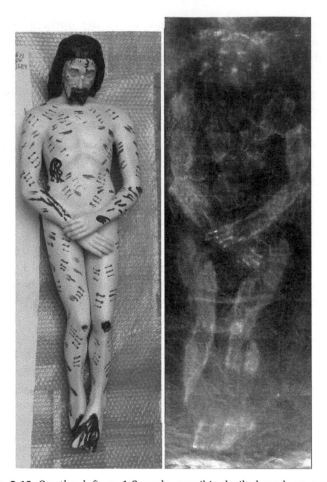

Figure 2.10 On the left, a 1:2 scale manikin built based on numeric experimental studies on the Shroud. On the right, the negative frontal body image obtained from a Shroud-like sheet wrapping a similar manikin covered with conductive paint and putting through a 300,000 V electric field. The negative pole has been, in this case, directly connected to the manikin foot. The ground consisted of a plate about 1 m (3 ft) over the manikin. Corona discharge happened in correspondence with the linen sheet.

Different kinds of sources of radiations have been proposed: For example, Rinaudo experimented on the effects of nuclear radiation (referring to the Resurrection described in the Gospels). According to Lindner, the image formed after electron radiation coming from the surface of the human body. He stated that the electrons and neutrons released during the "singularity" of the Resurrection must have interacted with Jesus' Shroud, and this happened according to nuclear physics and chemical laws. The American scholar A. Adler [1996], backing the image formation as a cause of the corona discharge, supposed the presence of a ball lightning in the sepulcher, referring to a one-of-a-kind phenomenon. According to the author [Fanti, 2010], corona discharge is the best hypothesis to explain several peculiar features of the Shroud image, see Fig. 2.10, but it is not sufficient to explain all we see in the Relic. Other factors, probably connected with the body fluids and the spices used during the burial, could have produced the so-called "photographic emulsion" that worked as "substrate" for the hypothesized "Divine Photography" [Fanti and Malfi, 2020].

The hypothesis of corona discharge triggered by an intense electric field seems to be the most reliable explanation because it produces characteristics that are close to the peculiar features of the Shroud. Nevertheless, the issue of how the image was formed is still unsolved and here the limit of science is reached. If, to explain the body image of the Shroud, we refer to an extremely unusual phenomenon, such as a miracle (like, for example, the Holy Fire [Fanti, 2019]), we would go beyond the realm of science.

2.3 The Blood Marks

While the body image is similar to a photographic negative, the blood stains are photopositive (Fig. 2.11) as they formed through direct contact with the corpse. UV fluorescence photographs show a pale aura of serum around these stains.

The human blood marks match with the position of the wounds on the body, taking into consideration the drapery of the cloth wrapping the corpse. Many of these blood and serum stains are difficult to be reproduced artificially, because this blood first coagulated on a wound in the skin and then dissolved again by fibrinolysis[f] after contact with the moist cloth [Malantrucco, 1992; Brillante et al., 2002].

---

[f]Fibrinolysis is a process that counterbalances blood coagulation and is in dynamic balance with it. Fibrinolysis breaks down fibrin and contrasts the platelet plug formation.

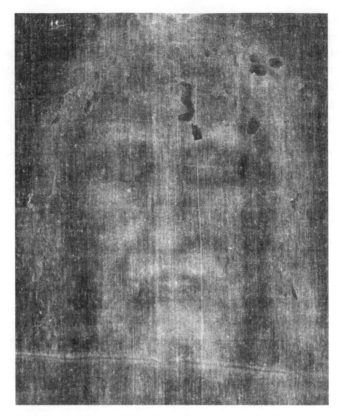

Figure 2.11 Face of Jesus of the Shroud: the image is photonegative; the red blood marks are photopositive.

The following description of the blood marks proves useful for the recognition of Jesus. According to the hypothesis (a sure fact, even if out of science, in the opinion of the author) suggesting that this Man is Jesus Christ, a number of blood marks suit the description in the Gospels of the sufferings He underwent in His Passion[g].

---

[g]The Four Gospels describe the Passion, the Death, and the Resurrection of Jesus Christ. He, betrayed by his apostle, Jude, was arrested by Romans and condemned to flagellation by the prefect of the province of Judaea, Pontius Pilate, on the Good Friday probably in AD 30 or 33. Immediately after, the crowd asked and obtained from Pilate the condemnation to crucifixion. He, then, was forced to carry on his shoulder the heavy cross on the way to Calvary, immediately outside Jerusalem's walls. There, He was crucified with nails through His hands and feet, and he died shortly afterward. A Roman centurion, to verify Jesus' death, pierced his chest

On the Shroud, there are clots of many lacerated and contused wounds distributed all over the body (the author counted more than 370 [Fanti and Malfi, 2020]). It is probable that they were caused by the flagrum, the Roman whip confirming the account of the scourging ("... *after he had Jesus scourged, he handed him over to be crucified,*" [Mt 27,26])

The following blood marks are evident on the face. On the forehead, the scalp, and the back of the head are several point and round shaped stains that would result from wounds produced by a crown of thorns, confirming the account of a "coronation" ("*And the soldiers wove a crown out of thorns and placed it on his head,*" [Jn 19,2]).

On both sides of the forehead blood formed two rivulets that flowed downward. Between these flows is one in the shape like the Greek letter epsilon (ε) or a reversed "3," (Fig. 2.11). According to the opinion of some physicians, it is consistent with the blood crossing the forehead wrinkles caused by frowning under intense stress [Barbet, 1953; Rodante, 1994] or, according to others, caused by a blunt object [Picciocchi and Picciocchi, 1979].

Some blood marks on the area of the hair could correspond to the cheek zone, if we consider that the Shroud wrapped the face during the blood mark formation, whereas it took a flatter configuration during the image formation [Lavoie, 2000].

Other blood stains are the following. Serious injuries associated with nail punctures are on the left wrist and on the feet. On the left forearm there is evidence of slight blood flow trailing down the elbow; on the right forearm a similar blood flow can be distinguished, probably related to a wrist injury (covered by the left hand) like that on the left forearm.

On the right side of the chest[h], a large oval wound can be seen. It can be deduced that it has been produced with a lance tip, which confirms the account that the Roman centurion verified in that way that Jesus was actually dead by crucifixion ("... *one*

---

with a lance. "Blood and water" came out from the chest, that is, blood and serum, which appears transparent like water. He was deposed in a sepulcher near Calvary in the evening of Good Friday, and there He remained until the following Sunday, when He rose from the dead, reappearing alive to many people.

[h]Remember that on the Shroud imprint, it is the left side, since the image is right-to-left reversed.

soldier thrust his lance into his side, and immediately blood and water flowed out," [Jn 19,34]). As typical of corpses, the chest wound margins remained enlarged and well outlined: the injury must have happened postmortem.

Another wound is the so-called blood belt, referring to the blood flow across the lower part of the man's back on the dorsal image. A number of scholars [Barbet, 1953, 1963; Vignon, 1938] associate this blood flow with blood running down from the chest wound while the body was on the cross.

This issue has been called into question [Fanti and Malfi, 2020], and some researchers [Zugibe, 2005] think that the blood flow on the dorsal image occurred when the corpse was laying down in the sepulcher.

In moving the body to put it down on the bench in the tomb, the position of some limbs could have changed, causing the runoff of some blood that was not coagulated yet. In this perspective, the blood belt formation is explained as due to the blood flow that occurred after the body was moved. Experiments, carried out by the author too, highlighted that this blood flow could come from the forearms, which would have dripped from the elbows. According to another explanation, this blood flow could be caused by a serious injury in the kidney area. On the Shroud, because of its peculiar wrapping, these kinds of injuries cannot be seen, but Jesus Christ could have been seriously injured in the kidneys during the heavy scourging He underwent.

2.4 A Long Journey

The journey of the Shroud is not easy to retrace during all of its 2000-year history. In fact, whereas it is relatively simple to find documents related to the Shroud's exhibition, travels, and preservation in the centuries closer to the present, it is obviously more difficult to trace it back to the remote past, when documents are rarer and reliable information and legends are difficult to distinguish.

This chapter begins with a brief description of this darker period related to its first centuries, beginning with the Resurrection of Christ. It then proceeds with sections focusing on the periods of interest for this book, in particular the Byzantine era, and it ends with a report of the most important events during the last seven centuries after the Sac of Constantinople in 1204.

2.4.1 Traces from the Remote Past

According to the Canonic Gospels, it was probably on Friday, April 3, in the year AD 33 or, according to someone, on Friday, April 7, in the year AD 30, Jesus' corpse was wrapped in a clean white linen, the Shroud. John the Apostle, who supervised Jesus' burial, reports that the Shroud, a sudarium, and the spices were used for the burial. On Easter morning this linen sheet was found empty by Him and he *"saw and believed"* [Jn 20: 8-9] in the Resurrection of Christ.

The apocryphal gospels talk about the burial cloths of Jesus; Jerome reports[i] a passage written in the Gospel of the Hebrews (second century) stating that Jesus gave a linen cloth to the servant of the priest preceding his appearance to James.

During the early centuries after Christ, direct references related to the Shroud are fragmentary and often history merges with legends. An interesting one is related to the Mandylion—a cloth on which the face of Jesus was reproduced. The image was considered *Acheropoietos*, that is "not made by human hand." A legend reports that King Abgar of Edessa asked Jesus to come and cure him of an illness. Jesus declined the invitation, but promised a future visit by his disciple Thaddeus of Edessa who went bearing the words of Jesus and the Mandylion that miraculously healed the king.

In the beginning of the history of the Church, Jesus' burial sheet was probably kept hidden for several reasons. First, it was a very precious "memory," having wrapped the One who sacrificed Himself on the Cross. Furthermore, Christians feared that someone could seize and destroy it: the Hebrews, in compliance with Mosaic Law, considered everything that had touched a corpse as impure.

---

[i]*De Viris Illustribus* (*On Illustrious Men*) is a collection of short biographies of characters of the New Testament and of the early centuries of Christianity, written in Latin by Eusebius Sophronius Hieronymus (Saint Jerome). He completed his work in Bethlehem around 392–393.

Nino, who evangelized Georgia under the Constantine Empire (306–337), inquired after the Shroud to Christian scholars of Jerusalem. He learned that the burial cloths had been for some time in possession of Pilate's wife, and after, Luke the evangelist stored them in a safe place known only to himself.

2.4.2   The Mandylion-Shroud

The weekly exhibition of the Shroud during its stay in Constantinople [Fanti and Furlan, 2019] is attested by the testimony of the crusader knight Robert de Clary, chronicler of the 4th Crusade [Dufournet, 2004]. He wrote about the wonders that could be seen before the fall of the city (April 12, 1204): *"Among these there was a church called St. Mary of the Blachernae, where the Shroud (Sydoines) was kept in which Our Lord was wrapped. Every Friday it was elevated all straight, so that it was possible to easily see the image of Our Lord."* [Savio, 1957, 1965].

Many historians [Antonacci, 2016; Guscin, 2009; Wilson, 2010; Zaninotto, 2002], by identifying the Shroud as the Mandylion, believe the Relic was in Edessa (currently named Sanliurfa in Turkey), in the early centuries and was in Constantinople until it fell in 1204. Others think that the Shroud and the Mandylion are two different relics and report that the Mandylion appeared in France where it remained in the Imperial Treasure until 1238 when Baldwin sent it to Louis IX. Nevertheless, they do not specify if the "Mandylion" in question was the original one or a copy. The author agrees with the hypothesis sustained by many historians [Guscin, 2009; Wilson, 2010] for the following reasons and therefore names it the Mandylion-Shroud:

- like the Shroud, the Mandylion showed not only the face but the full body;
- the Mandylion was also called tetradiplon which means doubly folded four times; when folding the Shroud eight times, only a face is visible like in the description of the Mandylion;
- like the Shroud, the Mandylion showed imprints of sweat and blood.

The Mandylion-Shroud or Edessa Image [Caccese et al., 2017] belonged in the first centuries to the Orthodox/Melkite Church. During festivities, the cloth was pulled out of a golden casket and venerated.

In the sixth century, in Edessa there existed an image of Christ, created by God. A tenth-century codex, named Codex Vossianus Latinus Q69 [Zaninotto, 1988] contains an eighth century account, coming from the Syriac area and translated by Smira archiater, saying that an imprint of Christ's whole body was left on a canvas kept in the cathedral of Saint Sophie at Edessa. The Codex Vossianus [Zaninotto, 1995] reports that it was in Mesopotamia of Syria. In the Second Council of Nicaea (787) there are various talks about the Image of Edessa, not produced by the hands of man.

2.4.3 The Constantinople Period

In the Narratio de Imagine Edessena [Guscin, 2009], attributed to Constantine VII Porphyrogenitus, Emperor of Constantinople from 912 to 959, we read that Abgar gave the order to destroy the statue of a pagan deity that was above the city door and replaced it with the Image of Edessa *"fixed to a wooden board and adorned with gold ...."*

Byzantine Emperor Romanus I Lecapenus, in 943, wanted to take possession of the Mandylion-Shroud and sent the army under the command of Armenian General Ioannis Curcuas. Some Islamic sources [Boubakeur, 1992] report both the permanence of the image in Edessa and the bargaining to give it to Byzantium, as well as how to transfer it to Constantinople. To receive the Relic with great honor, the emperor sent dignitaries bringing candles decorated with gold in their hands. The image was extracted from the reliquary and was venerated with great devotion [Guscin, 2009]. The Mandylion-Shroud came to Constantinople on the evening of August 15, 944 and it was placed in the upper chapel of the church of St. Mary of Blachernae.

The image did not have the characteristics of a well-recognizable painting, but of an ethereal imprint [Zaninotto, 1995]. The reliquary that contained the Mandylion-Shroud could have been opened during its long stay in Constantinople. The disclosure of the folded

Relic, also called Rakos Tetrádiplon, is confirmed by John Jackson who noticed on the Shroud the existence of folds consistent with the use of a mechanism used to lift the Mandylion-Shroud, so that the entire frontal figure was progressively visible [Jackson et al., 2000]. The existence of machinery and mechanical devices in the city of Constantinople is known [Brubaker, 2016]. Such a device could have been used to exhibit the Mandylion-Shroud to the faithful.

The Relic was then placed in the Sacred Imperial Palace in one of the main rooms for exhibition, called the Chrysotriklinos (literally "golden bed"). Machines were used to lift the throne of the Emperor. The scenery surrounding every emperor's public appearance was made even more impressive by the use of gold covered mechanical devices that were moved by hydraulic pumps. Perhaps such a mechanism was also used to impressively display the Mandylion-Shroud. Wilson [2010] argues that a possible exhibition of it, raised from a reliquary, can be inferred from the presence of a miniature in a Georgian manuscript of 1054 where it is possible to see a golden drape raised from a reliquary and on it, the Mandylion-Shroud decorated with red crosses.

A confirmation is given by the image painted by John Skylitzes[j] in his homonymous codex in which is depicted the arrival of the Relic in Constantinople in 944 (Fig. 2.12).

In Constantinople, the Mandylion-Shroud was probably opened and folded in four layers, showing not only the face but also part of the chest. Hence the birth, during the twelfth century, of *Imago Pietatis*[k] (Fig. 2.13), the representation of dead Christ at half-length protruding from its box bolt upright with crossed hands [Coppini and Cavazzuti, 2000, Pfeiffer, 1986].

Among the historical information of the Relic in Constantinople is that of Louis VII, King of France, during his visit, who venerated it in 1147 and that in 1171. Manuel I Comnenus showed to Amalric, King of Jerusalem, the relics of the Passion, among them, the Mandylion-Shroud.

---

[j]Biblioteca Nacional de Madrid (codex 26,2), the page came from a copy of the Chronicles of John Skylitzes, a Byzantine historian who lived under the reign of Alexius I Comnenius (1081–1118).

[k]Image of Pity, the representation of pity.

Figure 2.12 The arrival of the Shroud to Constantinople in AD 944 (Madrid Skylitzes, Biblioteca Nacional de Madrid).

Figure 2.13 Nineteenth century Russian icon of *Imago Pietatis* covered with metal riza.

A speech ascribed to Constantine VII Porphyrogenitus [Loconsole, 1999], Byzantine Emperor from 912 to 959 and an expert at painting, gives information about the Mandylion-Shroud, suggesting a new explanation of the image due to "a *liquid secretion*" without colors or paint[l].

In support of the identification of the Image of Edessa with the Shroud, Gino Zaninotto [1988] found in the Vatican Archive Codex Vatican Graecus 511 (tenth century) a report declaring that an image of Christ was brought from Edessa in 944[m]. This codex lists the colors used for drawing icon's faces[n] and states that the image has not been reproduced with artificial colors, as it is only "*reflection.*" Gregory explains the image as follows. "*This reflection, however—let everyone be inspired with the explanation—has been imprinted only by the sweat from the face of the originator of life, falling like drops of blood, and by the finger of God. For these are the beauties that have made up the true imprint of Christ, since after the drops fell, it was embellished by drops from his own side. Both are highly instructive—blood and water there, here sweat and image. Oh equality of happenings, since both have their origin in the same person.*"

Zaninotto underlines the unexpected element in this work: the detail of the side wound is senseless since the tradition sets the image formation after the crucifixion. The Image of Edessa, actually, did not depict only a face but also part of the breast at least up to the chest. By consequence we can observe that the image described by Gregory the Referendarius is the Relic and not a common depiction of Christ, otherwise the side wound detail would have no reason to be mentioned.

---

[l]How the form of a face could be imparted onto the linen cloth from a moist secretion with no paint or artistic craft, and how something made from such a perishable material was not destroyed with time and whatever else the supposed investigator of natural causes is wont to enquire into with curiosity: these questions he should yield to God's inscrutable wisdom.

[m]This is the text: "*A sermon by Gregory the Archdeacon and Referendarius of the great church at Constantinople, about how incredible things are not subject to the laws of praise, and about how three patriarchs have declared that there is an image of Christ which was brought from Edessa 919 years afterwards by the zeal of a pious emperor [Romanus I Lecapenus], in the year 6452 [AD 944]. Lord bless us.*" Translation from Greek by Marc Guscin of [*The Sermon of Gregory Referendarius*, 2004].

[n]It shows a sufficient knowledge of painting art and a discrete ability in discovering a potential fake.

2.4.4   After the Fall of Constantinople

In 1204, Robert de Clary, chronicler of the Fourth Crusade, writes in his work *La conquete de Constantinople* that before the fall of Constantinople (April 14, 1204), a Sydoine (the Mandylion-Shroud) was exhibited every Friday and on that cloth, the figure of Christ was clearly visible, but nobody knows what happened to the Relic after the conquest of the city. Some hints indicate that the Mandylion-Shroud was brought to Europe and perhaps kept by the Templars for one and a half centuries. Some clues indicate that before it was exhibited in Europe it passed through Greece. In France, in 1307, the Templars were persecuted and arrested by Philip the Handsome, who confiscated all their wealth.

The face venerated by the Templars (Fig. 2.14) has similarities with the face of the Mandylion-Shroud: it is a bearded face with blurred outlines. It is painted on an oak table, dated between the twelfth and fourteenth centuries.

Figure 2.14 The face venerated by the Templars, Templecombe (England), twelfth to fourteenth century [Wilson, 2010].

To sum up, referring to Fig. 2.15, the most reliable historical route of the Mandylion-Shroud is the following.

- From year AD 30 or 33 the Mandylion-Shroud was in Jerusalem in the Holy Sepulcher.

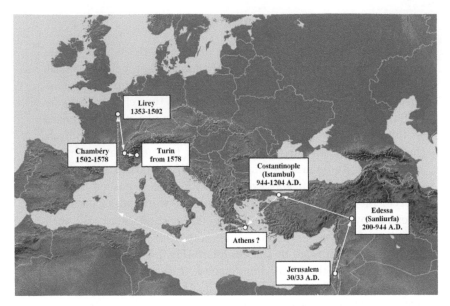

Figure 2.15 Presumable historical route of the Shroud during the centuries.

- Between approximately AD 200 and 944 it was exhibited several times and hidden for decades in the city walls of Edessa.
- From 944 to 1204 it was exhibited in Constantinople but after its fall it was brought to Europe.
- It was shown in Lirey, France, in 1353.
- It was in Chambery, France, in 1502.
- In 1578, it was brought to Turin, Italy, where it remains today.

2.4.5 Documents from the Recent Past

Thanks to a dispute that happened in the second half of the fourteenth century between Geoffroy de Charney who owned the Shroud, the canons of Lirey, Pierre d'Arcis, Bishop of Troyes, King Charles VI, and Antipope Clement VII, we have the first recognized historical documents related to the Shroud.

In 1389, the Bishop Pierre d'Arcis stated that the Shroud had been publicly displayed around 1355. In this letter the Bishop, irritated by the pilgrim's defection from Troyes because of their interest in the Shroud, wrote a long letter to Antipope Clement VII, in which he claimed that experts assured him that the Shroud of Lirey could not be authentic. This is because, if an image had been visible on Jesus' burial cloth, the Gospels would have certainly mentioned it[o].

He also claimed that a man had confessed to painting it. However, the bishop did not have documents or evidence corroborating his claims. In his defense, de Charney complained to the antipope about the bishop's behavior. Clement VII, fed up with the controversy, on January 6, 1390, issued a Bull and two additional letters discussing the Shroud. In these documents, he authorized the Shroud display and forbade any opposition by d'Arcis.

It is meaningful that the expression "*pictura seu tabula*" (painted table) written in the January 6, 1390, Bull was replaced with the phrase "*figura seu rapresentacio*" (figure or representation) because the term "paint" implicitly refers to something produced by an artist, while the terms "figure" or "image" are open to the possibility of something supernatural.

This documentation certifies that the Shroud was in France in the second half of the fourteenth century, but there was no other mention about the Shroud until 1418. On that date, Count Humbert de La Roche issued a receipt to the canons of Lirey listing the Shroud among the relics he took to Calabria (a region in Southern Italy) for safekeeping because of the disorders happening in the region of Lirey. He, married with Marguerite, granddaughter of de Charney, became Lord of Lirey. He died without returning the relics, among which was "*a cloth, on which is a figure or representation of the Shroud of our Lord Jesus Christ.*"

When the canons wanted to have their goods back from the widow Marguerite, they had to fight through the court. Marguerite handed the Shroud over to Anna of Lusignano-Chatillon (also known as Anna of Cyprus), wife of Louis, Duke of Savoy, on March 22, 1453. In 1502, Philibert II stored the Relic in Saint Chapelle of Chambéry castle. In Fig. 2.16 we see a rare lead medal discovered in France showing a Shroud exhibition performed

---

[o]It is likely that the Gospels did not mention the two body images on the Shroud because they were not visible at that time. Based on the hypothesis that the image was formed by an intense electric field (called a corona discharge), experiments indicate that the image would have become visible over a period of months to years. As a result, the Evangelists may have seen only the blood marks but not the image on the Shroud.

during these centuries. Contrary to the recent centuries, we see only half Shroud exposed and supported by three bishops.

Figure 2.16 Exhibition of the Shroud on a rare lead medal discovered in France datable from the fourteenth to the eighteenth century on the obverse; a faithful prays kneeling in front of the Cross on the reverse. On the top, for comparison, an embroided fabric of the eighteenth century showing a similar exhibition.

In 1506 Pope Julius II granted a specific liturgy for the Shroud [Garello, 1984] on May 4[p], with its proper Mass and office. From then on, the Relic, except for short pauses imposed by events, stayed in Chambéry until 1578, when Saint Charles Borromeo, archbishop of Milan, wanted to make a pilgrimage to Chambéry to venerate the Shroud in fulfillment of a vow. To spare him the rigorous trip over the Alps, Emmanuel Filbert, Duke of Savoy, brought the Holy Linen to Turin.

During the night of December 3–4, 1532, a fire burned the Saint Chapelle and seriously damaged the Holy Linen. Two years later, the Poor Clare nuns repaired the Sheet by sewing on about 30 patches and attached a linen cloth called the "Holland cloth" to the entire back of the Shroud for support.

On June 1, 1694, the Shroud was placed in the chapel built by the architect Guarino Guarini, adjacent to the Turin Cathedral and was exhibited to the public in various occasions (Fig. 2.17). That year, Blessed Sebastian Valfré strengthened its patches. From then on, no other restoration was undertaken until 2002,

[p]It is noteworthy that Pope Julius II approved not only the veneration of the Relic, but also its adoration. This was done because it contains Jesus' blood, thus part of the body of Jesus Christ.

when all the sixteenth-century patches were removed and the supporting Holland cloth was replaced. The Shroud is now kept in the Turin Cathedral in a reliquary (Fig. 2.18).

The first photograph taken by Secondo Pia in 1898 (Fig. 2.19) provoked an intense development of scientific research that continued up to now. The detailed photographs allowed scientists to carry out their studies in their own laboratories instead of being forced to observe the Shroud directly.

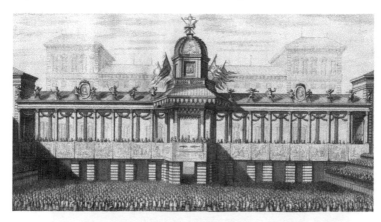

Figure 2.17 The Shroud during the exhibition of 1722 on the stage built in front of Palazzo Madama in occasion of the wedding between Carlo Emanuele III of Savoy with the princess Anna Cristina Sulzbach.

Figure 2.18 The Shroud in its present reliquary. On the removable fabric that covers the case, the traditional prayer: TUAM SINDONEM VENERAMUR, DOMINE ET TUA RECOLIMUS PASSIONEM (We revere Your Shroud, Lord, and [through it] we meditate on Your Passion) (Archdiocese of Turin).

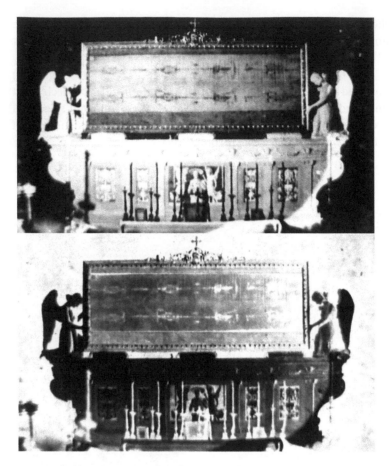

Figure 2.19 The first photos of the Shroud were taken in 1898 by Secondo Pia who highlighted the negativity of the image. Below, the negative photo better highlights the features of the human figure imprinted in the Relic.

On October 8, 1978, scientists from the STuRP team[q] spent 120 continuous hours conducting photography and experiments

---

[q]The STuRP (Shroud of Turin Research Project) team (www.shroud.com/78team. htm) officially composed of 33 American researchers, carried out in a methodical and detailed way various analyses on the Shroud, opening wide study and research opportunities in several scientific fields. The main purpose of this research was summarized in the following three questions: What is the Shroud body image composed of? How was the image produced? Is there blood on the Shroud? Different hypotheses about the body image formation have been articulated, but it was observed that hypotheses reliable from the chemical point of view were unreliable from the physical point of view and vice versa [Fanti and Malfi, 2020].

on the Shroud in order to accomplish a multidisciplinary scientific investigation. From these studies came out an official report in 1981, in which it has assumed that the Shroud wrapped the corpse of a man and that the body image was formed on the Relic in a way that is still unknown to science [Schwalbe and Rogers, 1982; Jumper et al., 1984].

A great number of scientific analyses have been done on the Shroud. Most of them are discussed in a private internet group called the Shroud-Science Group. The many scientific conferences and symposia on this theme, which cannot be listed in a few pages, show the current great interest of scholars in the Relic.

2.5   Dating the Shroud

The scientific research carried out up to now on the Shroud gives strong indication that the Shroud wrapped the corpse of Jesus, but the radiocarbon test performed in 1988 diverted the scientists from the way of scientifically proving what the Gospels ask to accept by faith. This section describes this test, explaining why these results are not statistically and scientifically reliable. Consequently, other alternative dating methods are therefore presented with the relative results thus arriving to determine an age of the Relic.

2.5.1   The 1988 Radiocarbon Dating

A strip 81 mm × 21 mm (3.19 in. × 0.83 in.) weighing 447.5 mg (0.01579 oz.) was cut from the Shroud in 1988 and radiocarbon dated [Salatino and Dubini, 2005]. About a half of it was taken by the Arcidiocesi of Turin for further analysis; the other half, was divided into three parts and given to the laboratory at the University of Oxford, to the Federal Institute of Technology in Zurich and to the Tucson Laboratory of the University of Arizona.

The samples were burned; the ratio between isotopes C14 and C12 in each linen sample was calculated and compared with previously determined plot in which an age corresponds to the calculated ratio. The outcome had been announced officially, by the director of the Vatican Press Office, M. D. Joaquin Navarro Valls, on October 12, 1988 stating, *"The calibrated calendar age range assigned to the Shroud cloth with 95% confidence level is from*

1260 to 1390 AD, ... [but] at the same time, the problems about the origin of the image still remain ... unsolved and will require further research and study. ..." The unexpected result is contradictory to all other scientific evidence in favor of the authenticity already discovered.

Someone observed that the Shroud is not the only fabric that could be contaminated by external environmental effects. For example, the radiocarbon dating of Egyptian mummy n. 1770 kept in the Manchester Museum [David, 1978] provided different ages for the bones and the bandages; these last, were 800–1000 years "younger" than the bones. Therefore if the radiocarbon dates were trustworthy, it would lead to the absurd conclusion that the corpse would have been wrapped in the bandages 800–1000 years after his death!

Statistical calculations of the radiocarbon results published by Nature [Damon et al., 1988] were checked, and serious mistakes were found. For example, engineer Ernesto Brunati [1997], observed that the statistical parameter of the significance level, published is not 5% but 4.17%; therefore the results should not have been combined with each other but carefully reexamined.

According to Remi Van Haelst [2000], the correct conclusion, which should replace the existing one [Damon et al., 1988], should be that the results yield a calibrated date with a significance level of only 1.2%. These results therefore furnish the conclusive evidence that the samples used by the three labs are not omogeneous[r] in C-14 content, so that the dates in [Damon et al., 1988] should not be trusted to be the true dates of the Shroud."

---

[r]In statistics, the independent *t*-test, also called the two-sample *t*-test for homogeneity, can be used to draw a conclusion about whether two unrelated populations, such as two independent sets of measurements, have a statistically significant difference between their means. The null hypothesis (what is assumed to be true) for the independent test is that the population means for the two unrelated groups are equal. In most cases, we are attempting to determine whether we can reject the null hypothesis and accept the alternative hypothesis, which is that the population means are not equal. To do this, we need to set a significance level that allows us to either reject or accept the alternative hypothesis. Most commonly, the acceptance criterion is a significance level of 0.05. In the present case for the 1988 carbon dating of the Shroud, since the significance level of 0.012 is less than the acceptance criterion of 0.05, we conclude that the radiocarbon dates measured by the laboratories for the three samples have statistically significant differences between their means. Thus, the three samples cannot be representative of the entire Shroud, so the average of the dates for the three samples can be significantly different from the date for the Shroud.

A group of professors of statistics headed by M. Riani, more recently demonstrated that the 1988 radiocarbon dating result is not reliable but rather is scientifically meaningless [Riani et al., 2013]. This statistical analysis shows a clear heterogeneity of the Shroud samples tested in 1988.

According to Bob Rucker [2020], *"the fact that the samples are heterogeneous indicates they are basically different from each other in their date, which should not be the case since they were cut from next to each other on the Shroud. Something strange is going on as though an unidentified factor, such as contamination, invisible reweave, or neutron absorption, was affecting the measurements to produce a systematic error in the measurements. This factor could change the dates of all the samples by an unknown amount, so that the only thing that can be done is to reject the conclusion that 1260–1390 is the true date of the Shroud. Thus, the dates published in Nature* [Damon, et al., 1988] *tell us nothing about the true date of the Shroud."*

2.5.2   Alternative Dating Methods

If you declare that the radiocarbon dating method is not applicable to a certain historical sample, you should indicate an alternative. After proper preliminary studies, two chemical methods based on vibrational spectroscopy and a mechanical multi-parametric method have been developed.

Some photochemical properties of the cellulose contained in flax fibers can be highlighted through the so-called vibrational spectroscopy based on FTIR (Fourier Transform Infra-Red) and Raman analysis, which use a laser beam to excite the various energy levels of the molecules present in the sample under examination.

In the flax fibers, which are mainly made of polysaccharides, cellulose is the main component. These components of the fibers deteriorate over time, thus modifying their chemical structure. FTIR and Raman spectroscopy allow analysis of the chemical substances present as the flax fibers age.

To understand what spectroscopy is, we can refer to a well-known example: the rainbow visible in the sky when the sun appears when raining. Sunlight passing through raindrops separates into different colors of light to form the rainbow that is characterized by seven colors, from red to violet. In physics, it is called the visible spectrum. A spectrometer such as FTIR works in a similar way, but the spectrum shows characteristic peaks of the chemical substances present in the tested material.

Professors Pietro Baraldi of the Modena University and Anna Tinti of Bologna University (Italy) carried out a study with the author [Fanti et al., 2013] on the samples of the Shroud. After correction of the FTIR result by 452 years due to exposure of the Shroud to the Chambéry fire, the FTIR analysis indicates an age of 300 BC ± 400 years at a confidence level of 95%.

The same authors performed a Raman analysis on the same samples. In this experiment, a laser beam either can pass through a sample or can be absorbed by it. In the latter case, part of the beam is scattered and the amplitudes of the different wavelengths of the beam are reported in Raman spectra. These amplitudes can be related to the chemical composition of the sample in question. These tests, which are focused on the molecular groups C–O–C and C–OH, furnished the Raman dating of the Shroud as 200 BC ± 500 years with a 95% confidence level.

A mechanical dating method [Fanti and Malfi, 2014] was performed at Padua University (Italy). This involved designing and calibrating, with engineer Pierandrea Malfi, a new machine for tensile tests on single textile fibers, see Fig. 2.20.

The following mechanical parameters have been measured for each single flax fiber: breaking strength, final elastic modulus, decreasing elastic modulus, loss factor, and inverse cycle loss factor. The multi-parametric mechanical method gave an age of the Shroud of AD 372±400 that was rounded to AD 400±400 years with a 95% confidence level [Fanti et al., 2015].

2.5.3 The Age of the Shroud

The unreliability of the radiocarbon dating carried out in 1988 which wrongly furnished an age from 1260 AD and 1390 AD, has been experimentally demonstrated by several alternative dating methods: two chemical, FTIR and Raman, based on vibrational spectroscopy, a multi-parametric mechanical method and a numismatic dating method.

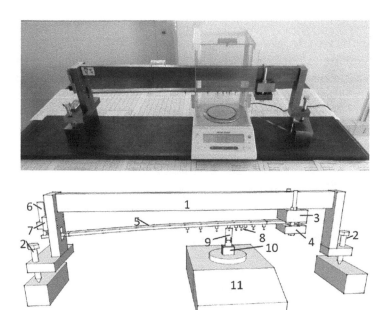

Figure 2.20 Photo (above) and sketch of the micro-cycling machine: (1) frame horizontally regulated by screws (2); (3) and (4) clamping blocks for the displacement reducer cantilever beam (5); (6) micrometer screw gauge, mounted on a coupling plate (7), which moves the beam (5). To one of the hooks (8) a polyester mask (9) is hung, indicating the fiber under test. The lower part of the mask is glued with two iron blocks (10) that lie on the plate of the analytical balance (11).

The FTIR vibrational spectroscopy determined an age for the Shroud of 300 BC ±400 years (after correction by +452 years to account for the Chambéry fire); the dating of the Relic from Raman vibrational analysis resulted in 200 BC ±500 years, the mechanical dating led to an age for the Relic of AD 400 ± 400 years. For all these three methods the uncertainty was evaluated at a confidence level of 95%.

The numismatic analysis that will be presented in the following chapters will show that the Shroud has been in existence at least since 692 AD.

The mean of the values from the two chemical dating methods and the mechanical method indicate that the most likely date of the Shroud is 33 BC ± 250 years with a confidence level of 95%. The lower uncertainty assigned to the final result comes from directly applying the statistical rules recommended by the current international standard [BIPM, 2008].

We should observe in Fig. 2.21 that there is a common time interval among these dating methods, which is precisely the first century AD. Hence, the final result is compatible with the era in which Jesus of Nazareth lived in Palestine.

The following chapters will evaluate the many correlations evident between the body image shown on the Shroud and the representation of Jesus Christ in both Byzantine coins and ancient icons.

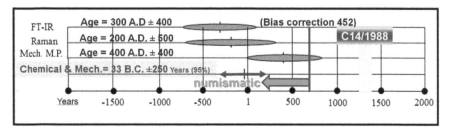

Figure 2.21 Age of the Shroud based on three types of analysis: Raman, FT-IR and mechanical methods. The combined date from the three results is 33 BC ± 250 years at a confidence level of 95%. This date is consistent with a numismatic analysis that indicates a period before 692, but contradicts the 1988 radiocarbon dating of the Shroud in the range from 1260 to 1390.

2.6 Author's Opinion

Outside of science, there is another aspect to consider. There are many indications in favor of the hypothesis that the Man of the Shroud is Jesus Christ, and none against it, but there is no certain evidence. Usually, when you study something deeply enough, some kind of proof comes out. Why is there no (indisputable) evidence in our case? The author considers this fact the best demonstration that the image of the Shroud comes from God. God proposes Himself but does not impose Himself; therefore everyone can decide according to their own free will. There are many clues in favor of the hypothesis that the Man of the Shroud is Jesus Christ, but in the end everyone is required to take the last step alone.

Chapter 3

Images of Christ in the Byzantine Age

In the previous chapters, a description of the Byzantine coinage showed the image of Jesus Christ along with a description of the Shroud of Christ that seemed related to the coins. Chapter 3 will consider in detail Christ's images during the Byzantine age in order to better understand the relationship between Byzantine coins and the Shroud.

This chapter is subdivided into four logically subsequent sections. The first section describes the kind of clothing in use at the time of Christ and in the Byzantine Empire.

The second one refers to the clothes of Jesus Christ shown on coins, mosaics, icons and ivories of the Byzantine age, coming to formulate new hypotheses on the influence of the Shroud on these clothes.

The third section discusses the development of ancient depictions of Jesus Christ at the light of the discovery of the Shroud.

The fourth section finally explores the images of Christ on Byzantine coins.

After investigating these four topics, the reader will be able to better understand the images of Christ reproduced on the Byzantine coins. These images (especially those of gold) are reliable and full of meaning in all their detail because they were controlled by the ruling Emperor before their production.

Byzantine Coins Influenced by the Shroud of Christ
Giulio Fanti
Copyright © 2022 Jenny Stanford Publishing Pte. Ltd.
ISBN 978-981-4877-88-6 (Hardcover), 978-1-003-21992-7 (eBook)
www.jennystanford.com

The fourth section is important also because, while the paintings of that age are relatively rare, there are many coins that reproduce similar images which allow us to study them in terms of their reproducibility.

3.1 Clothes at the Time of Christ and in the Byzantine Period

It is important to have a look at the clothing used in the Byzantine period because it will help the reader understand the meaning of the image of Christ. In fact, we must remember that the Byzantine artists were strictly bound to predefined canons full of intrinsic meaning [Hetherington, 1981] that had always to be respected.

Identification of the various parts of clothing used in the time of Christ and in the Byzantine period is neither easy nor unanimous. Also, the relative terminology is not the same for all the authors for various reasons, among them is the frequent failure of numismatists to understand the items and how they were worn [Grierson and Hendy, 1993–99, Vol. 2 Part 1 p. 70].

When referring to Roman or Greek terms, similar clothing assumed different names too, as in the case of the *pallium* that can be confused with the *loros* and even with the *stole* of our days. In addition, the terms *toga, robe, trabea or trabes* and *tunic* are frequently used specifying similar dress.

Clothing changed through the centuries especially during the seventh century, which is the period of major interest in this book because it coincides with the first minting of Christ's image. One example, the *chlamys* replaced the *paludamentum,* then after a long period of disuse, reappeared as the *loros*, perhaps someway influenced by the Shroud. Another example is the misunderstanding evidenced by Grierson and Hendy [1993–99] of Wroth [1908] who confused the old *paludamentum* with the *chlamys* (a mantle) used in this century and the *scarf* with a *"robe of lozenge pattern."*

The following section will clarify the description of some clothing with their various names [Fashion Era 2003, world4.eu]. Due to the specific interest of this book, we will obviously focus attention on the dress typical of emperors and of high-ranking priests, but will not forget to mention other kinds of clothes used by women too.

3.1.1 Paludamentum

The paludamentum of the Roman republican age is the solemn uniform worn by the general on the battlefield or in public ceremonies. This type of robe was used during the Roman Empire, only by the general in chief. The shape of the paludamentum is similar to the Greek *chlamys*, a red or white and red cloak (mantle) to be kept on the armor, short, draped and fastened on the left shoulder, see Fig. 3.1.

Figure 3.1 Barberini Ivory on display at the Louvre, Paris. It is a Byzantine ivory of the beginning of the sixth century representing the emperor, probably Justinian I as triumphant victor wearing a *paludamentum*. Above, Christ (Syriac representation with curly hair and beardless) flanked by two angels.

3.1.2 Colobium

The *colobium* or Greek *kiton* (or *chiton*) also called *tunica* by Romans is a form of tunic undergarment made of wool (silk or cotton) that is simple, rectangular in shape, about three times the circumference of the person and hangs from the neck to the knee. It is folded in half lengthwise and held on each shoulder by a fibula (clasp). A small belt fastens it around the waist, see Figs. 3.2 and 3.16. The Roman *colobium* is sewn on both sides, in which it only has the opening for the arms, while behind it is still often combined with the fibulae. It is also called a *subucula*, *interula* or *tunica interior* and was often worn under the heavier *himation*. If used without a *himation* it was called a *monochiton*.

Figure 3.2 On the left, an example of a Roman *colobium*, and on the right the *colobium Sindonis* (Shroud tunic) of the seventeenth century, a sleeveless white linen shift typical of the British Monarchs.

Analogous with the Shroud[a], it is interesting to note the *colobium Sindonis* (Shroud tunic), a sleeveless white linen shift typical of the British Monarchs of the seventeenth century that symbolizes divesting oneself of all worldly vanity and standing bare before God, see Figs. 3.2 on the right.

3.1.3   Tunic

The *tunic* (Latin *tunica*) is generally a simple garment going from the shoulders to the hips and sometimes to the knees. It was the basic garment worn by both men and women in Ancient Greece and Rome and it was generally worn under a *toga*. Jesus Christ wore a red woolen tunic made without sewing, which is supposedly conserved at Argenteuil, France, see Fig. 3.3.

Figure 3.3 Tunic of Argenteuil, France, supposedly wore by Christ during His Passion (saintetunique.com).

---

[a]The Bible mentions "… *the Son of Man, clothed with a long robe* (ποδήρη, a garment reaching to the feet)." (Ap 1,13) and "*When the soldiers crucified Jesus, … This garment was seamless, woven in one piece from top to bottom* (χιτὼν ἄραφος, a seamless chiton, see also § 3.1.4 and 3.2.2)." (Jn 19,23).

3.1.4 Toga

The toga, the ancient *trabea* or *trabes*, was a woolen cloth like a robe, worn draped over the left shoulder and around the body and was a distinctive garment of Ancient Rome. It was usually worn over a *tunic*. By the fifth century, it had been replaced by the more practical *pallium* (see Section 3.1.10) and *paenula*.

The toga was considered formal wear reserved for Roman citizens and reflected a citizen's rank in the civil hierarchy. Therefore, there were different kinds, among which were the *toga virilis* (toga of manhood) worn on formal occasions by adult males; the *toga praetexta* (hemmed toga), a white toga with a broad purple stripe on its border for magistrates, kings and pontifices; the *toga candida* (bright toga) worn by candidates for public office; the *toga pulla* (dark toga) used at funerals; the *toga picta* (painted toga) worn by consuls and emperors. For example, the *toga praetexta*, a white toga with a broad purple stripe on its border was worn over a tunic and it was the formal costume for some magistrates, see Fig. 3.4.

Figure 3.4 Example of *toga preatexta*.

Similar dress is the *laena*, a long, heavy cloak worn by priests and the *trabea*, a toga or mantle associated with citizens of equestrian rank. The *trabea triumphalis* (a purple toga embroidered with gold), worn typically by consuls, developed into the *loros* worn by the imperial family at the end of the seventh century when the title of consul had been abolished. At the beginning of the Byzantine Empire the Roman *toga* was still used in formal ceremonies, but in the seventh century it was replaced by the *tunica*, or long *chiton*.

3.1.5 Himation and Pallium

The *himation* among the Ancient Greeks from 750 BC continued into the Byzantine era and was the equivalent dress of the *pallium* (see Section 3.1.10) among the Ancient Romans. The *himation*, see Fig. 3.5, is the classic mantle worn only by adult males and females who put it above the *chiton*, which enveloped the whole person.

Figure 3.5 On the left, example of *himation*. On the right, example of a Roman *pallium*.

It was generally laid on the left shoulder so that one end fell in front, right under the calf, while the remaining part passed behind and then above or below the right arm, returning again to the left shoulder. It was different from the *chlamys*, in that it did not require being fixed by a fibula. Unlike a modern cloak, which is cut according to a given model, sewn and stopped with buttons, the *himation* was only a draped cloak.

It is very interesting to observe here that the *himation* consisted of a large rectangular sheet, about four meters (13 ft.) long by one and a half (5 ft.) wide [Battistini, 2020]. The Shroud is rectangular and just 4.36 m (14.3 ft.) long by 1.1 m (3.6 ft.) wide. It is easy to think that a Byzantine artist who was depicting Jesus Christ coming out of the sepulcher with His clothes considered representing Him wrapped in the Shroud dress like a *himation*. The *pallium* also consisted of a rectangular-shaped cloth that developed from the *toga* in the fourth century. It was simpler than the toga and was worn over the *tunic* or *chiton*, see Fig. 3.5. It was usually made of wool or flax; frequently it was white or reddish purple but other colors have been found.

3.1.6 Chlamys or Cloak

The *chlamys* is an ancient Greek cloak, a type of loose garment worn over indoor clothing, generally fastened at the neck or over the shoulder, see Fig. 3.6. During the Byzantine Empire, it was part of the Emperor's costume and survived after the twelfth century. In general, on the coins' depictions, the emperor wears the *loros* while either his son or the co-emperor wears the *chlamys*, thus leading one to think that this is a costume less important than the *loros*. Around the tenth century in the Byzantine Empire the *chlamys* was a magnificent full-length purple cloak fastened by a fibula at the right shoulder. It was the characteristic civil costume also [Reiske, 1829]. When coupled with the even grander *loros* it was the ceremonial costume for very formal occasions worn by both Byzantine emperors and high officials.

Figure 3.6 On the left, an example of a Roman *chlamys* (Photo Alexander); on the right, a *chlamys* wore by Constantine VIII, brother of Emperor Basil II (976–1025) on a gold solidus.

3.1.7 Mantle

The *mantle* (romanized *mandyas*, mentioned in Cicero [1991]), is similar to the current liturgical *chasuble* and *phelonion*. It is an episcopal outer garment worn like a cloak in service of the Eastern Orthodox Church and worn by monks too. It is a full cape worn over the outer garments that extends to the floor, joined at the neck. Christian knights also wear a similar mantle frequently showing crosses and Christian symbols.

The current *chasuble* worn by clergy during the celebration of the Eucharist in Western Christian Churches, see Fig. 3.7, derives from the Roman mantle. In general it is worn over the *alb* (a linen tunic) and *stole*. In the Eastern Orthodox and Catholic Churches the equivalent dress is the *phelonion*.

Figure 3.7 *Chasuble* worn during the celebration of the Eucharist in Western Christian churches (from www.artereligiosa.it).

3.1.8 Loros

The *loros* (from Greek λῶρος) evolved from the *trabea triumphalis* of the Roman consuls. It is a narrow, long and embroidered scarf worn over the *divetesion*, a long ceremonial silk tunic, see Fig. 3.8. The *loros* was worn only by the imperial family and a few other officials during imperial Byzantine ceremonies.

Figure 3.8 Byzantine ivory showing Christ blessing Emperor Constantine VII, 945 AD wearing a *loros* (Pushkin Museum, Moscow, Russia).

According to Moon and Bywater [2020], the precursor of the *loros* could have been the *tablion*, the rectangular linen altar-cloth mentioned in the fourth to seventh century which *"had a direct association with the burial cloth of Christ."* It was *"a piece of cloth inset in the front of the* chlamys *at the waist height"* worn by Byzantine Emperors such as Justinian I (482–565), see Fig. 3.9.

Figure 3.9 San Vitale (Ravenna, Italy) mosaic showing one gold embroidered *tablion* worn under the right arm of Emperor Justinian I (482–565) and other two ones worn by two high dignitaries of the court.

The way the *loros* was wrapped around the body was not simple. Grierson and Hendy [1993-99, Vol. 2 Part 1. p. 78] explains that the Emperor Justinian II wore the *loros* passing on his *"right shoulder, under his right arm, across the front of his body, over the left shoulder, across his back, and finally emerging from behind at his right side"* crossing *"the front of his body to hang down over his extended left forearm,"* see Fig. 3.10.

Figure 3.10 Example of the *loros* worn by Emperor Justinian II (692–695 AD) who keeps the cross in his right hand and the *akakia* (typical Byzantine roll containing dust) in his left hand.

The *loros* is probably related to the arrival of the Shroud in Constantinople in 944. Grierson and Hendy [1993–99, Vol. 4 Part 1. pp. 153–155] reveal evidence for the presence of two different forms of *loros* in the imperial depictions from the middle of the tenth century onward.

1. One is the traditional type of *loros* that remains like a richly decorated band wrapped around the body as reported in Figs. 3.9 and 10.

2. Another is the appearance of a simplified type of *loros* consisting in a band with a circular cutting for the head, going down to the ankles in front and going down to the waist in the back, ending on the left arm. The author of this book sees a probable connection with the Shroud of

Christ in agreement with Emperor Constantine VII who in *De Cerimoniis* [Reiske, 1829] writes that the *loroi* worn during the Feast of Resurrection recall God's burial and the splendor of the sun that was in the Resurrection of Christ. It is interesting to observe here that Constantine VII continued affirming that the wrappings of the *loroi* recall the burial wrappings of Christ. Curiously Grierson and Hendy [1993–99, Vol. 4 Part 1. pp. 153–155], who probably have no direct information on the Shroud, quote the description of Constantine VII affirming that, "*... the simplified form of loros is exactly that of a burial shroud .... as the loros had lost its original consular and secular significance... it acquired particular Christian ones.*" We finally must not forget that in the Klētorologion dated 899, [Bury, 1911] the symbolism of the *loros* is related to the burial and the Resurrection of Christ. This is due to the shape (burial) and the splendor (Resurrection) of the garment. For additional details, see Section 3.2.1.

Figure 3.11 Example of the *loroi* worn by Emperor Leo the Wise (886–912) on the left and by Constantine VII on the right.

3.1.9 Stole

The *stole* (From Greek στολή) corresponds to both a Roman dress also worn by women (see Section 3.1.11) and a liturgical vestment. Our interest here concerns the latter.

The corresponding dress in the Eastern Orthodox and Greek Catholic Churches is the *orarion* of a deacon and the *epitrachelion* of either a priest or a bishop. The latter wears an *omophorion* also. They are often decorated with embroidered crosses and equipped with decorative banding and fringe.

The current *stole* is a liturgical band of colored and decorated cloth common in the Catholic Church to deacons, priests and bishops. In general the center of the stole is worn around the back of the neck and the two ends hang down parallel in front, see Fig. 3.12. The *stole* is both a symbol of priestly authority and the sign par excellence of priestly dignity. The current ecclesiastical discipline prescribes its use in the mass, in the sacraments and in the sacramentals and whenever there is contact with the Holy Communion.

Figure 3.12 Example of a current *Stole* worn by Pope Benedict XVI (CC BY 3.0 br).

According to many authors, [Cabrol and Leclercq, 1922; Paci, 2008; Righetti, 1950] the shape and origin of the *stole* is uncertain and it is difficult to explain the strange passage from an ancient dress to the modern form similar to a scarf. From the fifth century (Isidore of Pelusa) up to the twelfth it was called *orarium, sudarium* or *linteum* (incidentally the Shroud too was named *sudarium* or *linteum* in the past).

Different interpretations have been furnished for the origin of the *stole* because it could symbolize:

- the light and gentle yoke of Christ;
- His humility when washing and drying the disciple's feet,
- the innocence of the priest;
- the sheep that the Good Shepherd carries on His shoulders;
- the cords used by the soldiers to drag Jesus Christ to Calvary.

But as we will see, according to the author, it may be connected with the Shroud that wrapped the dead body of Christ, see Fig. 3.13.

Figure 3.13 Image of benedictory right hand of Emperor Justinian II (692–695), partially wrapped in a sheet that could, according to the author, be interpreted as the Shroud, which could have inspired the current *stole* simulating the sepulchral sheet of Jesus (see also Fig. 3.16).

According to other authors [Cabrol and Leclercq, 1922], the *stole* is similar to the ancient *orarium (or orarion)*, a cloth that was used to clean the mouth, to wipe sweat or tears, like the current handkerchief. In the East, beginning from the fourth century, it was used by deacons as a liturgical garment and not as a simple handkerchief (see canons 22 and 23 of the Council of Laodicea). Before the third century the mention of *orarion* is rare in Latin authors, while in the western Church it is sometimes mentioned.

The *stole* appeared in the West during the sixth century in Gaul and Spain. During the eighth century we find Christ wearing a *stole*, see Fig. 3.14 on the so-called Altar of Duke Rachis (Cividale del Friuli, Italy, 737–744).

Figure 3.14 Jesus Christ wearing a *stole* (Altar of Duke Ratchis, Christian Museum of Cividale del Friuli Italy, 737–744). Note the tuft of hair in the middle of Jesus' forehead typical of Byzantine depictions and probably referring to the "reversed 3" visible on the Shroud.

The name *stole* first appeared in the sixth century just around the period in which the Emperor Justinian II coined the first image of Christ. His right benedictory hand is partially wrapped in a sheet that could be interpreted as the Shroud, the linen sheet that probably inspired the *stole*, see Fig. 3.13 and Section 3.2.5.

3.1.10 Pallium

The *pallium* has different meanings:

1. the Roman cloak described in Section 3.1.5;

2. a drape of fine fabric, used as a cover or banner;

3. in the Catholic liturgy the pallium is a circular band of white lamb's wool, which passes around the neck, adorned with 6 crosses. It has two pendants, one front and one rear, the ends of which have lead plates covered in black silk. When observed from the front or rear the pallium shows a letter "y." It is reserved for the pope, archbishops, patriarchs and primates. Someway connected with the *stole* is the *pallium* corresponding to its third definition, see Fig. 3.15.

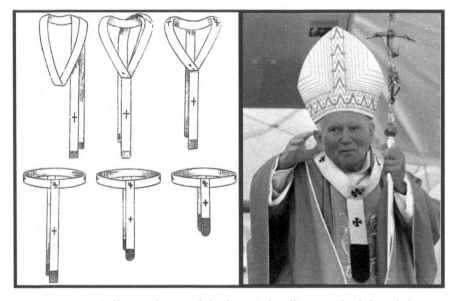

Figure 3.15 Different shapes of the liturgical *pallium* on the left and the Pope St. John Paul II wearing a pallium on the right (CC BY 3.0 br).

There are various hypotheses concerning the origin of the *pallium*. One of these suppose it was introduced as an imitation of its counterpart, the *omophorion*, already in use in the fifth century in the Eastern Church as a symbol of spiritual and ecclesiastical authority.

3.1.11   Feminine Dress

Before the end of this section, a synthesis of the feminine dress is presented here describing the *maforion*, the *palla* and the *stole.*

The *maforion* is a Roman outer long robe, from head to foot, used as a large shawl that covers almost the whole body, see Fig. 3.16. The Russian icons, see Fig. 3.17, usually show the Mother of God robed in a *maphorion* veil typical for married Jewish women. The original *maphorion* of the Mother of God was brought to Constantinople in 473 and kept in the ancient Church of Blachernae.

Figure 3.16 Anonymus *follis* of Class G [Sear, 1987] attributed to Emperor Romanus IV (1068–1071) showing on the obverse the bust of Christ wearing a nimbus cruciger (halo with cross) around His head, a *pallium* (according to the author the *pallium* could be interpreted as the Shroud) and *colobium,* while raising His right hand in benediction. On the reverse, the bust of the Virgin Orans Nimbate wears a *palla* or *pallium* (disposed differently than the obverse) and a *maphorion* [Sear, 1987].

The *stole* (in addition to the meaning of Section 3.1.9) is the traditional woolen garment of Roman women, corresponding to the *toga* worn by men. It was often used as a dress to walk outdoors, covered by the *palla*, see Figs. 3.16 and 3.18. In ancient times the *stole* was long to the feet and tightened by a belt, but it was subsequently shortened to the waist. *Palla* or *palliolum* is a traditional ancient Roman mantle worn by women and fastened by brooches. The shape of this overcoat is rectangular and it is the equivalent of the *pallium* for man.

Figure 3.17 On the left, a Russian Icon of the Mother of God Hodegetria (She who points the Way) of Tikhvin clothed in a large deep red *maphorion*, which is a symbol of life-giving energy and love. On the right, a gold *histamenon nomisma* of Theodora (1055–1056) shows the Mother of God Nimbate clad in an *ilium* and a *maphorion* holding with Her right hand the *labarum* (a vexillum displaying the "*Chi-Rho*" symbol ☧, a christogram formed from the first two Greek letters of the word Christ "Χριστός" symbolizing the crucifixion of Christ.).

Figure 3.18 Roman woman with *a stola* and *palla*, statue of Livia Drusila of Paestum (Museo Arqueol—gico Nacional de Espa–a, Madrid).

3.2   Dress of Jesus Christ

In the previous sections, we have had a look at the kind of clothes in use at the time of Jesus Christ. The following information will formulate some hypotheses regarding the recognition of the dress depicted by the Byzantine artists in order to represent Him.

3.2.1   Possible Connections between *Loros* and Shroud

It was mentioned in Section 3.1.8 that the simplified form of the *loros* could be in some way connected with the Shroud. Let's look at this hypothesis in some detail.

Maria G. Parani [2003, 2019] associate professor of Byzantine Art and Archaeology at the University of Cyprus wrote that she does not think there could be any direct connection between the *loros*, which was a civilian garment inherited from Roman antiquity, and the Shroud. The mystical symbolism that the *loros* acquires in the tenth century hardly justifies any association with the Relic. Nevertheless, she wrote in her book [2003, pp. 18–25] that the simplified form of the *loros-costume* which was developed out of the *trabea triumphalis*, was also adopted by religious art. By the tenth century it acquired a mystical dimension and it was worn on Easter Sunday. She also added that the scarf's convolutions remind us of the winding sheet of Christ's burial, while the golden trimming of the *loros* was a symbol of Christ's Resurrection.

Grierson and Hendy [1993-99, Vol. 2 Part 2. p. 570] instead wrote: *"The revival of the loros as the imperial costume on the coin was also the consequence of the representation of Christ since it was once connected with solemn and festive occasions of a religious or semi-religious nature (from the Book of Ceremonies)."* He adds [1993-99 Vol. 3 Part 1. pp. 78–80] that the traditional *loros* was in use up to the eleventh century but started from the middle of the tenth century. It was substituted by a modified *loros* that was simpler (the author notes that this happened just in conjunction with the arrival of the Mandylion-Shroud in Constantinople of 944).

Grierson and Hendy [1993-99, Vol. 4 Part 1. pp. 153–155] reported that in the period from 1081 to 1204 the *loros* was regularly worn only during Easter Sunday, as it is reported in *De Cerimoniis* [Reiske, 1829]. This information seems to confirm the strict relation with the Resurrection of Christ and the Shroud. The authors continue affirming that, while the *chlamys* was the most used imperial costume, the *loros* dominates the numismatic depiction of that period; although, "*No satisfactory explanation for this curious paradox has so far been advanced.*"

In 944 the Mandylion-Shroud (see Chapter 2) triumphantly entered Constantinople and Emperor Constantine VII wore the loros with twelve court dignitaries only during the ceremonies on Easter Day. In the tenth and eleventh centuries the *loros* had great splendor just when we see that most of the gold Byzantine coins represented the image of Christ.

While in agreement with Parani that there is an unclear connection between the *loros* and the Shroud, we could nevertheless think that the Byzantine artists were inspired by the particular way the loros wrapped around the human body when they had to depict the Shroud of Christ. In addition, the unclear change from the traditional *loros* to the simplified one, probably influenced by the Shroud in the Byzantine period, could be thought to have related to the arrival of the Relic in Constantinople.

It is interesting to observe the strict correlation between the revival of the *loros* with the Shroud. In 692 the first image of Christ resembling the Shroud face appeared on the gold *solidus* and the Emperor Justinian II wore a *loros* on the reverse. This was the first time that a Byzantine Emperor wore a *loros* on a coin, see Fig. 3.10.

3.2.2   The *Himation-Pallium*-Shroud Worn by Jesus Christ

Before to continue considering the *loros*, it seems important to have a look at the images of Christ portrayed few centuries earlier.

We have seen at the beginning of Section 3.1, that the identification of the various parts of the clothing is not easy or unanimous and that the relative terminology changes among the experts. The author agrees with these experts on the difficulty in identifying some forms of dress, but proposes a key for identification based on the Shroud for the interpretations of Jesus Christ's dress. A first numismatic depiction of Jesus Christ wearing a dress that can be a *himation-pallium*-Shroud is shown on the gold *solidus* of Justinian II (692–695), see Figs. 3.13, 3.16 and 3.19.

Figure 3.19 Detail of Christ on the gold *solidus* of Justinian II (692–695) (see also Figs. 3.13 and 3.16); on the right, the same image evidencing the robe in question that seems a *himation-pallium*-Shroud.

We see here the bust of Christ facing out with a cross behind His head, raising His right hand in benediction, partially wrapped in a kind of robe, and holding the book of Gospels in His left hand. While Wroth [1908] identifies the clothing worn by Christ as *mantle over tunic*, Sear [1987], Grierson [1999, Vol. 2, II] and others recognize them as *pallium* over *colobium*. Someone could also identify this dress as either *himation*, *loros*, *chlamys* or the Shroud. In Grierson and Hendy [1993–99, Vol. 5 Part 1. p. 74] we read, "*Christ is customarily described as wearing a tunic and a himation, a mantle worn over the tunic, but the details are usually obscure.*"

It is really not easy to recognize this clothing with accuracy from the image of a bust, but we can consider some iconographic interpretation of this very common image both in the Byzantine Empire and in the Orthodox tradition. For example, the mosaic representing the bust of Christ shown under the main dome of the Saint Sepulcher in Jerusalem, see Fig. 3.20, shows an image similar to that of Figs. 3.13, 3.16 and 3.19, where

Jesus Christ seems to wear a blue *himation-pallium*-Shroud over a red *tunic-colobium-chiton*[b].

Figure 3.20 Mosaic in the dome of the Saint Sepulcher in Jerusalem representing the bust of Christ wearing a blue (meaning transcendence and divine ineffability) *himation-pallium-Shroud* over a red *tunic-colobium-chiton*.

Let us now focus our attention to the outer dress of Jesus. In agreement with Section 3.1.6, when looking at the depictions of Byzantine coins, even if it can appear to be quite similar to the *chlamys*, this kind of clothing was worn by persons less important than the emperor. Therefore it is quite improbable to think that it was used in the representations of Jesus Christ who was named, *"King of rulers."*

---

[b]According to the rigid canons of Byzantine painters, the blue color signifies transcendence and divine ineffability and is typical for the *himation-pallium*. The red violet means royalty and is typical for the *tunic-colobium-chiton* of Christ and for the *maforion* of the Mother of God. The green means created life and is frequently used for the *tunic-colobium-chiton* too.

As Jesus Christ is frequently represented in the mosaics, icons and in general in the Orthodox tradition by wearing a *tunic-colobium-chiton* and the *himation-pallium* described in Section 3.1.5 see Fig. 3.21, we can make the following comments in reference to the outer dress.

- The outer garment evidenced in Fig. 3.19 seems to be a kind of *himation-pallium*. It seems to correspond to the image of Christ of Fig. 3.20.

- The way of wearing the *himation-pallium* was not unique, showing that a shroud could also have been used for the purpose. For example, the image of Fig. 3.21 shows it supported by a strap on the left shoulder.

- The *himation-pallium* of Figs. 3.13, 3.16 and 3.19 show Jesus Christ evidencing this garment posed over His blessing right arm, leading to think to an important object as it is the Shroud. The right hand of Fig. 3.20 does not even seem to bless, but it touches the important dress in question.

Figure 3.21 On the left, two images of Christ (one of them with *himation-pallium* evidenced) in the ivory (945) from the Pushkin Museum of Moscow, Russia. On the right is a Russian icon of Christ giving His hand to Adam in hell and wearing a green *tunic-colobium-chiton* under the red *himation-pallium*.

- In agreement with Section 3.1.5, the *himation-pallium* consisted of a rectangular sheet, about four meters long by one and a half wide [Battistini, 2020] with a size similar to that of the Shroud. It is therefore easy to think that Byzantine artists, while depicting Christ resurrected with His clothes, represented Him wrapped in the Shroud, used like a *himation-pallium*.

- The fact that the first image of Christ on coins, dated to 692, depicts Him with an apparent *himation-pallium* frequently reported then in the Byzantine art and always shown on the busts of Christ on coins, leads one to think of a well-defined canon already in place for the depiction of Christ in this age.

These findings therefore lead to identify the outer garment worn by resurrected Jesus Christ on the gold *solidus* of Justinian II (692–695) and on various Byzantine coins with a *himation-pallium* representing the Shroud.

Both the Pantocrator conserved in Saint Caterina's Monastery, (see Section 3.3.2 and Fig. 3.34) and the *"Crux Vaticana"* (see Section 3.3.3 and Fig. 3.36) show Jesus Christ wrapped in a *himation-pallium* too. Therefore we can suppose that this depiction of Christ was in use already from the sixth century.

3.2.3   The Simplified *Loros*-Shroud Worn by Jesus Christ

Few centuries later, a depiction of Jesus Christ wearing a dress different from *himation-pallium*-Shroud is that appeared around the tenth century consisting in the *simplified loros*-Shroud.

For example, the image of the Triptych Harbaville ivory (middle tenth century) of Fig. 3.22 shows the blessing hand of Christ partially wrapped in a scarf resembling something like the simplified *loros*-Shroud (see Section 3.1.8).

Images similar to that of the Harbaville ivory are frequent in Byzantine coins starting from the tenth century with Empress Theodora (1055–1056), see Fig. 3.23, and even lasting after the sack of Constantinople in 1204. This image, recognized as that of Christ Chalkite, shows something like a long scarf, very similar to a simplified *loros* (see Section 3.1.8), clearly wrapped around the blessing Christ, which leads you to think of the Shroud. Incidentally, the length of the sheet in question is comparable with the Christ's Relic. To clarify to the reader the way the linen sheet in question was wrapped around the body, a model of it has been represented in Fig. 3.24.

Figure 3.22 The right hand blessing of Christ partially wrapped by a scarf is shown on the Triptych Harbaville ivory of the middle tenth century at Louvre, Paris, France. On some coeval coins too, the blessing hand is partially wrapped in a sheet clearly different from the *himation-pallium*, but resembling the simplified *loros*-Shroud. On the left the real ivory; on the right the sheet in question is evidenced.

Figure 3.23 *"Christ standing facing on footstool"* according to numismatic experts, [Sear, 1987] or Christ resurrected from the Sepulcher, according to the author, on a gold *histamenon nomisma* of Theodora (1055–1056). The long sheet wrapping the body of Christ evidenced on the right seems a simplified *loros*-Shroud.

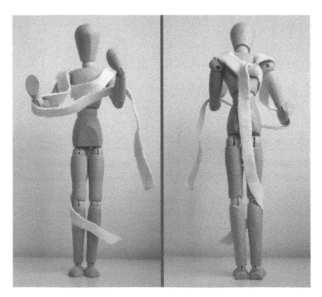

Figure 3.24 Model representing the way the linen sheet shown in Fig. 3.23 on the right is wrapped around a human body.

Also the Hyperpyron Magnesia of John III of Nicea (1221–1254) of Fig. 3.25, shows something like a long scarf or a simplified *loros* clearly wrapped around the blessing Christ seated on the throne. Again this leads the author to think of the Shroud. A model of this wrapping is shown in Fig. 3.26.

Figure 3.25 Image of Christ similar to that of Fig. 3.23: *Hyperpyron Magnesia* of John III of Nicea (1221–1254), showing the blessing Christ seated on throne, wrapped by a "scarf" that could be identified as the Shroud. On the right the sheet in question is evidenced.

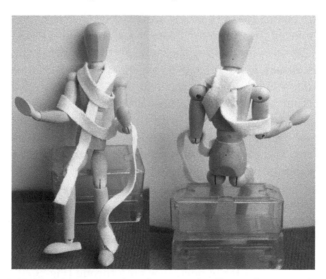

Figure 3.26 Model representing the way the linen sheet, evidenced in Fig. 3.25 on the right, is wrapped around a human body.

A bit different configuration is shown in Fig. 3.27 on the gold *hyperpyron* of Emperor John II (1118–1143) where the blessing Christ is seated facing the throne, wrapped by a long scarf or a simplified *loros.* This again leads the author to think of the Shroud.

Figure 3.27 Image of Christ similar to that of Fig. 3.25: gold *hyperpyron* of Emperor John II (1118–1143) showing the blessing Christ seated on a throne wrapped by a "scarf" that could be the Shroud. On the right the sheet in question is evidenced.

The three images of the blessing Christ on the *electrum aspron trachea*, minted by Emperor Manuel I Comnenus (1143–1180) of Fig. 3.28, are interesting because of the different positions of the simplified *loros*-Shroud wrapping Christ, in relation with the blessing right hand. On the left, we see an extended right blessing hand with the simplified *loros*-Shroud leaning on the shoulder and taken by Christ with His left hand posed over the Gospels. In the center, we see Christ's blessing hand partially wrapped by the simplified *loros*-Shroud. On the right, we see Christ wrapped by the simplified *loros*-Shroud in a different display, see Fig. 3.24, with His right hand tightly taking the simplified *loros*-Shroud and perhaps blessing too. Incidentally, in reference to this last coin, Sear [1987] gives evidence that strangely, "*Christ's right hand is not uplifted.*"

It is interesting to observe that, while we see the blessing hand of Christ when He is portrayed on a throne (Fig. 3.28 on the left and on the center), His right hand tightly takes the simplified *loros*-Shroud when He is portrayed coming out of the Sepulcher (Fig. 3.28 on the right).

Figure 3.28 On the top, three images of the blessing Christ wrapped by a sheet that could be the simplified *loros*-Shroud; on the bottom the same images with the sheet in question evidenced. It is interesting to note that the same Emperor Manuel I Comnenus (1143–1180) alternatively minted these three different *electrum aspron trachea* showing the blessing Christ with the right hand in three different positions.

Not only did Emperor Manuel I allow during his reign the production of different depictions of the blessing Christ, but other emperors after him minted alternatively, Christ with his right hand extended, or his right hand partially wrapped in a long sheet. For example, Sear [1987] again evidences that, *"Christ does not raise right hand in benediction,"* in a gold *hyperpyron* of Emperor John II (1118–1143), see Fig. 3.29, because He is holding the long simplified *loros*-Shroud in question.

Figure 3.29 Image of Christ holding a long simplified *loros*-Shroud: gold *hyperpyron* of Emperor John II (1118–1143) showing the blessing Christ seated facing out on a throne commented by Sear [1987], *"Christ does not raise His right hand in benediction."*

This poses a question. Knowing that the Byzantine canons were rigid and that the coin's engraver needed permission directly from the Emperor, along with his supervision, to produce depictions on gold coins, why did Emperor Manuel I and others allow such a variety of coins showing the blessing Christ?

Above all, why did such a long sheet that wrapped Jesus Christ's body like a simplified *loros*, hold the same significance as His benediction? The answer seems simple for the author. The long sheet in question could be the Shroud, and because it is such a significant object in the Resurrection of Christ, rightfully this Relic either took part in the blessing or was even directly evidenced by the right hand of Our Savior. Moon and Bywater [2020, p. 3] confirm the author's idea.

The three different images can be explained if we remember the great interest that was produced in the Byzantine people by the arrival at Constantinople of the Mandylion-Shroud in 944 (see Section 2.4.2) and its exposition in the Emperor's capital.

Therefore the Byzantine engravers, with the official approval, wanted to show on the coins that this Relic was very significant and of the same importance of Jesus' benediction. This could be the reason why, starting from the tenth century, we alternatively find these different depictions on the Byzantine coinage.

3.2.4 The Depiction of the Shroud of Jesus Christ

After validating the hypothesis that the Shroud is the sheet depicted in many images of Christ on Byzantine coins, we synthesize the study reported in Sections 3.2.2 and 3.2.3 concluding that the Relic was reproduced in two different ways.

1. Starting from 692, the Shroud was wrapped around the body of Christ like a *himation-pallium* in the images of many mosaics, ivories and icons like those of Figs. 3.20 and 3.21, and coins like those of Figs. 3.16 and 3.19.

2. About three centuries later, Jesus Christ is depicted wearing a different dress. In the Byzantine art, from the tenth century, the body image of Christ is wrapped by the Shroud like a simplified *loros*, see, for example, Fig. 3.22, and in the images of a great number of coins minted during many centuries of the Byzantine Empire even after the fall of Constantinople in 1204 shown in Figs. 3.23, 3.25, 3.27 and 3.28.

We remember that the representation of Jesus Christ resurrected, coming out of the sepulcher, started in the tenth century with Empress Theodora and continued for centuries after the fall of Constantinople in 1204. For example, the *mezzanino* coined by Andrea Dandolo of the Republic of Venice in the fourteenth century, see of Fig. 3.30, shows a typical Byzantine representation of Christ resurrected and dressed in His simplified *loros*-Shroud, the only clothing He had leaving the sepulcher (represented as a box). The banner taken by the right hand of Christ could be another reference to the Shroud too.

At this point, a self-defense seems necessary. Someone could affirm that the author "sees" the Shroud everywhere like someone sees "elephants in the clouds."

Figure 3.30 Silver *mezzanino* of Andrea Dandolo (Republic of Venice, 1343–1354) showing Jesus Christ resurrected, coming out of the sepulcher (represented as a box) dressed in His Shroud in a way very similar to the Byzantine representations.

After more than twenty years of study regarding this argument, it is possible the author does tend to "see" the object of his studies more easily than others. This could explain why many numismatists (who perhaps do not know the Shroud in detail) have not yet recognized the Relic depicted on many Byzantine coins, confusing it with other coverings.

There are no direct signs on the coins of Christ wrapped by His Shroud that undoubtedly attest that it is really the Relic in question, but was such a sign necessary for the Byzantine people looking at these coins? Perhaps it would be for us who believe only in a clearly demonstrated scientific fact, but probably it was not so for the very religious Byzantine people. They were happy to have in their capital of Constantinople the most precious Relic of Christ.

Incidentally, this explains, as suggested by Russ Breault, an American scholar on the Shroud, why the author, with Dr. Claudio Furlan of Padua University, detected on the Shroud the presence of many particles of *electrum*, probably coming from contact with Byzantine coins [Fanti and Furlan, 2019]. It is probable many Byzantine people rubbed their *electrum* coins showing Jesus Christ wrapped in His Shroud directly on the Relic, thus making these coins second-class relics, see Section 7.3.

It is well known that Byzantine images are full of details ruled by specific canons and it is clear that it is very important in the depiction of the blessing Christ. If someone is against the hypothesis formulated by the author, he would have to explain why the Byzantine coin engravers decided not to reproduce the right hand blessing of Christ, but instead preferred to reproduce his right hand holding a simple common cloth, as we can see, for example, on the image of Fig. 3.28 on the right.

3.2.5 Does the *Current Stole* Derive from *Loros* and Shroud?

We have seen how complex the recognition of clothes and fabrics depicted in Byzantine coins and icons is in general. Their development over the centuries also appears more intricate. From the discussion of the previous sections we have seen the following.

- Probably the Shroud played an important role in the depiction of Christ on the Byzantine coins.
- Two kinds of depictions of Christ have been evidenced: that of Christ wrapped in the *himation-pallium* appeared from 692 and found more frequently in the ancient Byzantine and Orthodox icons; that of Christ wrapped by a long sheet like a simplified *loros*-Shroud appeared about three centuries later, found more frequently in the Byzantine coins that began in the tenth century.

We have also seen that the advent of the simplified form of the *loros* could also be connected with the appearance of the Shroud in Constantinople. It is evident too, that the *loros* was frequently related to religious events, principally connected with Easter, in remembrance of Christ's Resurrection.

On the other hand, in Section 3.1.9, we have seen that the current *stole* is a liturgical band, symbolic of priestly authority, used whenever there is contact with the Holy Communion, the real Body of Christ. It is commonly worn in the Catholic Church by deacons, priests and bishops, and corresponds to the *Orarion* of the Eastern Orthodox and Greek Catholic Churches. We have also seen that the shape and origin of the *stole* is uncertain, and that its name first appeared in the sixth century just around the period in which the first image of Christ appeared, derived from the Shroud on Byzantine coins.

At this point, it seems legitimate to ask a question. Given that the origin of the *stole* is uncertain, is it possible from the analysis just performed to formulate a new hypothesis about the *stole* origin? To try to answer this question, we can comment on the proposed chart reported in Table 3.1, which considers the development of clothing with particular reference to Jesus Christ and His Shroud.

- Before the first century, we have the *consular loros* as the imperial dress, probably developed from *the trabea triumphalis*, while the *himation-pallium* was common for men up to the tenth century and later.

- In the first century, Christ resurrected from the dead, wrapped in the Shroud and the *loros* began to go out of use.

- In the fourth century, the disuse of the *loros* continued up to the tenth century. The first depictions of Christ appeared in art especially in the catacombs of Rome, but He is generally represented as a young man, callow, with short hair, different than the Shroud image.

- In the sixth-seventh century, remembering that the *himation-pallium* is a rectangular sheet having sizes similar to the Shroud, starting from the gold solidus of Justinian II (692–695) or earlier from the Pantocrator of Sinai of Section 3.3.2 and the "*Crux Vaticana*" (568–569) of Section 3.3.3 the *himation-pallium*-Shroud appears on coins as the dress of Jesus Christ. The Byzantine artists when depicting Christ, probably reproduced the way the *himation-pallium* was wrapped, but illustrated the religious importance of the Shroud that was taken by Jesus Christ in his right hand frequently in place of His blessing hand. From these centuries onwards, the image of Christ reproduced in the Byzantine coinage and in general was almost always Shroud-like as well.

- In the tenth century, the *loros* returned to use in two different forms as imperial dress, principally used in reference to liturgical feasts related to the Resurrection of Christ.

Table 3.1 Chart of the supposed clothing development

Age	Imperial and liturgical dress		Shroud of Christ and His dress in Byzantine art	Men's dress
Before 1st century	Probable development of *trabea triumphalis* to consular *loros*		-	*Himation-pallium*
1st century	Beginning of disuse of *loros*		Resurrection of Christ wrapped in the Shroud	*Himation-pallium*
4th century	Disuse of *loros*		First depictions of Christ	*Himation-pallium*
6th - 7th century	Disuse of *loros*		Appearance of the Shroud in Byzantine art. Christ wrapped in the *himation-pallium-Shroud*	*Himation-pallium*
10th century	*Traditional loros*	*Simplified loros* probably influenced by the Shroud	The Shroud is at Constantinople. Depiction of Christ Resurrected out of the sepulcher, also wearing the simplified *loros*-Shroud	*Himation-pallium*
Up to 21st Century	Orthodox *epitrachelion*	Catholic *stole*	The Shroud is at Turin, Italy	-

Note: Starting from *trabea triumphalis, consular loros, himation-pallium* in use before the first century, we see the probable influence of the Shroud of Christ in the first century. It appeared in Byzantine art, with its probable influence arriving at the *himation-pallium* of the sixth–seventh century, at the simplified *loros* of the tenth century, and to the current stole.

We have the traditional *loros* and a simplified version probably influenced by the way Jesus Christ was depicted, wrapped by His Shroud and coming out of the sepulcher. Therefore, the probable appearance of the Shroud in Byzantine art and at Constantinople (as the Mandylion-Shroud, see Section 2.4.2) seems to be responsible for the first development from the traditional *loros* to the simplified one, which was similar to the simple burial cloth of Christ. Therefore, from the sixth-seventh century, Jesus Christ is depicted first wearing the *himation-pallium*-Shroud, especially in the Byzantine mosaics and Russian icons, and later, from the tenth century, alternatively with the simplified *loros*-Shroud, especially on the Byzantine coins.

- After 1204, the Shroud was taken to Europe and exposed in France and in Italy, then ended up in Turin where it remained. The simplified *loros* of the tenth century, frequently used in religious ceremonies and the Shroud, were probably at the base of the development of the current liturgical *stole* of the Western Catholic Church, and of the *orarion* (*epitrachelion* and *omophorion* too) of the Eastern Orthodox Church.

The diagram in Table 3.2 shows the Shroud as the most probable origin for the *stole* and *epitrachelion* as well as the *himation-pallium*-Shroud appearing frequently in Byzantine art and on many Byzantine coins, and the simplified *loros*-Shroud of Byzantine coins and art.

Therefore, it's now possible to answer the initial question. Does the current *stole* derive from the *loros* and the Shroud? If we accept the hypotheses reported above, the answer seems yes. It seems probable that the current *stole*, with the corresponding garment used in the Orthodox Church, derives from both the Shroud and the simplified *loros,* which in turn was derived from the ancient *loros*. Incidentally, among Jewish liturgical clothing, there is nothing similar to the current *stole*, thus supporting the fact that this garment is only typical of Christian origin and linked to the Shroud.

Table 3.2 Diagram of the supposed dress origin based on the Shroud

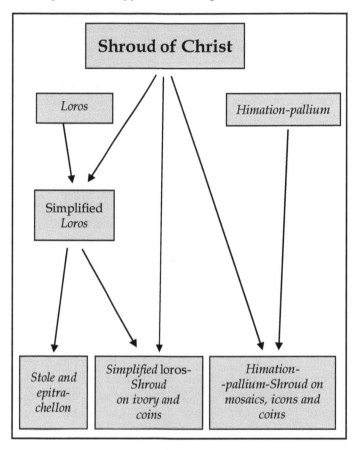

Note: We see the probable influence of the Shroud of Christ in the current stole, on the *himation-pallium*-Shroud of many Byzantine mosaics, icons and coins of the sixth-seventh century and on the simplified *loros*-Shroud of the tenth century, especially shown in Byzantine ivory and coins.

3.3 Ancient Depictions of Christ

After the analysis of the clothing used in the Byzantine age and in particular by Jesus Christ, we can now better analyze the various depictions of our Lord in art, starting from the first images discovered in the catacombs of the first centuries.

In the beginning of the history of the Church, the burial Sheet of Jesus was probably kept hidden for several reasons. First of all, it was a very precious "memory," having enveloped Him who sacrificed Himself on the Cross. Furthermore, Christians feared that someone could seize and destroy it. The Hebrews, in compliance with Mosaic Law, considered everything that had touched a corpse as impure. Thus, the reasons why the protectors of the Shroud wanted to keep it hidden are clear.

3.3.1   First Representations

During the first centuries, some symbols were used, like lamb, bread, and fish[c] to represent Jesus Christ. Results from iconographical studies [Marinelli, 2014; Fanti and Malfi, 2020] reveal Jesus Christ was initially depicted as young and beardless, with short hair, see Fig. 3.31, representing "The Good Shepherd" collecting sheep in pastoral scenes. But around the sixth century something changed.

One of the first representations of a bearded Christ that has survived till the present day is dated AD 290–310 where Jesus' blessing is depicted with a beard and bushy hair. In fact, there is a fragment of marbled plate with scenes from the New Testament that is conserved in the National Roman Museum—Palazzo Massimo alle Terme, see Fig. 3.32. This indicates that already by the end of the third century some information about the physiognomy of Jesus based on the Shroud image had even reached Rome. The young and beardless Jesus became bearded, with long hair.

Other examples of a majestic and bearded Christ can be found on the sarcophagi in the Lateran Museum, Saint Sebastian-Outside-the-Walls (around 370), Arles (before 370), and the Basilica of Sant'Ambrogio in Milan (380–390). Since then, throughout the centuries this kind of representation was not abandoned, and perhaps there was a good reason to keep it. The representations of Christ, even in the present day, relate back to the Shroud image.

---

[c]"Fish" in Ancient Greek is "ἰχθύς" (ichthys), ΙΧΘΥΣ in capital letters for "Ἰησοῦς Χριστός, Θεοῦ Υἱός, Σωτήρ" ("Iēsous Christos, Theou Yios, Sōtēr"), literally "Jesus Christ, the Son of God, our Saviour."

Figure 3.31 On the left, Jesus in the Catacombs of Rome, third century fresco from the catacombs of Callixtus of Christ as the Good Shepherd. On the right, Christ beardless with short hair healing a bleeding woman, catacombs of Marcellinus, and Peter (Rome), third century (M. Paolicchi).

Figure 3.32 Marbled representation of a blessing Jesus with a beard and bushy hair (290–310), National Roman Museum—Palazzo Massimo alle Terme, Rome.

During the early centuries we find the Mandylion, as reported in Section 2.4.1, which corresponds to the image of Edessa. It is a relic consisting of a rectangular cloth upon which a miraculous image of the face of Jesus had been imprinted [Wilson, 2010]. According to a legend, King Abgar of Edessa asked Jesus for an image of Himself, so Jesus wetted his face and put it on a sheet to produce such an image. From this came the tradition of, *"Christ with a wetted beard,"* that is reported in many pictorial reproductions of the Mandylion where Jesus has a long wetted beard. The gold histamena coin minted by Michael VII (1071–1078) is an example see Fig. 3.33 and also Section 1.3.18.

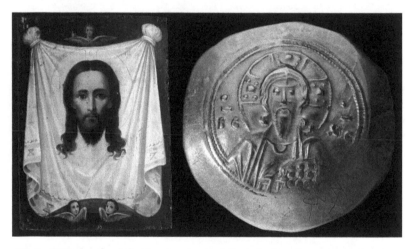

Figure 3.33 On the left, Russian icon of the nineteenth century showing an example of Mandylion; on the right, gold *histamenon nomisma* minted by Michael VII (1071–1078) showing Christ with a long beard.

3.3.2   The "Syrian" and the Shroud-Like Faces

As we have seen in Section 1.3.2, the manner of depicting Jesus was not uniform around the sixth century. In particular, two kinds of Jesus' faces circulated. The first one, a "Syrian" or "Semitic" form, shows a short-bearded Jesus with short frizzy hair, see Fig. 1.16. The second one shows a bearded Jesus with hair parted in the middle, frequently longer on the left side, and according to some scholars [Breckenridge, 1959] was similar to the manner in which the god Zeus was depicted, but according to others [Marinelli, 2014; Fanti and Malfi, 2020] was very similar to the Shroud.

The second depiction of the face of Christ shows some asymmetrical and irregular features, hardly to be ascribed to the artist's imagination. In particular, we can observe:

- long, parted, and often asymmetrical hair along the face; a lock of short hair, with different ends on the forehead;
- pronounced eyebrow arches; a V-shaped mark on the bridge of the nose;
- big, deep wide open eyes, and big orbits; a long and straight nose;
- pronounced cheekbones;
- a little mouth, not hidden by the mustache, which is often droopy; a hairless area between the lower lip and the beard;
- an asymmetrical beard.

The first example of this kind of iconography is the Pantocrator, conserved in Saint Caterina's Monastery, at the foot of Mount Sinai, Egypt, which was painted in the sixth century by order of Emperor Justinian I, see Fig. 3.34. The Shroud bibliography [Whanger and Whanger, 1985, 1998] found many points of congruence between the Pantocrator icon and the Shroud face, demonstrating that whoever painted the icon saw the Shroud.

The author noted while observing the eyebrows of the Pantocrator of Saint Caterina, there is a noticeable difference between the right face and the left one that contributes to a diversification in the facial expression, see Fig. 3.35. Some scholars commented on this dissimilarity, affirming that the iconographer wanted to represent two faces of the Lord in the same icon, one more gentle (the left half) and one more severe (the half on the right).

Actually, this asymmetry of the left eyebrow corresponds to the same irregularity of the Shroud face; it has, in fact, a more raised left eyebrow with the same sharp outline due to a swelling caused by one of the many blows he came under.

Figure 3.34 On the left, Christ Pantocrator conserved in Saint Caterina's Monastery, painted in the sixth century compared with the Shroud image on the right.

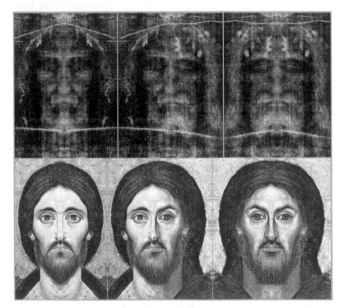

Figure 3.35 Shroud face on the top and Christ Pantocrator in Saint Caterina's Monastery in Sinai on the bottom. In the center are the original images; on either side the symmetrical images of the right and the left side of the face, highlighting the asymmetry.

3.3.3 The *"Crux Vaticana"*

Of particular interest is the Cross of Justin II also known as *"Crux Vaticana"* (*"Vatican Cross"*) dated around 568–569. It is kept in the Treasury of St. Peter's Basilica, in Vatican City and is perhaps the oldest staurotheke (reliquary of the Christ's Cross). It is a jeweled cross in gilded silver 35 cm (13.8 in.) tall, given to the Roman people by the Emperor Justin II, see Fig. 3.36.

Figure 3.36 On the center, Cross of Justin II also known as *"Crux Vaticana"* (568–569). The front of the Cross (lower left) contains a Relic of the Christ's Cross while the back is interesting because shows two medallions with busts of Christ similar to the Shroud (upper and lower right in the figure). The medallion on the center (upper left) shows the Lamb of God as it was used to represent Christ at that time.

While the front of the Cross shows a Relic of the True Cross with precious jewels, the back shows five medallions. The medallion in the center shows the Lamb as it was customary to represent Christ at that time. At the top and the bottom of the Cross are two medallions showing images of Christ (but someone suggests that the bottom one could be of John the Baptist even if the faces are very similar). The upper medallion shows a nimbate blessing Christ holding the book of the Gospels, while the lower one shows Christ with a cross and a scroll in His hands.

The Cross is quite enigmatic [Rezza, 2013] and interesting because its back shows the face of Jesus Christ at a time when the church was beginning to favor the representation of the human figure of Christ. It is important for the present study because we find one of the first images of Christ with some characteristics similar to the Shroud; the bust of blessing Christ on the top of the Cross has unsymmetrical long hair, moustaches and beard, swollen cheeks and large eyes. In addition, it seems perhaps the first image of Jesus Christ wrapped in a *himation-pallium*-Shroud.

3.3.4   Other Examples

One of the first examples depicting the face of Christ, is the one painted on the vase from Emesa, the modern Homs in Syria, dated between the sixth and seventh century. On this vase, a man with a mustache, beard, and Shroud-like long wavy hair can be observed, see Fig. 3.37. Furthermore, the cheekbones are pronounced, the right one more than the left one, and the area under the inferior lip is hairless. These features are analogous to those of the Shroud face.

The face of Christ on various objects like the cameo of the sixth century, the silver plaque and ring shown in Fig. 3.38, and the silver ampule of Fig. 3.39, have features similar to the above-mentioned ones of the Shroud face. The inscriptions "IC XC NIKA" (Jesus Christ conquers) on the ampule are common on coins of the eleventh century, see Fig. 3.40.

The iconoclast debate in the eighth century forbade all the depictions of Jesus Christ and the representation of the Savior under the guise of a lamb was pretty common and used for several centuries. A thirteenth century example of this is in the

Figure 3.37 Christ Pantocrator reproduced on a silver vase of the sixth to seventh century from Emesa, the modern Homs in Syria (Louvre, Paris).

Figure 3.38 On the left, the face of Christ on a cameo once conserved at the National Museum in Vienna, today regained by the ancient Polish family Lanckoronoski (sixth century). The cameo was found by the Viennese Shroud-scholar Gertrud Wally in the museum archives. In the center, an eighth to tenth century Byzantine silver plaque (Pars Coins, USA). On the right a Byzantine ring, around the tenth century (Felix_Aedius, Spain).

Soisson Cathedral in France: there is an interesting image of
the lamb wrapped in the Shroud, borne by two angels. This is
also another sign that the Relic was already known in those
years, see Fig. 3.41.

Figure 3.39 Silver Byzantine ampule, eleventh century, perhaps once
containing Holy water, probably a pilgrims' souvenir from a S. George
shrine. The lid shows "*IC XC NIKA*" (Jesus Christ conquers, see Fig. 3.40)
followed by "*Georgos*" (George). On the left Jesus Christ nimbate with
right hand blessing and holding the Gospels in His left hand; on the
center S. George nimbate holding a spear in His right hand (Pars Coins,
USA; expertise by Shroud-scholar Paul Maloney.)

Figure 3.40 On the left, a bronze *follis* of Romanus IV (1068–1071)
showing the bust of Christ with inscriptions "IX XC" (Jesus Christ)
and "NI KA" (Conquers). On the right a bronze *follis* of Michael IV
(1034–1041) showing again the same inscriptions.

Figure 3.41 Depiction of the Lamb enveloped in the Shroud. Soisson Cathedral, France, 1200 (photo Shroud-scholar Traudl Wally).

This overview of the face of Christ iconography from the first millennium, shows the close connection of the typical features of these depictions with those of the Shroud face. The results clearly demonstrate the Relic had often been a model for the representations of Christ.

3.4   Images of Christ on Coins

After an overview of the garments and the images of Christ from the Byzantine art in this chapter, and after the analysis of Byzantine coins presented in Chapter 1, a synthesis of the different kinds of Christ's images on coins seems necessary before finishing this presentation. This will assist the reader by showing that relatively few different depictions of Christ were produced in the more than five centuries of the Byzantine Empire under analysis.

This fact confirms that the artist's fantasy though was reduced to a minimum, because there were rigid canons to be respected for the representations of religious men and scenes referring to particular events.

3.4.1 The Most Frequent Image of Christ: His Bust

We have seen in Chapter 1 that the first image of Jesus Christ appeared in the gold solidus of Justinian II in 692 and continued without appreciable variations to the sack of Constantinople in 1204 when the Shroud disappeared from there, and later: it is the blessing image of His bust with the Book of Gospel in the other hand.

The image shows the right hand blessing and wrapped in the *himation-pallium*-Shroud evidenced in Section 3.2.2, and the left hand holding the book of the Gospels. In the first centuries we see a cross behind the head of Jesus, then starting from Emperor Basil II (976–1025), the head is surrounded by a halo.

We see here how the most important Christian symbols connected with Man-God like the cross-halo, Shroud, book of the Gospels and blessing are well integrated together in a very beautiful image that was also frequently reproduced in icons, mosaics and other objects of the Byzantine and Orthodox art.

Figure 3.42 shows as an example some of these very numerous coins which appeared during these centuries minted by various Emperors starting from Emperors Justinian II (692–695) to Manuel II (1391–1423) through Michael III (842–867), Basil II (976–1025) and John I (969–976).

Figure 3.42 Some representations of the bust of Christ from 692 to 1423 on Byzantine coins. From the left to the right, *solidi* of Justinian II (692–695), Michael III (842–867) and Basil II (976–1025), bronze *follis* of John I (969–976) and silver *half stavraton* of Manuel II (1391–1423).

3.4.2 The Image of Christ on a Throne

Another important representation of Christ on Byzantine coins is that representing our Savior on the throne, see Fig. 3.43. This depiction first appeared with Emperor Basil I in 867 and continued in the centuries thereafter, even after the Sack of Constantinople in 1204. For example, we find this kind of depiction on the anonymous *basilikon* attributed to Andronicus II or III (1282–1341), see Fig. 1.77.

Figure 3.43 Example of depictions of Christ on the throne. From the left: gold *solidi* of Basil I (867–886) and Leo VI (886–912); gold *histamenon* of Romanus III (1028–1034); *electrum histamenon* of Alexius I (1081–1118) and old *hyperpyron* of John III (Nicea Empire, 1222–1254).

The image of Christ on a throne of Fig. 3.43 contains features similar to those of the bust of Christ of Section 3.4.1, but it adds an interesting detail. Almost the totality of these depictions represent, analogous with the Shroud image, the right foot of Christ smaller than the left one and tilted, leading one to think of the tradition of "Jesus lame" discussed in Section 3.4.8. We again observe that on the second and third gold solidi from the left, the right blessing hand of Christ is partially wrapped by a sheet, which indicates this sheet must be as important as the blessing. Thus, the author has recognized the sheet to be the *himation-pallium*-Shroud discussed in Section 3.2.2.

3.4.3 The Image of Christ Chalkites

An interesting depiction is that of Christ Chalkites that belongs to those images, like the Camuliana[d] image that was visible

---

[d]The Camuliana image of Christ in Cappadocia was mentioned [Zacharias Rhetori, sixth century] during the reign of Justinian I (527–565 AD). It was exhibited around cities to protect them from barbarian attacks and it was one of the earliest images described as a miraculous imprint on cloth.

during the Byzantine Empire, but was later lost. The name derives from the Chalke Gate, the main ceremonial entrance to the Great Palace of Constantinople and it means "Bronze Gate," because of the bronze portals.

Above the main entrance of the Chalke, there stood an icon of Christ, the *Christ of the Chalke.* During the iconoclastic period of the eighth century it was removed by Emperor Leo III and restored by Empress Irene (about in 787), but it was again removed by Emperor Leo V at the beginning of the ninth century.

The exact depiction of the icon is not clear, but it seems similar to the image of some Byzantine coins, see Fig. 3.44, like those of Empress Theodora (1055–1056), Emperor Romanus IV (1068–1071), Emperor Manuel I (1143–1180) and Alexius III (1195–1203), [Grierson, 1982; Bellinger and Grierson, 1973; Goodacre, 1967]. These gold coins show the image of Jesus Christ standing on a so-called "footstool" that, in agreement with Section 1.3.14, seems instead to be the sepulcher from which Jesus Christ is exiting during His Resurrection. As discussed in Section 3.2.3, Christ seems dressed in the simplified *loros*-Shroud.

Figure 3.44 Four examples on coins of the image of Jesus Chalkites coming out of the sepulcher [Grierson, 1982; Bellinger and Grierson, 1973; Goodacre, 1967], see also Fig. 3.23. From the left, gold *histamena nomisma* of Theodora (1055–1056) and Romanus IV (1068–1071), *electrum aspron trachy* of Manuel I (1143–1180) and gold *hyperpyron* of Alexius III (1195–1203).

3.4.4 The Image of Christ Antiphonetes

Another important depiction on Byzantine coins is that of Christ Antiphonetes (it means "guarantor," One who guarantees). The original image was located in the Church of the Theotokos Chalkoprateia, one of the most important churches of

Constantinople dedicated to the Virgin Mary. Over the centuries the image has been lost, but some copies refer to it, see, for example, Fig. 3.45 and that on a bronze *follis* of Fig. 3.46.

Figure 3.45 Byzantine image of Christ Antiphonetes (about 1350) reproduced on a 7 cm steatite plaque. The right hand is blessing while the left one shows the Book of the Gospels (Rogers Fund, 1979, www. metmuseum.org/art/collection/search/466046).

Empress Zoe (1028–1050) commissioned a copy of it and a contemporary historian, Michael Psellus [1018-after 1078], described the fervent piety of Zoe toward this icon copy. He reports that she foretold the future with it, as the icon was capable of responding to questions by changing color. The Empress commissioned a precious marble floor at the chapel of the Antiphonetes in the church of Theotokos Chalkoprateia and she chose that chapel as her personal burial place. The icon of Christ Antiphonetes also appeared on her coins.

Figure 3.46 Anonymous bronze *follis* attributed to Michael IV (1034–1041) showing three-quarter length figure of Christ Antiphonetes standing facing out raising his right hand in benediction (see also Fig. 1.36).

It must be noted that while the plaque of Christ Antiphonetes Fig. 3.45 shows the Book of the Gospels on the left arm of Jesus, the coin of Fig. 3.46 also shows a sheet that seems to be the lower part of the simplified *loros*-Shroud. This raises a question. Why did the artist prefer to put that sheet so in evidence? The sheet must have been considered important. The answer is simple for the author because the sheet in question must have been the Shroud, the garment which portrays Christ's Resurrection.

3.4.5 The Image of Christ Crowning the Emperor

A less common depiction of Christ on Byzantine coins represents Him crowning an emperor, see Fig. 3.47. While other saints like Saint Alexander appear on coins crowning Emperor Alexander (912–913), the first depiction of Christ crowning an emperor appears on Byzantine coins starting from 924 with Emperor Romanus I, see Fig. 3.47 on the left.

Another example of Christ crowning the Emperor is the scyphate *billon aspron trachy* of Andronicus I (1183–1185) on the right of Fig. 3.47, indicating a sheet on the left arm of Christ that could be identified with the simplified *loros*-Shroud.

Figure 3.47 Examples of images of Christ crowning the emperor. On the left is a gold *solidus* of Constantine VII with Romanus I and Christopher (924–931). Emperor Romanus I is standing facing out with his left hand extended towards Christ who is standing facing out with a cross behind the head crowning the Emperor [Sear, 1987]. On the right, scyphate *billon aspron trachy* showing Christ crowning Emperor Andronicus I (1183–1185).

3.4.6   The Image of the Infant Christ in the Depiction of Our Lady of the Sign

Another depiction of Christ on Byzantine coins is that representing the Infant Jesus on the icon of "Our Lady of the Sign." On Figure 3.48, we can see two images of the Virgin holding the Infant Jesus.

Figure 3.48 Two depictions of the icon of Our Lady of the Sign. On the left, *electrum tetarteron nomisma* of Michael VII (1071–1078) showing the bust of the Virgin facing out holding before Her the Infant Jesus facing out, whose nimbate head is depicted alone. On the right, *electrum aspron trachy* of Alexius I (1081–1118) showing the Virgin enthroned facing out, holding the same head of the Infant Jesus.

We find the first depiction of this type with Emperor Basil I (976–1025). It continued for centuries in the Byzantine Empire and in Bulgaria, then later in the Nicea Empire.

3.4.7   Right Shoulder Lowered

Another interesting detail of the bust of Christ shows His right shoulder lowered, not common in reproductions of flawless men, but of Jesus Christ shown on the Shroud.

A recent study [Bevilacqua et al., 2014], disclosed that the Man of the Shroud has just the right shoulder lowered because it was probably dislocated after a fall while carrying the cross to Calvary. An anthropometric analysis report confirms glenoidal dislocation of the humerus of nearly 3 cm (about 1 in.).

In agreement with this dislocation visible on the Shroud, some Byzantine coins report this peculiar feature in the depictions of Christ, see, for example, Fig. 3.49. In particular, the first coin from the left shows evidence of the protuberance of the lowered shoulder typical of a dislocation, while the third coin accentuates this feature.

Figure 3.49 Examples of Christ showing the right shoulder lowered in agreement with the Shroud body image. From the left, gold *solidus* and gold *semissis* of Justinian II (692–692); gold *solidus* of Constantine VII (955–959); gold *histamenon nomisma* of Romanus III (1028–1034).

3.4.8   Christ Enthroned, Smaller Right Foot Tilted

The Orthodox Cross, depicting the lowest of the three horizontal crossbeams, slanted see Figs. 3.50 and 3.51, is in compliance with the representation of Christ on the Byzantine coins. Probably it was thought that Jesus was lame [Cazzola and Fusina, 1983] and it is likely that this belief is derived from the fact that the body image of the Shroud shows the feet of Jesus as deformed. The feet remained fixed in that position because of *rigor mortis* (death rigidity), after Jesus Christ was removed from the Cross.

Figure 3.50 On the left, a Byzantine cross with the third crossbeam slanted. On the right, is a gilded silver cross 12 cm × 9 cm (4.7 in. × 3.54 in.) ascribed to Charlemagne, twelfth century from Aachen Cathedral Treasury, Germany. www.bildindex.de/dokumente/html/obj20460173#—home. Picture by Marburg, registration Nr. 1.086.066.

In fact, in the Shroud image the left foot[e] is in an anomalous position, which can wrongly lead one to think He was a lame man if no references are made to Him being nailed to a cross, and then afterward wrapped in a sheet with the feet extended and partially overlapped. The anomaly of the Byzantine coins depicting the right foot thinner compared to the left foot is very common in the Eastern iconography.

---

[e]Apparently the right foot, since the image is specular. The knowledge about the image formation in that age was insufficient, and probably not so many people thought that the Shroud image was specular, being consistent with the corpse wrapping; so the left foot seemed the right; thus it is represented in this way in many iconographic depictions, also numismatic.

Figure 3.51 On the left, a Russian icon of the nineteenth century showing a brass Byzantine cross; on the right, a detail of the icon showing the deposition of Jesus Christ wrapped in the Shroud.

Figure 3.52 Examples of coins showing the right foot tilted and smaller than the left one: from the top left, gold *solidi* of Basil I and Constantine VII (867–886), of Leo VI and Constantine VII (886–912) and of Constantine VII and Romanus I (921–931), gold *histamena* of Constantine IX (1042–1055) and of Constantine IX (1042–1055) and *electrum aspron trachy* Manuel I (1143–1180).

The twelfth-century cross ascribed to Charlemagne and conserved in the Aachen Cathedral Treasury in Germany, seems to confirm this too, see Fig. 3.50. In fact, even if the third slanted crossbeam is not represented, the right foot is inclined without any logical explanation if the Byzantine tradition recalling the Shroud is not taken into consideration.

As mentioned in Sections 1.3.4 and 3.4.2, from a numismatic point of view, the depiction of *"Jesus lame"* with His right foot tilted and smaller than the left one, is frequent on coins starting from Emperor Basil I (867–886), who first represented Christ on the throne, see Fig. 3.52.

3.4.9 Faces of Christ

The faces of Christ obviously varied in their details according to the subjectivity of the engraver who prepared the coin, although, like all other Byzantine icons, in general they followed particular predefined canons. Therefore, for each face of Christ, it is relatively easy to go back to the corresponding Byzantine canon to which they referred. During the many centuries in the period ranging from the first coin of Christ of Justinian II in 692 to the sack of Constantinople in 1204, we essentially can find five different kinds of faces of Christ like those shown in Fig. 3.53.

1. The most common face that was reproduced in similar forms for many centuries, not only in the Byzantine Empire, but also in many other states, is certainly that inspired by the Shroud. It is shown on the gold *solidus* of Justinian II, first period (692–695) shown in Fig. 3.53A.

2. Rarer than this is the face reproduced in Fig. 3.53B of the gold *solidus* of Justinian II, second period (705–711) recovered by Alexius III (1195–1203) on the *billon aspron trachy* of Fig. 3.53E. This coin shows the so-called Syrian Christ beardless with curly hair, see Section 1.3.2. As mentioned in that section, the Syrian type of Christ was probably more common during the first centuries AD when the Shroud was protected and hidden to the public. The Shroud type of Christ though was preferred by the Byzantine Emperors from the discovery of the Mandylion-Shroud conserved at Edessa, see Section 2.4.2.

Figure 3.53 Different faces of Christ depicted on Byzantine coins. (A) The most common face was inspired by the Shroud, gold *solidus* of Justinian II (692–695). (B) Syrian face, gold *solidus* of Justinian II (705–711). (C) Christ with "wet beard" of the Agbar's legend on an *electrum histamenon nomisma* of Michael VII (1071–1078). (D) Christ Emmanuel on a gold *hyperpyron* of Manuel I (1143–1180). (E) Later Syrian face on a *billon aspron trachy* of Alexius III (1195–1203). (F) Infant Christ on an *electrum aspron trachy* of Alexius I (1195–1203).

3. As presented in Section 1.3.18, the face of Christ, see Fig. 3.53C showing an *electrum histamenon nomisma* of Michael VII (1071–1078), displays evidence of an elongated beard in reference to the "wet beard" of Agbar's legend. This kind of image of Christ was widely minted by Emperor Michael VII after a first issue made by Empress Theodora (1055–1056), see Fig. 1.40a.

4. During the reign of Manuel I (1143–1180), another iconographic type of Jesus Christ appeared: the face of Christ Emmanuel or Immanuel, like the face on the gold *hyperpyron* of Fig. 3.53D. It is a Hebrew name, which appears in the book of Isaiah as a sign that God will protect the house of David. The Gospel of Matthew (1:22–23) quotes *"a virgin shall be with child, and shall bring forth*

a son, and they shall call his name Emmanuel." The icon of Christ Emmanuel is frequent in the Orthodox art and represents Christ with the somatic traits of an adolescent who is beardless and almost an adult. This depiction is a sign of reverence to the Man-God who is indeed wise like an old man. Perhaps Emperor Manuel I preferred this kind of image because of the correspondence with his name.

5. Last we must remember the face of the Infant Jesus presented in Section 3.4.6, seeing, for example, the *electrum aspron trachy* of Alexius I (1081–1118) where the Infant Jesus is shown by the Virgin enthroned, see Fig. 3.53F.

Following this overview on the images of Christ in the Byzantine Period, we will discuss in the next chapter the details of the faces of Christ reproduced on coins. In particular, we will show evidence for the large number of details typical of the Shroud reproduced on these coins.

Chapter 4

Details of Christ's Face on Coins

After a general overview of the Byzantine coins and of the Shroud, we have seen the clear influence of this Relic on the depiction of Christ in the coinage of the seven centuries between the seventh century and the thirteenth century and even later.

We have also seen the strict relationship between the images of Christ depicted on coins and the body image on the Shroud. Lastly, we have observed the depiction of the so-called "Jesus-lame" with the right foot smaller and tilted due to the Byzantine interpretation of the Shroud image, and the depiction of the right shoulder of Christ on coins showing a dislocation evident on the Shroud.

Now we will focus our attention on the face of Christ depicted on Byzantine coins, performing a direct comparison with the face visible on the Shroud. These coins demonstrate, from a general point of view, that the most important Relic in the world has greatly influenced the Byzantine face of Christ on coins.

4.1　Christ's Face on Byzantine Coins

The face of Christ on coins presents many peculiar details typical of the Shroud image, which shows a tortured man. This chapter will explore, one by one, these details. As reported in Section 1.3.1,

Byzantine Coins Influenced by the Shroud of Christ
Giulio Fanti
Copyright © 2022 Jenny Stanford Publishing Pte. Ltd.
ISBN 978-981-4877-88-6 (Hardcover), 978-1-003-21992-7 (eBook)
www.jennystanford.com

from 692, under the reign of Emperor Justinian II, the Byzantine artists began to depict the face of Jesus Christ on coins, see Fig. 4.1. Apart from the iconoclastic period, this kind of coin continued also after the sack on Constantinople of 1204. Many states in the world copied this subject that will be described in Chapter 5. The depiction of the whole figure of Christ, that is of the face and bust, is the most frequent subject reported on the Byzantine coins, and not only on them, but also on icons, mosaics, ivories, statues and so on.

Figure 4.1 Face of Christ on two gold *solidi* of Justinian II, First Period (692–695).

The very religious Byzantine people gave such great importance to Christ's face that they often posed it on the front of the coins, by placing the emperor's effigy in the reverse. This importance is also confirmed by the fact that in some cases like that of Fig. 1.49, some anonymous coins were minted without the depiction of the Emperor (Romanus IV in this case) but showing the bust of Christ on the obverse and that of His Mother on the reverse.

Before going into the details of this description, we must note that the majority, but not all of these coins, show a face very similar to that of the Shroud. The following inspection will be based on a selection of these significant coins, knowing that not all the reproductions of the face of Christ were possible by looking directly at the Relic. This was either because not all the

Byzantine engravers had the possibility of seeing His face on the Shroud, which was hidden to the public during various periods, or because the engravers of some "*officinae*" (factories where the coins were prepared) were too far from Constantinople. The latter is also the case of coins minted by states far from the Byzantine Empire, as will be shown in Chapter 5.

The first engravers probably observed the Relic directly and manufactured the most faithful depictions, whereas others just copied the previously minted coins, or some available images painted from the Shroud. This made the human features less similar to the tortured face of the Relic and more similar to a perfect man. The number of peculiar features that made the face unique, with the clear marks of Jesus' Passion therefore decreased; for example, the swelling on the cheeks caused by the suffered blows, the asymmetrical torn beard on the right side, and the asymmetrical hair shape became less evident.

4.2 List of the Types of Details

This Section shows a list of the most significant details of the face of Christ present on some Byzantine coins evidencing a similarity to the peculiar details of the Shroud face.

A preference for the analysis is given to the gold coins because these were subjected to more rigid controls in part by the Emperor, who based his decision to conform to precise rules [Hetherington, 1981] defined by the Byzantine canons.

It is interesting to observe the extreme accuracy of the production and the skill of the engravers, who succeeded in reproducing details approximately one-tenth of a millimeter (0.004 in.). Nevertheless, it is obvious that the coin engravers were not able to reproduce with sufficient details all the peculiar features of the face of Christ on the Shroud. It is therefore interesting to observe and compare the variety of coins, which alternatively show some of these details visible on the Relic[a].

---

[a]We have seen that in Chapter 2 that the double body image of the Shroud, front and back, is mirror reversed. In many cases, the Byzantine engravers did not consider this fact and therefore they copied the body image as they saw in the Relic. To avoid some possible misunderstanding in the following description, we will always refer to right and left directly to the human being there described.

To simplify the comparison between the Byzantine coins and the face of Christ visible on the Shroud, Fig. 4.2 indicates the details that will be discussed on the face, according to the last number of each of the following sections.

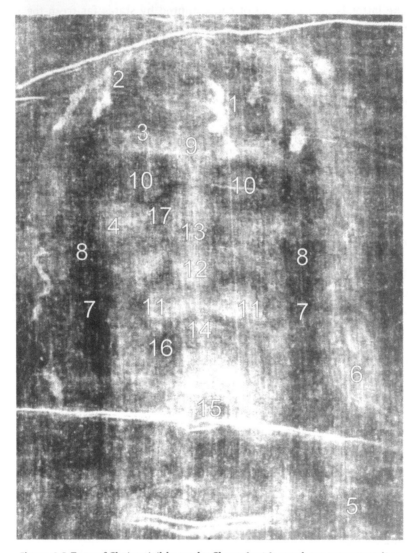

Figure 4.2 Face of Christ visible on the Shroud with numbers corresponding to the details hereafter discussed, numbered according to the last number of each of the following sections.

The reader will note a millimeter scale on the bottom of many of the photos indicating the real size of the engraved result. It was obviously not simple to reach such a level of detail reported on Byzantine coins, which were never surpassed by other coins of the same age, as will be seen in Chapter 5.

4.2.1 Tuft of Hair on the Forehead

We remember that in 692 the canon n. 82 of the Council in Trullo (or Quinisextum) decreed that Christ had to be exhibited in human form images instead of the lamb, as the custom was at that time. In the same year, Justinian II minted the first coin officially recognized in numismatic history showing the bust of Christ, the gold *solidus* of Fig. 4.1.

Observing the hair of Christ, on all the coins of Fig. 4.3 we note the particular tuft of hair on the forehead, which is characteristic of almost all the coins reproducing these faces. This detail very probably derives from the famous *"reversed 3"* sign of the Shroud produced on Christ's forehead by a blood flow.

Figure 4.3 Various faces of Christ on gold *solidi* of Justinian II, of the First Period (692–695) showing the tuft of hair on the forehead.

As reported in Section 1.3.1, the canon n. 82 of the Trullan Council or Quinisextum, (692) stated that the image of Christ had to be exhibited in human form images instead of the ancient lamb. It is written: *"Thou shalt not paint a lamb for the type of Christ, but himself."* Nevertheless, Jesus Christ had to be represented as Himself but without the signs of His Passion. It is therefore easy to think that the engravers, when trying to reproduce that particular trace of blood characteristic of the Shroud image, exchanged it for a tuft of hair.

This tuft of hair on the forehead of Christ's face is not only evident on the gold *solidi* of these images, but it is a very common sign reported on many representations of Christ during the centuries of the Byzantine Empire and later.

The strict connection of this tuft of hair with the Shroud image is also confirmed by the fact that none of the faces of "Syrian Christ" (that were not Shroud-like) coined under the same Emperor Justinian II during his Second Period (705–711) show this peculiar detail.

4.2.2   Tufts of Hair All Around the Head

The tuft of hair on Christ's forehead represents the wound on His face as seen on the Shroud. This was previously mentioned in Section 4.2.1 and shown in Fig. 4.3. Some rarer Byzantine coins add other signs of bloodstains as tufts of hair. The gold *solidus* of Justinian II, of the First Period (692–695) of Figs. 4.4 and 4.5, shows many tufts of hair representing the wounds visible on the Shroud in their specific location. There are so many tufts of hair on that face that the Man appears dishevelled.

Figure 4.4 Rare gold *solidus* of Justinian II, of the First Period (692–695) showing various tufts of hair corresponding to the bloodstains on the Shroud.

Figure 4.5 Detail of head of the gold *solidus* of Justinian II of Fig. 4.4 comparing the various tufts of hair evidenced in red with the corresponding bloodstains of the Shroud. The reversed *"V"* shape of the swollen right eyebrow mentioned in Section 4.2.3 is evidenced too.

It is obvious to think here that the coin engraver wanted to represent more than one bloodstain visible on the Shroud, but in agreement with the prohibition of canon n. 82 of the Trullan Council mentioned in Section 4.2.1, he avoided representing Jesus with the signs of His Passion, interpreting them as many tufts of hair.

It is important to evidence that the various tufts of hair all around the head that are a clear interpretation of the bloodstains, also sustains the hypothesis of Section 4.2.1 regarding the *"reversed 3"* sign of the Shroud.

4.2.3   Reversed "V" Shape of the Swollen Right Eyebrow

The face of Christ on the Shroud shows various swellings due to the torture suffered during His Passion. Among them it is evident a swelling of the right eyebrow probably produced by a blow caused by either a rod or a punch.

The rare gold *solidus* of Fig. 4.4 shows another detail typical of Christ's face on the Shroud. This is the right swollen eyebrow in a reversed "V" form evidenced in dark in Fig. 4.5. The gold *solidus* of Justinian II shown in Fig. 4.6 instead shows a different engraver's interpretation of the same swollen eyebrow with a bump.

Figure 4.6 Gold *solidus* of Justinian II (693–695) showing Christ's right eyebrow swollen visible on the Shroud as a bump instead of the interpretation of the reversed "V" form evidenced in dark in Fig. 4.5.

4.2.4 Swelling on the Right Cheekbone

The Gospel of Mark (15, 19) states, "*Again and again they struck him on the head with a staff and spit on him.*" This is evident with the swelling of the right cheekbone in the Shroud image.

Figure 4.7 Two gold *solidi* of Constantine VII (949–959) showing the bust of Christ with evident swelling in correspondence of the right cheekbone.

This detail has been evidenced on many coins reproducing Christ, especially those of Constantine VII, see Fig. 4.7. It is noted that the coins were minted in 949–959, just a few years after the arrival of the Mandylion-Shroud in Constantinople in 944. It is therefore easy to understand that the engravers had access to the Relic enabling them to provide additional details to the image of Christ because they were looking at it directly.

4.2.5 Long Left Hair

The body image on the Shroud had to be more evident in the first centuries than it is now because the flax background was certainly whiter; in fact, with the passing centuries, the yellowing of the flax reduced the contrast with the yellow-brown body image. It was therefore easier in the Byzantine epoch than now to detect the body features of the image.

Among these features, it is important to focus on the hair: it is wavy, shoulder-length, asymmetric and appears longer on the left side than on the right. Currently, we can better detect the major length of the hair on the left if we increase the contrast on a photo of the Shroud. Nevertheless, in the Byzantine epoch, this feature had to be such an evident detail that many engravers underlined this hair asymmetry on the face of Christ on their coins just to better characterize Him, see, Figs. 4.7 and 4.8.

Figure 4.8 Three gold *solidi* showing the bust of Christ with left hair longer than the right one, minted, respectively, from the left, by Michael III (842–867) Constantine VII (949–959) and Basil II (976–1025).

Someone could ask for an explanation of this asymmetry of the hair. It is possible that Jesus Christ's hair was not disposed in a symmetric position in the sepulcher, but we can also see evidence of the tortures endured by Jesus Christ described in the next Section 4.2.16. It is in fact possible that the hair was partially torn.

It is interesting to observe that some of the first engravers preferred to partially hide this non-symmetry to embellish the face of the Savior by intermingling the left long hair with the dress collar (see Figs. 4.1, 4.3, 4.4 and 4.6).

We must remember (see Note of Section 4.2) that on occasion some Byzantine engravers, when minting coins of minor importance, like the *aspron tracky* on the left of Fig. 4.9, probably without the emperors' control, forgot the fact that the Shroud image is reversed, thus exchanging the right with the left side of the face.

Figure 4.9 Two cases of *aspron trachea* of Manuel I (1143–1180) on which, contrary to the normal, the right hair is longer than the left one.

4.2.6 Ringlet in the Lower Left Hair

Typical of the Shroud image of the face, the hair on the left side is not only longer than the right side, but displays a ringlet at the level of the beard near the mouth. This detail has been frequently depicted on the Byzantine coins representing Christ; three examples are shown in Fig. 4.10.

4.2.7 Detached Hair

Typical of the Shroud, is the fact that the hair appears to be detached from the face probably because of the presence of a chin band used to close the mouth. The coins shown in Fig. 4.11 are examples of this non-typical peculiarity for a common face.

Figure 4.10 Three examples of Byzantine coins showing an evident ringlet in the lower left hair: from the left, gold *tremissis* of Justinian II (692–695), gold *histamenon nomisma* of Basil II (976–1025) and bronze anonymous *follis* of Class B attributed to Basil II and Constantine VIII (976–1028).

Figure 4.11 Some examples showing the hair of Christ detached from the face and the lack of ears. From the top left to the bottom right, gold *Solidus* and *tremissis* of Justinian II (692–695); gold *solidus* Michael III with his mother Theodora (856), *histamenon nomisma* of Michael VII (1071–1024), bronze *follis* of Crusaders at Antioch under Tancred (1101–1112) bronze *follis* of Artuquids in Anatolia, Arabian Empire under Fakr Al-DinQara Arslan, with countermark on the right (1148–1174).

4.2.8 Lack of Ears

The Shroud face shows no ears and some Byzantine coins reproduce this feature. This is the case, for example, of the six coins shown in Fig. 4.11 and 4.12. Someone can doubt this detail stating that the engraver may not have been able to include the ears because they are very small facial features. Nevertheless, we have seen that in many other cases, the Byzantine engravers were able to include at least a sign representing the ears on the side of the face in their very detailed images. We detect the lack of this detail of ears when we observe another detail typical of the Shroud image: the detached hair mentioned in Section 4.2.7.

Figure 4.12 Two examples of faces of Christ showing the lack of ears. Detail of the faces, of the gold *solidus* and *tremissis* of Justinian II (692–695) shown on the top left Fig. 4.11. The richness of details of the face on the right that is only about 6 mm (0.24 in.) tall must be noted.

Some could also think they see a small sign of ears, for example, where the hair curls around the face on the gold *solidus* of Justinian II (692–695) shown on the left of Fig. 4.12. There could be two problems with this interpretation. First, the hypothetical ears are in a position too low with respect to the face and second, more important, the hair is well separated from the face. Therefore, if the engraver had the intention to reproduce the ears, it is not easy to explain why he reproduced them in that abnormal position and detached from the face.

4.2.9 "T"-Shaped Nose-Eyebrows

Under Emperor Constantine VII (920–959) and after the triumphal arrival in Constantinople of the Mandylion-Shroud in 944, (see Section 2.4.2) another feature typical of the Shroud face appeared in the depiction of Christ's face on Byzantine coins.

Especially when observing the positive image of the Shroud face, a "T"-shape in correspondence with the nose and the eyebrows appears evident and it was reproduced on the Byzantine coins.

Figure 4.13 Three examples of gold *solidi* showing a "T" shape in correspondence of the nose and the eyebrows. On the top two coins of Constantine VII with Romanus (920–959), on the bottom one of Basil II (976–1025) compared with the Shroud face.

In fact some coins show the appearance of a "T"-shaped cross on the face, see Fig. 4.13.

4.2.10   Closed and Big Eyes

The image of Christ on the Shroud shows relatively big eyes that appear closed. Even if a proper image processing can show the left eye sligtly open, the resolution on the Shroud image of 4.9±0.5 mm [Fanti and Basso, 2008] does not allow the ability to detect whether the eyelids are open or closed.

It is obvious that the Byzantine engravers were unable to perform such numerical analysis, and thus frequently interpreted the Shroud image as showing Christ with closed eyes. This is demonstrated by the three coins of Emperor Justinian II (692–695) on the left of Fig. 4.14.

It is quite strange to see the face of a man with his eyes closed on a coin if we do not think of the Shroud as the reference image. This explains why in some cases we find the eyes of Christ open like that on the right of Fig. 4.14.

Figure 4.14 Three examples of gold coins (from the left, *tremissis* and two *semisse*) of Justinian II (692–695) showing Christ with closed eyes, to be compared with the gold *solidus* of the same Emperor on the right instead showing Christ with open eyes.

4.2.11   Long Moustaches

Similar to the Shroud image, the face of Christ on the Byzantine coins very frequently shows long and thick moustaches that almost completely cover the upper lip and tend to emphasize the protruding lower lip, see Fig. 4.15.

Figure 4.15 Three examples of gold coins showing the face of Christ with long moustaches covering the upper lip. From the left, *solidus* of Justinian II (692–695) and two *histamena nomisma* of Basil II (976–1025).

4.2.12 Nose Longer than the Normal and Asymmetric

The Shroud face of Christ is in agreement with the reproduction of many Byzantine coins showing a prominent nose, which, in some coins of Constantine VII, see Fig. 4.16 on the left, was sometimes curiously connected with the moustaches.

The asymmetry of the nose of Christ, typical of the Shroud, has been reproduced by evidencing the left nostril, see Fig. 4.16 on the right.

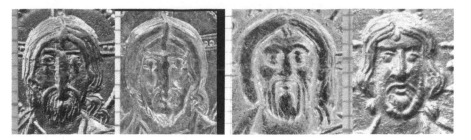

Figure 4.16 On the left, are two examples of a prominent nose connected with the moustaches on gold *solidi* of Constantine VII with Romanus (913–959). On the right are two examples of the left nostril more evident on a gold *solidus* of Michael III (842–867) and a gold *histamenon nomisma* of Basil II (976–1025).

4.2.13 Crooked Nose

As reported in Section 4.2.4, in agreement with the Gospel of Mark (15, 19) "*… they struck him on the head with a staff …*" we see that the nose of Christ on the Shroud is crooked probably due to a blow produced by something like a club which broke the nose's cartilage.

Some coins, for example, those minted by Justinian II (692–695), see Fig. 4.17, display an interesting feature: the nose is twisted to the right as evidenced on the Shroud face which shows the deviated nose due to the septum fracture. Someone could perhaps affirm that the crooked nose could have been either due to a minting flaw or to damage on the coin produced during its circulation, but we must observe that this feature is not so rare on the Byzantine coins that reproduced Jesus Christ.

Figure 4.17 Gold *solidus* of Justinian II (692–695) showing a crooked nose voluntarily reproduced by the engraver.

The twisted nose voluntarily produced by the engraver of the gold *solidus* of Justinian II as he looked at the Shroud, is compared with another one showing instead a crooked nose produced by an evident strike or blow to the coin. The difference of the two examples is clear. By Contrast, an engraving continuity of the crooked nose is well evident while observing a magnification of it, see Fig. 4.18 on the left. This continuity cannot be attributed to damage during circulation or similar defects, as is the case reported in the same figure on the right.

Finally, the fact that the nose is usually twisted to the right on coins and not to the left makes this detail not common like either a minting flaw or a blow could be.

Figure 4.18 Details of two gold *solidi* of Justinian II (692–695) showing on the left the crooked nose voluntarily made by the engraver of Fig. 4.17, compared with a "crooked" nose produced by an accidental blow, on the right.

4.2.14 Protruding Lower Lip and Gap in the Beard below It

Typical of the Jews is the protruding lower lip. Jesus Christ, a Jew, shows this peculiar feature on the Shroud body image that is evidenced by the gap in the beard below the lower lip.

The Byzantine engravers noticed this detail on the Shroud body image and reproduced it on their coins depicting our Savior. See some examples reported in Fig. 4.19.

Figure 4.19 Three examples of faces of Christ showing a prominent lip evidenced by the lower gap in the beard. From the left, respectively, gold *solidus* and silver *hexagram* of Justinian II (692–695); gold *histamenon nomisma* of Basil II (976–1025).

4.2.15 Bipartite[b] Beard

Some faces of Christ on Byzantine coins, especially those reproduced on the bronze *follis* did not always receive the direct approval from the Byzantine Emperor. As a result, they show a greater variety of depictions when reproducing some details like the beard on Christ's face, see Figs. 1.3, 1.32, 1.40, 1.49, 1.55 and 1.57.

Some coins reproduce the bipartite non-symmetric beard of the Shroud image, especially those of Justinian II (692–695) and of Michael III (1071–1078), see Fig. 4.20. Others show a more common form of beard like those of Fig. 4.13 indicating that the engraver of these coins focused his attention in the reproduction of other details of the face, which he considered more significant.

Figure 4.20 Three examples of bipartite beard on Byzantine coins. From the left, respectively, gold *solidus* and *tremissis* of Justinian II (692–695); *electrum histamenon nomisma* of Michael VII (1071–1078).

4.2.16 Right Beard Sparse

Isaiah in the Bible (50:6) wrote "*I offered … my cheeks to those who pulled out my beard.*" On Christ's Shroud, we see a partial lack of the right beard on the image of the face, in agreement with Isaiah's prophecy.

---

[b]By bipartite we mean the beard divided into two parts; in fact, the lower end of the beard of Jesus Christ of the Shroud ends with two rounded shapes separated from each other by a void.

This detail, perhaps less evident than others on the Shroud body image, has been observed by some Byzantine engravers that minted some coins by adopting different techniques, as shown in Fig. 4.21, to evidence this peculiar feature.

Figure 4.21 Different techniques were used by the Byzantine engravers to reproduce in a relatively small area the right sparse beard of Christ's face. From the left, gold *solidus* Constantine VII with Romanus (945–959); gold hista*menon nomisma* of Basil II (976–1025) and anonymous *follis* attributed to Basil II with Constantine VIII (976–1028). It is interesting the technique used on the right image, where the asymmetric display of the discs shows the sparse right beard.

4.2.17 Tears and Right Eyelid

As already reported, the details of the Shroud body image were probably more visible during the Byzantine Empire, and it is therefore easier to explain why some engravers included details that are a bit more difficult to detect today. This is the case of the tears visible on the coins reported in Fig. 4.22.

In addition to the tears, let us observe the face of Christ on the *folles* attributed to Emperor Nicephorus III (1078–1081) of Fig. 4.23, where the bipartite beard with other details typical of the Shroud face are evidenced too.

The detail of the right eye of the *follis* shown on the left of Fig. 4.23, indicates another curious feature of the Shroud image. In agreement with a result obtained by the author, the right eyelid of Christ's face seems sheared, probably due to a scourge blow. It is hard to attribute this sign to a defect of the coin.

Figure 4.22 Various coins showing the face of Christ in tears. From the top left to the right bottom: three different gold *solidi* of Constantine VII with Romanus (920–944); bronze anonymous *follis* of Class A2 attributed to Basil II and Constantine VII 976–1028); two bronze anonymous *folles* of Class I, attributed to Nicephorus III (1078–1081).

Figure 4.23 Detail of face of the two bronze anonymous *folles* of Class I, attributed to Nicephorus III (1078–1081) shown in Fig. 4.22. On the left *follis*, it is curious to see the right eyelid of Christ's face apparently sheared, probably due to a scourge blow, as it seems to result from the Shroud.

4.2.18 Faces of the Byzantine Emperors

We have seen many peculiar details of Christ's face on the Shroud evidenced by the Byzantine engravers when reproducing the face of Christ on coins. We have also seen the practical impossibility for these engravers to reproduce all these details on each coin showing an image of the face generally variable from 6 to 10 mm (0.24–0.39 in.) in height.

The consequence of this is the fact that we find Byzantine coins showing different faces of Christ, each evidencing a restricted number of details coming from the Shroud of Christ, subjectively selected by each engraver.

The greater or lesser richness of the Shroud details reported on each coin leads to imagine if the engraver in question had the possibility of looking directly at the Relic, or if he copied the face from previous paintings.

Nearing the end of this chapter, it is interesting to make a comparison between the faces of Christ depicted on the obverse of the Byzantine coins with those of the Emperors reproduced on the reverse side to show how different are the Emperor's faces from the Christ's ones in the reproductions. Figure 4.24 shows some examples that highlight the variability of the face of the Emperors in contrast with the almost invariable face of Christ, which was clearly copied from a particular model: the Shroud.

The impossibility for the Byzantine engravers to reproduce all the peculiar features of the Shroud image of the face on one coin only is also obviously against the following hypothesis. Someone affirmed that the body image of the Shroud was reproduced (perhaps in the Middle Ages!) by copying the face of Christ reproduced on the Byzantine coins. If so, how was the hypothetical artist capable of doing so, if the Byzantine engravers were not able to reproduce all the peculiar details present on the Shroud on one of their coins? This argument will be more deeply considered in the details of Chapter 8.

Chapter 4 has shown how significant the Shroud was in inspiring the Byzantine coin engravers when they reproduced the face of Christ. The influence of the Relic spread to many other states more or less connected with the Empire, when they decided to depict images of Christ on their coins.

Figure 4.24 Various faces of Byzantine Emperors show a clear difference among them. From the top left to the right bottom: gold *solidus*, of Justinian II, II Period (705–711); gold *solidus* of Michael III with his mother Theodora (856); gold *solidus* of Constantine VII with Romanus I (913–959); gold *histamenon nomisma* of Constantine VIII (1025–1028); gold *histamenon nomisma*, of Michael IV (1034–1041); gold *histamenon nomisma* of Constantine IX (1042–1055); *electrum histamenon nomisma* of Michael VII (1071–1078); *electrum aspron trachy* of Manuel I (1143–1180).

This topic will be treated in Chapter 5, which will present the different depictions of Christ's face on the medieval coins of the world.

Chapter 5

Christ in the World's Medieval Coins

The previous chapter discussed the peculiar features of the face of Christ reproduced on Byzantine coins, which showed strict connection with the Shroud image. These peculiar features have not only been reproduced in the Byzantine coinage, but many States connected with the Empire for cultural or commercial purposes were influenced by this image of Christ and they reproduced it on their coins in similar forms.

This chapter explores how many states in the Middle Ages copied the Byzantine canons in reproducing the face of Christ, and how the Christian creed was spread in the world.

5.1 Christ's Face in the World's Coins

This section considers many of the world's medieval coins showing the face of Christ. It evidences how, over the course of the centuries and depending on the distance from Constantinople, many of the details of the Byzantine canons were gradually, but not completely abandoned. The depictions of Christ were less and less comparable with the Shroud face because of the difficulty for the engravers to see first-hand either the most important Christian Relic in the world, or a good copy of it.

Byzantine Coins Influenced by the Shroud of Christ
Giulio Fanti
Copyright © 2022 Jenny Stanford Publishing Pte. Ltd.
ISBN 978-981-4877-88-6 (Hardcover), 978-1-003-21992-7 (eBook)
www.jennystanford.com

Figures 5.1 and 5.2 show the map of the coinages (stars) with the effigy of Christ in the period between 600–1400, produced by states bordering the Byzantine Empire. Some of these states continued this tradition in subsequent centuries as well. For example, as we will see in Section 5.1.3, the Maritime Republic of Venice continued its coins of Christ up to 1800 with both the resurrected Christ and the "*Almond Christ.*" It is impressive to see that the interest of the effigy of Christ on coins was far reaching and extended for thousands of kilometers (or miles).

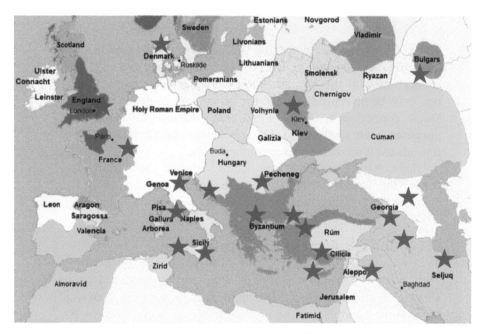

Figure 5.1 1100-Map[a] of the coinages (stars) with the effigy of Christ in the period 600–1400. Among them, we find the following: Merovingian, Anglo-Saxon, Georgia, Anatolia, Syria, Russia, Venice, Bulgaria, Palermo and Denmark.

As reported in Section 1.3, the Byzantine Empire under Emperor Justinian II (692–695), was the first in the world that officially minted coins showing the image of Jesus Christ. Nevertheless, some ceremonial gold *solidi* already appeared in 437 for the wedding of Licinia Eudoxia and Valentinian III, see Fig. 1.7;

---

[a]Map taken from http://geacron.com/home-en/.

these images reproduced the face of Christ with short curly hair and beardless [Breckenridge, 1959].

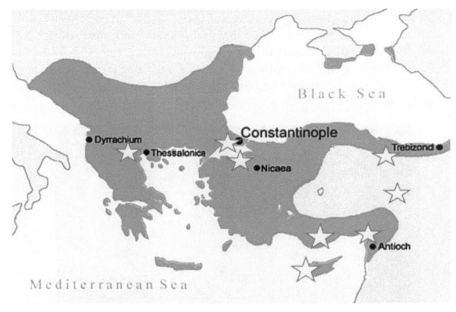

Figure 5.2 Map of the Byzantine Empire under Manuel I in 1180 with the indication of the places (stars) where coins with the effigy of Christ were minted.

According to a scholar [Travaini, 2003], Christ's image was present before the reign of Justinian II in the Merovingian reign around 625, see Fig. 1.8. These coins only sketched the face of Christ, thus neglecting many details typical of the Shroud.

Many coins in the Middle Ages showing the effigy of Christ are grouped in the following sub-sections according to their geographical area:

1. Anglo-Saxon sceattas
2. North-European coins
3. Coins of the Republic of Venice
4. West Balkan coins
5. Russian coins
6. Arab-Anatolian coins
7. Sicilian coins
8. More recent coins

5.1.1 Anglo-Saxon Sceattas

Excluding the coins of the Byzantine Empire, perhaps the most interesting ones showing an effigy of Christ similar to the Shroud image are the *sceattas*. They are very small and rare silver Anglo-Saxon coins minted in East Anglia or Mercia from 715–720 [Metcalf, 1993; Gannon, 2011, 2013, 2015; Abramson, 2012], see Figs. 5.3–5.9. The name *sceat* derives from Old English sceat, meaning "wealth" or "money."

Figure 5.3 Sceat of series Z, Type 66 [Abramson, 2012], from East Anglia o Mercia (715–720). Similar to the Shroud, the face of Christ shows a sign of the tuft of hair, moustache arranged in a "reversed W" shape, long hair, pronounced annulets forming the eyes and an evident asymmetry in the correspondence of eyes and beard.

Figure 5.4 Sceat of series Z [Abramson, 2012], from East Anglia or Mercia (715–720). Similar to the Shroud, the face of Christ shows the tuft of hair, "T"-shaped nose-eyebrow system, relatively long nose, prominent cheeks and right eyebrow, pronounced annulets forming the eyes and long hair.

Figure 5.5 Sceat of series Z [Abramson, 2012], from East Anglia or Mercia (715–720). Similar to the Shroud, the face of Christ shows forked beard, relatively long nose, pronounced annulets forming the eyes, a complex shape of the moustache and long hair.

Figure 5.6 Sceat of series W [Abramson, 2012], from East Anglia or Mercia (715–760). The probable blessing Christ, with a very rare face in profile, shows a relatively long nose and hair similar to the Shroud.

Apart from the Merovingian coins that have not as yet fully identifiable face of Christ, these sceattas are the first coins depicting this face of Christ produced outside the Byzantine Empire, only about two dozen years after the first coins of Emperor Justinian II (692–695).

Figure 5.7 Sceat of series BZ, type 29bi [Gannon, 2011; Abramson, 2012], from Essex or East Anglia. Rudimentary head of Christ showing a forked beard and a T-shape of nose-eyebrows similar to the Shroud image[b].

Celtic Christianity developed and spread to both Ireland and Great Britain, especially in the sixth and seventh centuries. Some elements of Celtic Christianity had already been introduced to Ireland by the Briton St. Patrick in the fifth century. These coins are interesting because of some refined details reported in these effigies. Looking at them (even if some of them can be a bit posterior or hybrid) we can see the following:

1. As reported in Chapter 2, the forked beard like that of the Shroud is evident on the coin of Figs. 5.3, 5.4, 5.5 and 5.7.

2. Figures 5.3 and 5.4 show a lock of the typical tuft of hair on the forehead of Christ's face on the Byzantine coins, corresponding to the "reversed 3" bloodstain on the Shroud (see Section 4.2.1).

3. The "T"-shaped nose-eyebrows configuration is evident in Figs. 5.4 and 5.7 as it appears on the positive image of the Shroud face, see Section 4.2.9.

4. The relatively long nose typical of the Shroud is visible on Figs. 5.4, 5.5 and its evidence is exaggerated as seen in Fig. 5.6.

---

[b]A. Gannon [2011] wrote: "... *the thin face, long nose and intense gaze may in fact reproduce an ancient icon of the Holy Face.*" That is the Mandylion-Shroud mentioned in Section 2.4.2.

5. Fig. 5.8 shows a full frontal figure of a man, probably Christ, again with a long face evidencing the smaller right leg and tilted foot on the coin. It is interesting to observe that such a Shroud-like detail will be minted only two centuries later in the Byzantine Empire (see Section 3.3.2).

Figure 5.8 Sceat of series U [Abramson, 2012] from East Anglia or Mercia (715–760). The full frontal figure of a man, probably Christ, with a long face, smaller right leg and tilted foot and a bipartite beard.

Figure 5.9 Various levels of superimposition of the Shroud face with that of the *sceat* of Fig. 5.4 shows their clear analogies.

6. Figure 5.6 probably shows, according to the author, a quite rare blessing Christ with His face in profile, recognizable for pronounced nose long hair. We must advance many centuries up to the Vatican States to find other faces of Christ in profile.

7. The Shroud-like face with prominent cheeks is well depicted on coins of Figs. 5.4 and 5.5.

8. The Shroud-like prominent right eyebrow is well reproduced on the face of coin of Fig. 5.4.

9. The pronounced annulets forming the eyes on the coins of Figs. 5.3, 5.4 and 5.5 give a hieratic expression to the face like that of the Shroud. Similar to it, the annulets alone without the depiction of the eyeball of Figs. 5.3 and 5.4, lead a viewer to think it is a man with closed eyes.

10. Like the Shroud, all the faces on the *sceattas* in question show long hair.

11. Figs. 5.3 and 5.5 show a complex shape of the moustache and beard arranged in a "reversed W" shape similar to the Shroud face.

12. While other faces of Christ on the sceattas are quite symmetric, that of Fig. 5.3 shows evident asymmetry corresponding to the eyes and beard analogous to the Shroud face.

According to John W. Williams [1999] "*Direct transmission of a Justinian II Pantocrator coin to Britain is not out of question. Some contemporary Byzantines have been found in the Anglo-Saxon hoards of the period, although rarely.*" We therefore must admit that the face of Christ reported on the *sceattas* show various similarities with the face of Christ shown on the Shroud and reproduced in the Byzantine coins. They also depict additional details like the "T" shape of the eyebrows and nose, and the right foot smaller and shorter, which are not present on the Justinian II coins. These were typical of the Shroud image that were coined centuries later in the Byzantine Empire by Basil I, starting from 867.

This fact is again in favor of the hypothesis that the images of Christ shown in the Anglo-Saxon silver *sceattas* and in the Byzantine gold *solidi*, came from a common model, the Shroud.

The general likeness to the Shroud is evident in some of the faces of Christ depicted on the *sceattas.* Figure 5.9 shows the superimposition of the Shroud face with that of the *sceat* of Fig. 5.4. This demonstrates how well the Anglo-Saxon engraver interpreted in a few lines the peculiar face of Christ on the Relic.

The reverse of the *sceattas* of Figs. 5.3–5.8 are not yet well interpreted by experts, but some depictions are recurrent; for example, Figs. 5.3, 5.4 and 5.5 seem to represent the same subject in similar forms. The interpretation of these images by a numismatic expert is interesting in view of a religious perspective [Gannon, 2011] that affirms these images seem to be referring to a long-legged quadruped with lowered muzzles and short horns like stags drinking water.

The expert supposes that the depicted scene invokes baptism and renewal representing stags drinking from the waters of Paradise, in agreement with Psalm (42:1–2) saying, "*As the deer pants for streams of water, so my soul pants for you, my God. My soul thirsts for God, for the living God.*" It can also refer to other passages of the Bible like John (3, 5), who presents Jesus Christ, "*talking figuratively about thirst as a spiritual quest and proclaiming Himself as the only one who can quench our spiritual thirst.*" [Gannon, 2011].

The numismatist continues, "*Looking more closely ... the tip of the 'tail' is zoomorphic. On some specimens ...* (author's note: like that of Fig. 5.4) *the tip is bifurcated and suggests jaws, whereas on others ...* (author's note: like that of Figs. 5.4 and 5.5) *a little dot by the tip represents an eye. ... There the 'tail' appears to be totally independent of the stag. I would suggest that what is interlacing between the stag's legs is actually a serpent. ... The combination of stag and snake suggest that the origin of this imagery ... goes back to the spiritual allegories ...* (where), *a stag could find and kill snakes; therefore, allegorically, it was said to stand for Christ, who defeats Satan.*"

Lastly, there is interesting unpublished evidence: The sceat declared from East Anglia or Mercia (715–760) of Fig. 5.10 sketches a face quite different from those of Christ shown in the previous figures of *sceattas* and it is supposed similar to that of a local divinity, the Wodan/Monster [Gannon, 2015; Abramson, 2012]. Due to the presence of the Christian crosses on the reverse of this coin, the author believes that perhaps a representation similar to that of Wodan/Monster was for some reason also used for the depiction of Christ.

Since this coin is very similar to another very rare lead coin found at Apolonia, Fier in Albany, see Fig. 5.11, this leads us to think these kinds of depictions were quite common in a large area comprising the British Islands and the Balkans, influenced by the Byzantine Christian culture. The author therefore supposes that the two faces in question may be of Christ, but not Shroud-like faces. They could instead resemble the Syriac Christ of Figs. 1.13–1.15 and 1.17–1.19, in fact, Justinian II coined the Syriac face of Christ in these years during his second reign period (705–711).

Figure 5.10 Sceat from East Anglia or Mercia (715–760). The sketchy face, probably of Christ, because of the crosses shown on the reverse, is very similar to a lead coin found at Apolonia, Fier in Albany (see Fig. 5.11).

Figure 5.11 Lead coin found at Apolonia, Fier in Albany very similar to the *sceat* of Fig. 5.10 showing a Syriac face of Christ comparable with that minted by Justinian II during his second period of reign (705–711), of Figs. 1.13–1.15 and 1.17–1.19.

5.1.2 North-European Coins

Starting from the eleventh century, we find coins showing Christ on the throne influenced by the body image of the Shroud.

In Denmark, where relationships with the Byzantine Empire were already documented in the tenth century, King Lund, Sweyn II Estridsson Ulfsson (1047–1075) reported on a silver *penny* the image of the blessing Christ on the throne similar to the Byzantine type.

Even if some Shroud features appear deteriorated like the absence of an evident beard, thus demonstrating that the engraver did not have direct access to the Relic, we still note the long hair and right foot smaller than the left and rotated on this coin, see Fig. 5.12.

Figure 5.12 Danish silver penny of King Lund, Sweyn II Estridsson Ulfsson (1047–1075) showing Christ on the throne.

During the Second Bulgarian Empire, we find various coins minted from the fourteenth to the fifteenth centuries showing Christ on the throne. For example, the silver *penny* or *grosso* of King Theodor Svetoslav (1300–1322), see Fig. 5.13, depicts the blessing Christ on the throne with a face not so well refined, but still quite similar to the Shroud image. In fact, we note the long hair and beard, the right foot tilted and the tuft of hair on the forehead that are typical of the Shroud body image.

Figure 5.13 Silver *penny* or *grosso* of King Theodor Svetoslav (1300–1322) of the Second Bulgarian Empire depicting the blessing Christ on the throne.

Starting from the fifteenth century, some states of Germany produced coins showing Christ on the throne like that of Fig. 5.14. It is a gold *goulden* of King Ludvig III of Bacharach, Germany (1410–1436) vaguely showing a Shroud-like face of Christ with long hair and bipartite beard.

Figure 5.14 Gold *goulden* of King Ludvig III of Bacharach of Germany (1410–1436), mint of Pfalz, vaguely showing a Shroud-like face of Christ.

5.1.3 Coins of the Maritime Republic of Venice

The Maritime Republic of Venice kept tight commercial relations with Constantinople for a long time, and consequently, it acquired its styles and habits. Under Doge Enrico Dandolo (1192–1205), this Republic, taking perhaps inspiration from the Danish penny of Fig. 5.12, started a series of mintages of Christ that lasted for several centuries until the fall of the Republic in 1797. Figure 5.15 shows the first coin of this lucky series of the silver *ducat* named *grosso* or *matapan*.

Figure 5.15 Silver *ducat, grosso* or *matapan* of Doge Enrico Dandolo (1192–1205) of the Maritime Republic of Venice showing Christ on the throne with evident Byzantine features. The probable *himation-pallium-*Shroud must be noted.

The engraved image is in accord with the Byzantine canons which show the rotated right foot, but the face becomes more symmetrical and round. The marks of the Passion, like the swollen cheekbones, are less evident, but some features like the big eyes, right sparse beard, mustache, and long, often asymmetrical hair remain. In agreement with Section 3.2.2, the blessing right hand is partially covered by the probable *himation-pallium-*Shroud wrapping the shoulders of Christ, passing over the book of Gospels, and falling on His left side.

The Venetians not only copied the Byzantine depictions of Christ on the throne on their *grossi* but also went further by minting new and different representations, always in coherence with the Byzantine canons acquired through the observation of the Shroud image, or a good copy of it.

An example, see Figs. 3.30 and 5.16, is the *mezzanino* minted by Doge Andrea Dandolo (1343–1354) depicting the resurrected

Christ wrapped in His Shroud showing Shroud-like asymmetrical long hair and bipartite beard, though the face size is only 3 mm.

Figure 5.16 Silver *mezzanino* of Doge Andrea Dandolo (1343–1354) of the Maritime Republic of Venice showing the resurrected Christ wrapped in His Shroud with a Shroud-like face.

The gold *sequin* (Italian *zecchino*) or *ducat*, see, for example, the one minted by Francesco Dandolo (1329–1339) on Fig. 5.17, shows a new image of Christ within an oval "*Almond Christ*" or "*Vesica Piscis*" (fish bladder), called "*Mandorla*" in Italian for almond. This coin depicts Christ with faces not always respecting the Byzantine canons, but maintaining the general features of the Shroud image.

Figure 5.17 Gold *sequin* of Francesco Dandolo (1329–1339) of the Maritime Republic of Venice showing the "*Almond Christ*" or "*Vesica Piscis.*"

The almond or *"mandorla"* is an oval frame with decorative function enclosing the sacred figure of Christ. This Romanesque-Gothic decorative element has a double value: It refers both to the almond fruit and to the seed in general. It is a clear symbol of life and therefore an attribute for the Man who is *"the Way, the Truth and the Life"* [Jn 14,6].

The intersection of two circles of the almond represents the communication between the two worlds, the material and the spiritual one, respectively related to the human and the divine sphere. Jesus, made Man, becomes the only mediator between the two realities, therefore He is depicted within the intersection thus as a means of communication between the spiritual and the material world.

Like the silver *grosso*, the gold *sequin* was a famous coin too that was minted for centuries not only in the Maritime Republic of Venice but also in other states like the Ducat of Milan and the Papal State. For example, Fig. 5.18 shows a gold *sequin* minted by the Crusaders of the Chios Maona Society (Greece) about in 1350.

Figure 5.18 Gold *sequin* of Crusaders of the Chios Maona Society (Greece, ca. 1350), imitation of the Venetian gold *ducat*.

Another interesting coin was produced by the Maritime Republic of Venice in the sixteenth century, the silver *lira* of Doge Mocenigo, see Fig. 5.19, showing the blessing Christ resurrected from the sepulcher in a depiction similar to the Byzantine coins, see Fig. 3.44. The long hair and the bipartite beard are again Shroud-like features.

Figure 5.19 Silver lira Mocenigo of the Maritime Republic of Venice, minted by Doge Pietro Lando (1539–1545) showing Christ resurrected.

5.1.4 West Balkan Coins

In the fourteenth century, the West Balkan states like Serbia and the Dalmatian Maritime Republic of Ragusa (or Dubrovnik) were influenced in their coinage by their cultural contact with the Byzantine Empire and the Venetian Maritime Republic. Serbia and Ragusa produced various images of Christ on their coins sometimes very similar to the Shroud body image.

Figure 5.20 Silver *dinar* or *grosso* of Stefan Uros I of Serbia (1243–1276) showing Christ on the throne. The tilted right foot and the long non-symmetric hair are analogous with the Shroud.

For example, the silver *ducat* named *grosso* or *matapan* produced by the Venetian Maritime Republic was taken as reference for the silver *dinar*, or *grosso* minted by Stefan Uros I of Serbia (1243–1276). Figure 5.20 depicts Christ on the throne. The right foot is tilted and the bearded face of Christ has long non-symmetric hair detached from the face, analogous with the Shroud body image.

The silver *dinar* or *grosso* of Stefan Uros V of Serbia (1355–1371), see Fig. 5.21, instead takes its reference from the Byzantine depiction of Christ resurrected from the sepulcher like those of Fig. 3.44. Again, this coin shows a Shroud-like face.

Figure 5.21 Silver *dinar* or *grosso* of Stefan Uros V of Serbia (1355–1371), showing a Shroud-like Christ resurrected from the sepulcher.

Figure 5.22 Silver *dinar* or *grosso* of the Republic of Dubrovnik (or Republic of Ragusa, 1284–1372) showing Christ in an almond with a Shroud-like face.

The Republic of Dubrovnik (or Republic of Ragusa), in the Balkans, in the thirteenth to fourteenth century, coined a silver *dinar* reproducing an image of Christ in the almond, see Fig. 5.22. This depiction is similar to that of the Venetian *sequins*, see Fig. 5.17. In this case, the face of Christ, like that of the Shroud, is more elongated than the normal, with long hair, bipartite beard and pronounced cheekbones.

5.1.5 Russian Coins

Czar Vladimir Sviatoslavich (958–1015), called the Great, was Prince of Novgorod, Grand Prince of Kiev and ruler of Kievan Rus'. Also known as Saint Vladimir, originally a follower of Slavic paganism, he converted to Christianity in 988 and Christianized the Kievan Rus'. From this information, we better understand the image of Christ on the silver ruble of Fig. 5.23 depicted to evangelize the area of his reign. The evident "T-shape" of the nose-eyebrows is clearly a Shroud feature.

Figure 5.23 Silver *ruble* of Srebrennik coined by Vladimir I the Great of Kiev, Russia (980–1015).

In addition, the bronze *follis*, probably of Prince Jaroslav II of Novgorod and Vladimir (1215–1246), shows a face of Christ with signs typical of the Shroud, like beard, moustache and long hair.

Figure 5.24 Bronze *follis* probably of Prince Jaroslav II of Novgorod and Vladimir (1215–1246) showing a face of Christ typical of the Shroud.

5.1.6 Arab-Anatolian Coins

A relatively great number of different coins [Goodwin, 2006], mostly quite rare, have been found in the Arab-Anatolian area showing an image of Christ derived from both the Byzantine canons and the Shroud. They demonstrate that the tradition of Christ on the coins continued for centuries after the Sac of Constantinople of 1204 when the Shroud disappeared from the Byzantine area.

The following list of coins is an example of the many Arab-Anatolian coins showing faces of Christ, the blessing Christ on the throne and Christ resurrected according to the Byzantine canons respectively shown in Figs. 3.43 and 3.44. Some of these coins had been minted after 1204 when the coin-engraver had not the opportunity to look directly at the Shroud and therefore some typical features of the body image of Christ were lost. Notwithstanding this, these coins frequently show many features amenable to the image of the most important Relic of Christianity.

1. NICEA. Gold *hyperpyron* of Michael VIII (1272–1282), minted about seventy years after the fall of the Byzantine Empire. Here Christ appears on the reverse, crowning the Emperor with the Archangel Michael. On the obverse the Constantinople walls with the Mother of God are reproduced, see Fig. 5.25. The still Shroud-like face of Christ shows long asymmetric hair and long nose.

Figure 5.25 Gold *hyperpyron* of Michael VIII of Nicea (1272–1282) showing Christ on the reverse (see arrow); Constantinople walls with the Mother of God on the obverse.

2. TRABZON or TREBIZOND. The *electrum histamenon nomisma*, of Andronicus I (1222–1235) shows the resurrected Christ holding in His right hand an important sheet that can be identified in the simplified *loros*-Shroud that agrees with the study performed in Section 3.2.3, see Fig. 5.26.

3. ANATOLIA. Bronze *dirham* or *follis* of Fakhr al-Din Qara (or Kara) Arslan (1144–1174), Artuqid dynasty, with the countermark on the obverse, showing Christ on the throne having a face very similar to that of the Shroud: long wavy hair detached from the face, prominent cheeks, absence of ears, and eyes like rounded buttons, as if they were closed, but expressive. It is interesting to observe that the Arab scripture is inverted going from the right to the left, and the Byzantine depiction of Christ on throne, similar to those of Figs. 3.43, is inverted too, showing Christ holding the simplified *loros*-Shroud, with His left hand, see Fig. 5.27.

4. ANATOLIA. Bronze *dirham* or *follis* minted by Sebastia (1164–1172) of the dynasty of Danishmend (or Danishmendid), minted in Cufic style, showing Christ on the throne with Shroud-like long hair and right leg-foot shorter than the left one, see Fig. 5.28.

Figure 5.26 *Electrum histamenon nomisma*, of Andronicus I Emperor of Trabzon or Trebizond (1222-1235) showing on the obverse the Mother of God standing and on the reverse the resurrected Christ holding the simplified *loros*-Shroud in His right hand and the Book of Gospels in His left hand.

Figure 5.27 Bronze *dirham* or *follis* of Fakhr al-Din Qara (or Kara) Arslan (1144–1174, Artuqid dynasty, Anatolia Turkey), with countermark on obverse, showing Christ on the throne with a face very similar to that of the Shroud. Like the Arab scripture, the Byzantine depiction of Christ on the throne is inverted too.

5. SELJUK EMPIRE. Bronze *dirham* or *follis* of Nur al din Mahmud ibnZangi of the Zangids dynasty of Aleppo in Syria,

(1146–1173) showing Christ on the throne holding the book of the Gospels. We note some remembrance to the Byzantine canons of Fig. 3.43 with the Shroud falling down from the left arm, see Fig. 5.29. In agreement with the Arab scripture, the symbol "XC" for Jesus Christ is inverted too.

Figure 5.28 Bronze *dirham* or *follis* minted by Sebastia of the dynasty of Danishmend (or Danishmendid), Anatolia (1164–1172) written in Cufic style, showing Christ on the throne.

Figure 5.29 Bronze *dirham* or *follis* of Nur al din Mahmud ibnZangi of the Zangids dynasty of Aleppo Syria, Seljuk Empire (1146–1173) showing Christ on the throne. In agreement with the Arab scripture, the symbol "XC" for Jesus Christ is inverted too.

6. CIPRUS. *"White bezant"* (that is a scyphate *electrum* coin based on Byzantine *trachea* minted in the Kingdom of Cyprus) of Henry I, Lusignan Kingdom, (1218–1253) showing Christ on the throne. His face, while stylized and more symmetric, conserves some Shroud features like the beard, long hair longer on the left side and the tuft of hair on the forehead, see Fig. 5.30.

Figure 5.30 *"White bezant"* (scyphate *electrum* coin based on Byzantine *trachea* minted in the Kingdom of Cyprus) of Henry I, Lusignan Kingdom, Ciprus (1218–1253) showing Christ on the throne.

7. ANTIOCH Principality. Follis of Tancred (1104–1112) showing the face of Christ similar to the Shroud image with long wavy hair detached from the face and without ears, see Fig. 5.31.

8. Count of EDESSA. Baldwin II (1100–1104), see Fig. 5.32, and Joscelin I de Courtenay (1119–1131), see Fig. 5.33. The busts of Christ on bronze *folles* show that the cult of Christ was still active at Edessa, probably in memory of the Shroud-Mandylion there preserved some centuries ago, as reported in Section 2.4.2. The face of Christ face of Fig. 5.32 is very similar to the Shroud showing long hair, eyes like rounded buttons and bipartite beard.

9. ARMENIAN CILICIA. Silver coin of Levon I of Armenia (1198–1219) showing Christ crowning the king. Eyes like rounded buttons, long nose and hair of this face make it similar to the Shroud, see Fig. 5.34.

10. GEORGIA. Silver *dirham* of Rusudan (1223–1245), see Fig. 5.35, showing the bust of the blessing Christ in the Byzantine style of Fig. 4.19 with the Book of Gospels in His left hand.

Figure 5.31 *Follis* of Tancred (1104–1112) of Antioch Principality showing the face of Christ similar to the Shroud image.

Figure 5.32 Bronze *follis* of Baldwin II (1100–1104), Count of Edessa showing the bust of Christ with a face similar to the Shroud: long hair, eyes like rounded buttons and bipartite beard.

Figure 5.33 Bronze *follis* of Joscelin I de Courtenay (1119–1131), Count of Edessa showing a bust of Christ.

Figure 5.34 Silver coin of Levon I Armenia (1198–1219), king of Cilician Armenia showing Christ crowning the king.

Figure 5.35 Silver *dirham* of Rusudan (1223–1245) of Georgia showing the bust of the blessing Christ.

5.1.7 Sicilian Coins

Sicily (Italy) had strict relationships with the Arabs and the Byzantine Empire in the twelfth century and this culture frequently prevailed in the Sicilian Rulers. We find various coins depicting Jesus Christ having a Shroud-like appearance and even texts written in the Arab language.

Examples are King Roger II of Palermo (1130–1140), see Figs. 5.36, and King William I of Palermo (1131–1166), see Figs. 5.37, who minted silver scyphate *ducats* depicting the blessing bust of Christ with the book of the Gospels in His left hand like the Byzantine style of Fig. 4.19. These Shroud-like faces show long wavy hair, moustache, bipartite beard and in some cases a tuft of hair on the forehead.

Different from the above-mentioned silver ducats, the bronze *follaro* of Fig. 5.38 minted by King Roger II of Messina (1105–1154), shows the blessing Christ with His right hand extended in the Byzantine style shown in Fig. 3.28 (on the left). This posture was depicted during the same time period by Emperor Manuel I Comnenus (1143–1180). Arabic influence is present in the inscriptions written in this language on the reverse.

Figure 5.36 Silver *ducat* of King Roger II of Palermo (1130–1140) showing a Shroud-like bust of Christ.

Figure 5.37 Silver scyphate *ducat* of King William I of Palermo (1131–1166) showing a Shroud-like bust of Christ.

Figure 5.38 Bronze *follaro* of King Roger II of Messina (1105–1154) showing the blessing Christ. Arabic influence is evident in the inscriptions of the reverse.

5.1.8 More Recent Coins

Christ's depictions endured over the centuries in different states until the present years, but never with the same frequency of representation that appeared during the Byzantine Empire. For example, for celebrating the Great Jubilee in 2000, some states minted coins with the face of Christ and, among them, the gold coin of 500 *schillings* minted by Austria, see Fig. 5.39, in which a "modern" Christ is depicted showing some Shroud-Byzantine reminiscences. A faint sign of Byzantine tradition, linked to the Shroud, reflected in this Austrian coin is visible in the beard and mustache. In addition, the Byzantine Shroud details of still wavy hair and the swellings in correspondence to the cheekbones have been handed down during the centuries but are still evident in the tradition regarding the features of Christ.

Figure 5.39 Gold coin of 500 *schillings* minted for the 2000 Jubilee. The face of Christ has still a weak Byzantine-Shroud reminiscence, for example, long wavy hair, but now more symmetric.

Commemorating the Shroud exhibition of 2015, the State of Vatican City minted a celebrative gold coin of 10 *euro* representing again a Shroud-like face, see Fig. 5.40. The hair longer on the left, the tuft of hair on the forehead, the bipartite beard, the swollen cheekbones and the elongated face, typical of the Byzantine canons related to the Shroud image of face, should be noted on this coin.

All these features, but in particular the tuft of hair on the forehead, very typical of the Byzantine canons, lead to think that the Vatican engraver made reference to the Shroud.

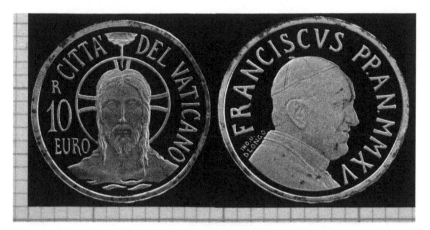

Figure 5.40 Celebratory gold coin of the State of Vatican City minted for the occasion of the Shroud exhibition in 2015. There are many features of the face typical of the Byzantine canons related to the Shroud image.

5.2 Highlights of the Analysis

Section 5.1 has shown the relatively large number of different coins minted in the Middle Ages by various states. Even though these states were separated by thousands of kilometers from the Capital of the Byzantine Empire, they copied the Byzantine canons in reproducing the face of Christ on their coins, thus demonstrating how the Christian culture spread throughout world. The following list shows interesting facts which have emerged from this analysis.

5.2.1 Variety of Depiction of Jesus Christ

Almost all the coins considered in Section 5.1 show many Shroud-like features such as an asymmetric face, long hair with the typical tuft on the forehead, corresponding to the reversed "3" bloodstain on the Shroud, "T"-shaped nose-eyebrows, pronounced annulets forming the eyes, relatively long nose, prominent cheeks, bipartite beard, smaller right leg and tilted foot.

States far from Constantinople, where the Shroud was conserved and exposed during that period, reproduced Shroud-like faces of Christ having a reduced number of typical features.

This confirms the hypothesis that the engravers had difficulty directly observing the Relic.

The great majority of coins showing Christ refer to the Byzantine canons derived from the Shroud. Depictions like the bust of the blessing Christ, Christ on the throne and the resurrected Christ are typical of the Byzantine tradition. In addition to these depictions, others appear, like the Venetian Christ in the almond or "*mandorla,*" see Figs. 5.17 and 5.18, confirming the increased interest by many people in Jesus Christ and the Christian religion.

5.2.2 Bust of Christ

Many rulers, like those reigning in Antioch (see Fig. 5.31), Georgia (see Fig. 5.35), Edessa (see Fig. 5.32), Palermo (see Fig. 5.36), Russia (see Fig. 5.23) and others, minted coins showing busts of the blessing Christ typical of the famous Byzantine type begun with Justinian II (692–695), see Fig. 5.41, where many of the above-mentioned Shroud-like features are evident.

Figure 5.41 Busts of Christ similar to the Byzantine type begun with Justinian II (692–695, on the top left) produced by various rulers like those (from the top left to the right bottom) of Antioch, Georgia, Edessa, Palermo and Russia.

This fact underlines the great cultural influence, other than commercial, the Byzantine Empire had on neighboring States.

5.2.3 Christ on Throne

Other rulers like those in Denmark (see Fig. 5.12), Bulgaria (see Fig. 5.13), Cyprus (see Fig. 5.30), Venice (see Fig. 5.15), Syria (see Fig. 5.29) minted coins showing the image of Christ on the throne, common in the Byzantine coinage begun with Basil I (867–886), see Fig. 5.42. Many of the above-mentioned Shroud-like features are evident on these depictions, again confirming the great cultural influence, other than commercial, of the Byzantine Empire.

Figure 5.42 Christ on throne similar to the Byzantine type begun with Basil I (867–886 on the top left) produced by various leaders like those (from the top left to the right bottom) of Denmark, Bulgaria, Cyprus, Venice and Syria.

Among the various depictions of Christ on the throne minted by the various states, noteworthy is the bronze *dirham* or *follis* of Fakhr al-Din Qara (or Kara) Arslan (1144–1174, Artuqid dynasty, Anatolia Turkey) of Fig. 5.27 showing the classic Byzantine depiction of Christ on the throne, but reversed like the direction of Arabic writing, see Fig. 5.43.

Figure 5.43 Typical Byzantine depiction of Christ on the throne of Romanus III (1028–1034 on the left) compared with a bronze *dirham* or *follis* of Fakhr al-Din Qara (or Kara) Arslan (1144–1174, Artuqid dynasty, Anatolia Turkey) of Fig. 5.27 showing Christ on the throne similar to the Byzantine one (on the right) but reversed. In the center, for comparison, the same image is reversed.

5.2.4 Resurrected Christ

Many countries like Trabzon or Trebizond (see Fig. 5.26), Serbia (see Fig. 5.21), Venice (see Figs. 5.16 and 5.19) and others minted coins showing the image of the resurrected Christ also typical of the Byzantine coinage begun with Theodora (1055–1056), see Fig. 5.44.

While these coins again confirm the great cultural influence of the Byzantine Empire on neighboring areas, we detect a certain freedom of choice in the depiction of the Resurrection scene. While the empire of Trabzon or Trebizond minted coins more similar to the traditional Byzantine type of Theodora (1055–1056), the Maritime Republic of Venice proposed two quite different and new depictions of the resurrected Christ. The depictions always reproduced a face of Christ similar to that of the Shroud with long hair bipartite beard and without ears.

Figure 5.44 Resurrected Christ starting from the Byzantine type begun with Theodora (1055–1056, on the left) coined by various empires like those (from left to the right) of Trabzon or Trebizond, Serbia, Venice and Venice.

5.2.5 Faces of Christ

We have seen the great variety of depictions of the face of Christ on many coins minted by different states far from Constantinople, capital of the Byzantine Empire.

Figure 5.45 compares some examples of these faces with that of the Shroud (shown on the top left). Starting from the Shroud, to the bottom right, in order of similarity with the Relic, we respectively see the following faces minted by: Justinian II (692–695, see Fig. 4.1 on the left), Venice (see Figs. 5.17 and 5.16), Anatolia (see Fig. 5.27); on the second row, Dubrovnik (see Fig. 5.22), Anglo-Saxon (see Fig. 5.4), Edessa (see Fig. 5.32), Messina (see Fig. 5.38), Bulgaria (see Fig. 5.13); on the third row, Palermo (see Fig. 5.36), Cyprus (see Fig. 5.30), Trebizond (see Fig. 5.26), Venice (see Figs. 5.15 and 5.19).

As already stated, all these images indicate some correlation with the Shroud image, but while some of them show many features of it, others only vaguely show these features. This is probably because the coin engraver did not have the chance to observe directly either the Shroud image or a good copy of it.

The variability of these faces will be discussed further in Chapter 8. They depend upon the subjectivity of the engraver who interprets and puts in some features according to the subjective feeling the Shroud image produces in the artist. For example, even if the faces produced by Venice, Anatolia and Dubrovnik (in the first row) shown on Fig. 5.45 appear very good copies of the Shroud face, they seem quite different from each other.

Instead, some faces like those of Bulgaria, Cyprus and Trebizond, shown in the third row of Fig. 5.45 are quite different from the reference model of the Shroud. Again, this can be explained by the engraver's inability to see the Shroud directly because in that period it was taken away by the Crusaders from Constantinople.

Figure 5.45 Faces of Christ derived from the Shroud starting from the top left to the bottom right in order of similarity with the Relic. The following faces are respectively shown: that minted by Justinian II (692–695), those of Venice, Anatolia; on the second row, Dubrovnik, Anglo-Saxon, Edessa, Messina, Bulgaria; on the third row, Palermo, Cyprus, Trebizond Venice and Venice.

5.2.6   Faces of Christ on the Anglo-Saxon Sceattas

As reported in Section 5.1.1, the *sceattas* showing the face of Christ, minted from 710–715, about two dozen years after the first coins of Justinian II (692–695), are interesting because many of them show features typical of the Shroud, but follow models quite different from the Byzantine ones.

These coins, see Fig. 5.46, show on one hand how far the Christian culture had spread in the world during this period, and on the other, that the distance from Constantinople released the Anglian engravers from some Byzantine canons thus allowing them more freedom in their interpretation.

Figure 5.46 Faces of Christ minted on Anglo-Saxon sceattas showing some Shroud-like features.

5.2.7   Connection between Anglo-Saxon and Albanian Coins

An apparently interesting and unpublished comparison between the two coins of Figs. 5.10 and 5.11 was performed in Section 5.1.1. An evident similarity resulted in both the obverse and reverse of a silver *sceatta* coming from East Anglia or Mercia and a rare lead coin found at Apolonia, Fier in Alban. This similarity demonstrates the cultural closeness between these two distant lands, which were more than 2000 km (1200 mi.) from each other. Perhaps some historical connections between these regimes should be reconsidered.

Following this presentation of the coins of Christ in the medieval world, we shall consider in the next chapter only one coin of Justinian II (692–695). Through a probabilistic evaluation, we shall see if a hypothetical Byzantine engraver could have obtained the resulting face of Christ seen on that coin without having observed either the Shroud or a good copy of it.

Chapter 6

Probabilistic Analysis Applied to a Coin

The previous chapters have presented the numerous coins that show the face of Christ, minted both in the Byzantine Empire and in other states.

We have also seen that the great majority of these faces of Christ show peculiar features strictly connected with those of the Shroud body image. This demonstrates that the most important Relic in Christianity was the primary reference source for the Byzantine engravers. It was known in the Empire at least from 692 when Emperor Justinian II coined the first official gold solidi depicting the blessing Christ.

This chapter takes into consideration only one of the many coins showing a face of Christ molded by the Byzantine engravers. It will be analyzed to determine the probability of the peculiar features on the face being minted without the engraver viewing the Shroud.

6.1 Coin Description

The coin selected for the probabilistic analysis is shown in Fig. 6.1. It is a 19 mm gold *solidus* minted by Emperor Justinian II during

Byzantine Coins Influenced by the Shroud of Christ
Giulio Fanti
Copyright © 2022 Jenny Stanford Publishing Pte. Ltd.
ISBN 978-981-4877-88-6 (Hardcover), 978-1-003-21992-7 (eBook)
www.jennystanford.com

his first period (692–695) and shows the face of Christ on the obverse and the Emperor on the reverse. An image processing of the gold *solidus* in question has been performed in Fig. 6.2 to show the evidence for the similarity of this face of Christ with that of the Shroud.

Figure 6.1 Coin considered for the probabilistic analysis: gold *solidus* minted by Emperor Justinian II in 692–695. On the obverse: the blessing bust of Christ probably wrapped in the *himation-pallium*-Shroud (see Section 3.2.2) with cross behind head. He has long non-symmetric hair, bipartite beard, long nose, raising right hand in benediction and holding the book of Gospels in left hand. On the reverse Emperor Justinian II is wearing a crown and loros standing facing and holding cross with his right hand.

Many of the faces of Christ produced by the same Emperor Justinian II during this relatively short time range (692–695) are shown in Fig. 6.3, providing evidence that each engraver subjectively depicted some features typical of the Shroud face, but neglected others. For example, while almost all the faces of Christ show a tuft of hair on the forehead, the *solidus* on the left bottom of the figure neglects it. Also, if we ignore the coin on the top right of Fig. 6.3 because the area of the nose was deformed by something hitting it, some of the coins show a straight nose while others show the nose skewed to the left as it appears on the Shroud.

Before proceeding with the probabilistic analysis, it is necessary to analyze the style of the faces in use during the Byzantine Empire. This initial analysis must be done to avoid considering features that can appear typical of the Shroud face, but are also typical on coins of many, if not all, the important persons of the Empire. For this reason, Fig. 6.4 shows some faces of Byzantine Emperors that must be used for comparison with the features of the face of Christ on the coin in question.

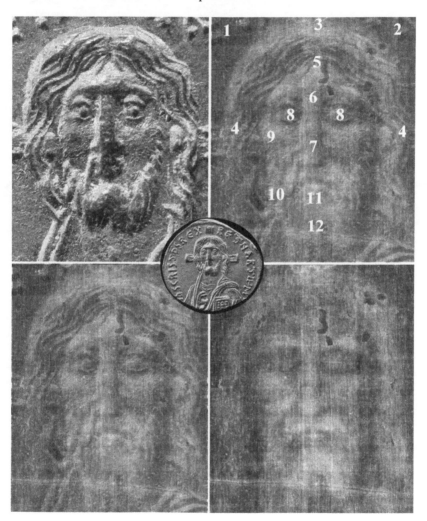

Figure 6.2 Image processing of the face of Christ (on the top left) depicted on the gold *solidus* of Fig. 6.1 of Justinian II (692–695), compared with the Shroud face (on the bottom right). The other two images are given by overlapping the two faces, with the indication of the 12 peculiar features considered in the probabilistic analysis.

Figure 6.3 Variety of faces of Christ minted on gold *solidi* during a relatively short time range (692–695) by Emperor Justinian II. From the top left to the bottom right, the typical features of the Shroud-like image seem to dampen.

Figure 6.4 Faces of Byzantine emperors reported on gold coins that must be used for comparison with the features discussed in the probabilistic analysis applied to the coin of Fig. 6.1. From the top left to the bottom right the following Emperors are respectively shown: Justinian II (692–695); Michael III (842–867); Johannes I (969–976); Basil II (976–1025); Michael IV (1034–1041); Constantine IX (1042–1055); Michael VII (1071–1078); Manuel I (1143–1180).

6.2   Probabilistic Analysis

The goal of this calculation is to answer the following question. What is the probability for the engraver to reproduce the face of Christ on the coin of Fig. 6.1 without having referred to the Shroud image or a good copy of it?

As already stated, other Byzantine coins depicting the face of Christ show additional features similar to the Shroud, but the probabilistic analysis is performed to consider only the following features of the coin in question. This is done both because it is simpler from a probabilistic point of view and because the result appears clearly conclusive without the need to consider other coins.

By using special concepts and theorems of probability calculus reported in the Appendix 1, we can calculate the probabilities of detecting the following features. Each of them is assigned an appropriate event probability. It is assumed there is no external influence on the artist in reference to the detail of the Shroud in question by any part, but that the artist arbitrarily decided to reproduce that particular feature.

1. *Unattractive face.* From Psalm 45:2 we read, "*You are the most handsome of men; ....*" We can remember the beauty of Jesus described in the Byzantine canon by the three Eastern Patriarchs: Christopher of Antioch, Job of Alexandria and Basil of Jerusalem. Also later in the Byzantine era, Nicephorus Callistus in 1330 confirmed that Jesus Christ was very beautiful in stature and face. However, the face of Christ on the Shroud is not beautiful because He had been tortured. Therefore, if the Byzantine engraver depicted Jesus Christ with such a tortured face when Psalm 45:2 refers to Him as "*the most handsome of men,*" then the engraver must have received his inspiration from the Shroud. In addition, we must remember that any possible defect or subjective variation in the depiction of Christ's face would not have had the approval of the Emperor.

   Probability: 1 chance in 500.

2. *Asymmetry of face.* A comparison with the almost entirely symmetrical faces of the Byzantine emperors shown in

Fig. 6.4 evidences the distinctiveness of the face of Christ in question. As the face of the Shroud is not symmetric, 1 chance in 100 could be assigned for this feature, but a small correlation could be detected with Feature #1. For this reason, accounting for this possible correlation, the results are as follows.

Probability: 1 chance in 20.

3. *No crown or decorations.* As we can see in Fig. 6.4 and as indicated by Grierson [1973], all the emperors were depicted with crowns or diadems with pendilia reported as *"a vertical line of fine dots on either side of the face ending in a trefoil ornament shown as three pellets."* These head ornaments were used in antiquity to emphasize the dignity of the rulers and symbol of sovereignty. The Shroud face of the so-called *"King of kings"* is instead depicted without any kind of crowns and pendilia. Only the cross appears behind His face. This evident difference demonstrates a clear connection with the Shroud.

Probability: 1 chance in 200.

4. *Long and wavy hair.* Like the Shroud, the hair is long and wavy. Nevertheless, the face of Justinian II of Fig. 6.4 has relatively similar hair which is a bit different in the lower part. Therefore the probability must account of this fact.

Probability: 1 chance in 30.

5. *Tuft of hair.* As discussed in Section 4.2.1, this detail seems connected with the famous reversed *"3"* sign of the Shroud produced on Christ's forehead by a blood flow. It seems typical of the Shroud face and perhaps never reported on the emperor's faces.

Probability: 1 chance in 200.

6. *T-shaped nose-eyebrow.* The nose-eyebrow configuration frequently forms a *"T"* shape in many depictions of Christ on Byzantine coins and this is a typical feature of the Shroud face. Nevertheless, rarely does this *"T"* shape appear on the faces of the Byzantine emperors too. Therefore, the probability must take account of this fact.

Probability: 1 chance in 10.

7. *Long nose.* If we look at the Emperor's face shown in Fig. 6.2, we see that the Byzantine engravers anatomically studied the nose in the details because it varies from face to face. Nevertheless, the long nose typical of both the image of Christ in question and the Shroud, also appears on the face of Justinian II. Therefore, the probability must account for this fact.

Probability: 1 chance in 10.

8. *Closed, large and round eyes.* The relatively low resolution of the face of the Shroud does not allow detecting the eyelids and so it seems that Christ has His eyes closed. In agreement with many Byzantine engravers, in this coin too we find open eyes because the engraver wanted to depict Christ present and alive after the Resurrection. The eyes are peculiar because they are large and expressive, round and without iris and pupil. These features have not been accounted for in the probabilistic analysis, because they are typical of many emperors' faces too, like those shown in Fig. 6.4. Instead, in agreement with the study performed in Chapter 7, the peculiarity of this face considered here is that, like the Shroud, the eyes are closed and the ratio of nose to eyes is higher than the normal.

Probability: 1 chance in 10.

9. *Swollen right cheek.* Like the Shroud image, the swelling of the right cheek, is probably evident due to a blow from a reed as reported in the Gospel of Mark (15, 19).

Probability: 1 chance in 100.

10. *Beard sparse on the right.* In agreement with both the Shroud image and the Bible (Isaiah 50:6), the beard appears sparser on the right side of the face of Christ, depicted on the gold *solidus* in question. Considering this feature alone, it would produce a rarer probability, but in some rare cases, emperors also show this characteristic. Due to this consequence, the probability has been reduced.

Probability: 1 chance in 50.

11. *No beard under lower lip.* Like the Shroud image, there is a gap in the beard below the lower lip. This could be thought

of as a rare occurrence, but various emperors shown in Fig. 6.4 report the same feature. Therefore the probability must take account of this fact.

Probability: 1 chance in 4.

12. *Bipartite beard.* Not only is the beard bipartite, but Christ's face on the gold solidus in question has the same shaped beard as that shown on the Shroud image. This depiction is therefore rather improbable for an engraver who did not see the Relic.

Probability: 1 chance in 300.

Other peculiar features, like the following, could be considered in the probabilistic evaluation, but the author prefers to neglect them for the following reasons. The face of Christ on the gold *solidus* in question shows:

- *Long moustache,* but all the emperors of Fig. 6.4 show this feature.
- *Flattened and slightly curved nose,* but in some cases reported in Fig. 6.4, the shape of the nose is not always straight; in some cases flattening could also be due to the wear of excessive handling.
- *High-arched left eyebrow* and *swelling next to the right eye* are evident on the Shroud image due to probable contusions and hematomas, but these details do not appear evident on the image of the gold *solidus* in question, while they are well evidenced in other similar coins.

6.3 Probabilistic Results

Probabilistic analysis is not trivial. It requires that the probabilities of 12 independent events in which the engraver decided to reproduce some peculiar features of the face of Christ on the gold *solidus,* be combined in such a way that all the possible mixed combinations[a] are excluded.

---

[a]As described in the Appendix 1, the probability resulting from the combination of multiple events may seem at first, to always correspond to the product of the probabilities of each event. For example, the probability that the number 6 occurs twice in a roll of two dice is the product of the probabilities $(1/6 \times 1/6) = 1/36$. Instead, in the present case for an engraver to produce the image of the face from

The evaluation of the unknown probability is therefore performed by applying the Bayes formula where three kinds of probabilities appear. They are the a priori, the a posteriori probability, and the likelihood. This calculation, which is based on mathematical formulas, is reported in the Appendix 1.

This calculation indicates that the probability that the engraver reproduced the coin in question without knowing anything about the Shroud image is:

$$1.13 \times 10^{-19}, \text{ or } 0.000000000000000000113$$

In other words, the hypothesis that an engraver was able to mould the face reported on the coin without having seen the Shroud, or a good copy of it, results in 1 chance over 10 billion billion. Obviously, this is not impossible, but extremely improbable.

If we consider the uncertainty of the probabilistic values assigned in the Appendix 1, the hypothesis under consideration results in the range between 5 chances over 1 million billion billion and 2 chances over 10 million billion. A previous statistical analysis [Fanti and Malfi, 2020] performed on different features reaches a different result *"seven chances over 1 billion billion"* but within the estimated uncertainty range, confirming the robustness of the probabilistic results.

A better understanding of the meaning of this result, *"1 chance over 10 billion billion"* can be seen in the example referring to a roulette game (see Appendix 1 for the calculations). It would correspond to the chance of hitting the same number, *12* consecutive times. Similarly, in the roll of a dice with six faces, it would correspond to the chance of having the same number, *24* consecutive times.

---

the Shroud on a coin, we have to eliminate the probabilities corresponding to mixed events (for example, we have to exclude the probability that it considers an event marked as True coupled with an event marked as False). Similarly, in the dice example, it corresponds to determining the probability that the number 6 will occur twice in a roll of two dice, with the constraint that it is only possible for pairs of equal values (1-1, 2-2, 3-3, 4-4, 5-5 or 6-6) to occur. The corresponding probability is not 1/36 as above, but it increases to 1/6." (Because all mixed possibilities such as 1-2 or 5-6 are excluded).

In general, if we have two possibilities as in the coin under consideration, whether it is True or False, we must exclude the probability considering an event marked as True to be coupled with an event marked as False.

In support of the probabilistic result obtained, there are also more than 100 points of congruence determined by the scholars A. and M. Whanger [1985, 1998, 2007] on a similar coin and the studies of the numismatist M. Moroni [1983, 1986, 2000]. This confirms that the Byzantine engravers, who molded the face of Christ on the gold *solidus* of Justinian II, certainly saw the Shroud or a good copy of it.

6.4 Conclusive Remarks

The probabilistic analysis performed on a gold *solidus* of Justinian II (692–695), which shows the face of Christ, among the many others coined during the Byzantine Empire, demonstrates that the Byzantine engraver almost surely had the occasion to view the Shroud before molding the coin. In fact, the analysis based on the Bayes formula indicates a probability of 99.99999999999999999% that the image of Christ on the coin in question was copied either from the Shroud or from a good copy of it.

Appendix 2 shows a new medal coined to directly compare the face of Christ on the Shroud, on the obverse, with the face of Christ of Fig. 6.1 minted by Justinian II in 692, on the reverse.

A more complicated probabilistic analysis considering many kinds of faces of Christ from those minted during the Byzantine Empire would be more complete, but seeing the clear result obtained here, the author thinks the results are significant and conclusive without continuing with additional calculations.

The reader could ask if we have seen everything regarding the faces of Christ depicted on the Byzantine coins. Obviously, we have not, because many other aspects can be studied in detail. One of them is regarding the possibility of performing a quantitative analysis on the various faces of Christ molded during the centuries in order to seek additional information. This is the task of the following chapter that will also confirm that the Shroud was exhibited to visitors during the Byzantine period, based on evidence, still present today, that many pilgrims very probably put their gold Byzantine coins in contact with the Shroud to make second-order relics.

Chapter 7

Quantitative Analysis and *Third-Class Relics*

We have just seen that it is practically impossible to think that the face of Christ on the gold solidus of Justinian II was molded without copying the Shroud. Even if the probabilistic analysis, by definition, is based on subjective evaluation of the degree of confidence relative to the occurrence of a specific event, this and the following chapters will confirm the result from quantitative points of view.

In this chapter, the Byzantine coins are treated following two avenues in order to reach a more objective result. The first one regards the shape of the face of Christ on the coin measured by the so-called nose-to-eye ratio; the second one treats the comparison of the alloys of the Byzantine coins with the composition of some metal particles found on the Shroud.

7.1 Quantitative Analysis of Christ's Face

If we look at the face of Christ on the Shroud, we see that it appears somewhat elongated with a long nose and eyes closed to each other. Some Byzantine coins, but not all, reproduce these features. The present study is addressed to show evidence of a possible correlation between the reproduction of these features on coins

Byzantine Coins Influenced by the Shroud of Christ
Giulio Fanti
Copyright © 2022 Jenny Stanford Publishing Pte. Ltd.
ISBN 978-981-4877-88-6 (Hardcover), 978-1-003-21992-7 (eBook)
www.jennystanford.com

with the fact that the Byzantine engravers had the occasion to directly view either the Shroud or a good copy of it.

Scientific analysis [Bevilacqua et al., 2008; Soyel and Demirel, 2007] suggests the measurements of several features of the human face, some of which are not so easy to identify on the face of Jesus Christ on the Shroud. Among the most evaluated parameters, there are those related to the length of the nose and the distance between the eyes. These will be considered in the present analysis. A dimensional analysis of computerized images is therefore carried out in order to measure the R-ratio between the length of the nose and the eyes of the various faces.

The nose and eye length parameters used to evaluate the R-ratio, are shown in Fig. 7.1 on three examples of images of Christ. From left to right, the Shroud image with R-ratio = 1.28, a gold *solidus* of Justinian II (692–695) with R-ratio = 1.04 and a miraculous image of Christ obtained at Gimigliano, Ascoli Piceno, Italy with R-ratio = 1.17.

Figure 7.1 Length parameters (length of the nose and distance of the eyes) on three images of Christ. From the left to the right, the Shroud image with R-ratio = 1.28, that of a gold solidus minted by Justinian II (692–695) with R-ratio = 1.04 and that of a miraculous image of Christ obtained at Gimigliano, Ascoli Piceno, Italy with R-ratio = 1.17.

To understand the meaning of this ratio variation, Fig. 7.2 exemplifies a comparison of the real Shroud face where the R-ratio is 1.28, with the same face distorted obtaining an R-ratio respectively equal to 1 and to 0.7 which corresponds to the ratios of some faces of Christ shown on some Byzantine coins.

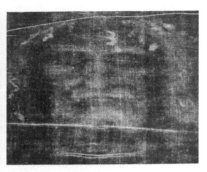

Figure 7.2 Original Shroud face (on the left) with an *R*-ratio equal to 1.28, compared with the same distorted faces, respectively obtaining an *R*-ratio equal to 1 (in the center) and to 0.7 (on the right).

The accuracy of the computer evaluation of *R*-ratio on digitized images of faces depends both on the image resolution (segments of at least 200 pixels have been considered) and on the definition of the points delineating the segments of nose and eyes in question. Therefore, only two decimal digits have been considered and an uncertainty of ±0.03 has been assigned to the resulting *R*.

7.1.1 *R*-Ratios of Reference Images and of Byzantine Emperors

Six contemporary reference images of face have been selected (among which is that of the author) to evaluate the common range of variability of the *R*-ratio. A mean value of 1.00 resulted with a standard deviation of 0.07. Respectively, the maximum and minimum value results are of 1.08 and 0.90.

The *R*-ratio of the eight images of the Byzantine Emperors shown in Fig. 6.4 has been evaluated in order to determine the range of variability of this ratio for the faces of emperors shown on the Byzantine coins. A mean value of 0.96 resulted with a standard deviation of 0.25. Respectively, the maximum and minimum values resulted of 1.38 and 0.70 showing a great variability, more than three times that of the reference images. Table 7.1 and Fig. 7.3 report this data. These mean values of 1.00 and of 0.96 will be taken as reference.

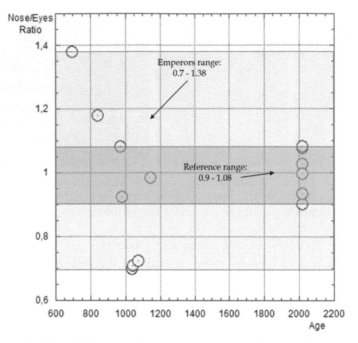

Figure 7.3 Plot of R-ratios of six contemporary reference faces and of the eight faces of Byzantine Emperors shown in Fig. 6.4.

Table 7.1 R-ratios of six contemporary reference faces and of the eight faces of Byzantine Emperors shown in Fig. 6.4

Age	Type	Nose/eyes ratio
2020	Reference 1	1.03
2020	Reference 2	0.90
2020	Reference 3	1.08
2020	Reference 4	0.93
2020	Reference 5	1.00
2020	Reference (Author)	1.08
692–695	Justinian II	1.38
842–856	Michael III	1.18
969–976	John I	1.08
976–1025	Basil II	0.92

(Continued)

Table 7.1 (*Continued*)

Age	Type	Nose/eyes ratio
1034–1041	Michael IV	0.70
1042–1055	Constantine IX	0.71
1071–1078	Michael VII	0.73
1143–1180	Manuel I	0.98

We can note a tendency to decrease the *R*-ratio relative to the Byzantine Emperors with the age increasing especially around 1000–1100. These results are useful comparisons with those coming from the faces of Jesus Christ on coins, which will be discussed in the next section.

7.1.2   *R*-Ratios of Images of Christ Minted by Justinian II

The first images of Jesus Christ on the coins of Justinian II (692–695) have in general the same shape and style but there are many small differences in some details, like the shape of nose and eyes. For this reason, a separate analysis of the corresponding *R*-ratio has been performed and the results are reported in Table 7.2 and Figs. 7.4 and 7.5.

Table 7.2 *R*-ratios of 18 faces of Christ on gold and silver coins of Justinian II (692–695)

Fig./Ref.	Type	Nose/eyes ratio
Fig. 4.2	SHROUD	1.28
Fig. 6.1	Solidus	1.20
Fig. 4.12-1	Solidus	1.22
Ref. 110	Solidus	1.17
Fig. 4.19-1	Solidus	1.03
Fig. 1.9	Solidus	0.88
Fig. 4.3-5	Solidus	1.04
Fig. 4.17	Solidus	0.94
Fig. 4.6	Solidus	1.18
Fig. 4.4	Solidus	1.28

(*Continued*)

Table 7.2 (*Continued*)

Fig./Ref.	Type	Nose/eyes ratio
Ref. 113	Solidus	1.07
Fig. 4.14-2	Semissis	1.15
Fig. 1.9	Semissis	1.04
Fig. 4.14-3	Semissis	1.02
Ref. 385	Semissis	1.06
Fig. 4.3-2	Tremissis	1.01
Fig. 4.10-1	Tremissis	1.05
Fig. 1.11	Tremissis	1.17
Fig. 1.12	Hexagram	1.12

Note: The second digit of a figure number indicates which coin, starting from the top left. Some coins not reported in this book have been numbered with the corresponding reference. For comparison, the *R*-ratio of the face of Christ on the Shroud is reported too.

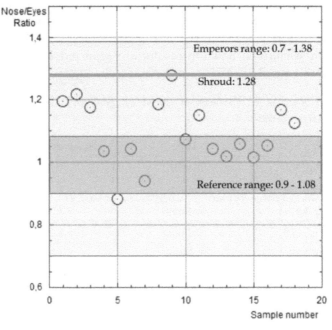

Figure 7.4 Plot of *R*-ratios of 18 faces of Christ on gold and silver coins of Justinian II (692–692) reported in Table 7.2. For comparison, the *R*-ratio of the face of Christ on the Shroud is reported too.

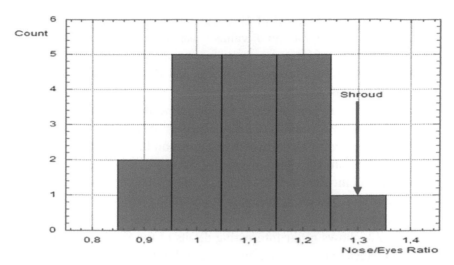

Figure 7.5 Histogram of the values of *R*-ratios relative to the 18 faces of Christ on gold and silver coins of Justinian II (692–692) reported in Table 7.2, and Fig. 7.4. For comparison, the *R*-ratio of the face of Christ on the Shroud is reported in the arrow.

These ratios have to be compared with that of the Shroud which results in *R* = 1.28 and perhaps with that of the supposed image of Christ of Gimigliano shown in Fig. 7.1 which results in *R* = 1.17. A mean value of 1.09 resulted with a standard deviation of 0.10. Respectively, the maximum and minimum values are of 1.28 and 0.88. This shows that all the values are smaller or equal than that of the Shroud, but the mean value of 1.09 is quite high with respect to the reference mean values of 1.00 and 0.96.

In light of the Shroud, the following considerations may be extracted.

1. The relatively high variability of *R* can be explained by the fact that not all the engravers working in officinae (work places) distant from the place where the Shroud was displayed, had the possibility to look at the Relic in order to make a good copy of the face of Jesus Christ.

2. The influence of the face of the Shroud having *R* = 1.28 on the engravers copying it increased the mean value to *R* = 1.09 from the reference ones of 1.00 and 0.96.

3. Among the 18 faces of Christ taken into consideration, only one of them has an *R*-value equal to that of the Shroud, and two of them greater or equal to 1.20, probably corresponding to engravers who had the occasion to view the Relic or a good copy of it.

4. The gold *solidus* of Fig. 4.4 having a ratio *R* = 1.28 equal to that of the Shroud is the rare coin described in Section 4.2.2, showing various tufts of hair corresponding to the wounds visible on the Shroud in their specific location. Instead of a coincidence, it is easier to think that the engraver of this coin had the occasion to study the Relic carefully.

5. The gold *solidus* of Fig. 4.12 (left) having a high *R*-value of 1.22, shows other interesting details of the Shroud face like the lack of ears, thus indicating a probable direct observation of the Shroud on the part of the engraver.

The histogram of the 18 *R*-values relative to the measured faces of Christ on the coins of Justinian II of Fig. 7.5 showing roughly a Gaussian behavior summarizes these considerations.

7.1.3   *R*-Ratios of Images of Christ Minted by Byzantine Emperors

The first images of Jesus Christ on the coins of Justinian II (692–695) show, in general a greater variation in the details of the face—and therefore of the ratio *R*—compared to the images of Christ coined by other Byzantine emperors. This variation can be due to the fact that the first engravers did not have a well-defined canon to follow because the image was relatively new and the engravers of the various *officinae* (at least 10 have been noted scattered throughout the Empire [Sear, 1987]) had greater possibility of subjective interpretation.

The following analysis of the *R*-ratio relative to the various Byzantine Emperors is here simplified by studying a reduced number of coins per Emperor. Therefore, one to four different coins per each Emperor have been considered, depending on the variability of features of the faces of Christ molded on the various coins.

Table 7.3 *R*-ratios of faces of Christ on 36 coins of Byzantine Emperors from 842 to 1376

Figure	Age	Emperor	Type	Nose/eyes ratio
1.20	842–856	Michael III	Solidus	1.10
1.21	857–886	Michael III	Solidus	1.29
1.23	886–912	Leo VI	Solidus	1.20
1.24	921–931	Romanus I	Solidus	0.90
1.25	921–931	Romanus I	Solidus	0.87
1.26	949–959	Constantine VII	Solidus	1.11
1.27	963.969	Nicephorus II	Solidus	0.90
1.28	969–976	Tsimisches	Solidus	0.94
1.29	976–1025	Basil II	Histamenon	1.30
1.30	976–1025	Basil II	Tetarteron	0.98
1.31	976–1025	Basil II	Follis	0.98
1.32	976–1025	Basil II	Follis	0.99
1.33	1025–1028	Constantine VIII	Histamenon	1.21
1.34	1028–1034	Romanus III	Histamenon	1.20
1.35	1028–1034	Romanus III	Follis	0.82
1.36	1034–1041	Michael 4	Histamenon	0.96
1.38	1042–1055	Constantine IX	Histamenon	0.87
1.39	1042–1055	Constantine IX	Tetarteron	0.79
1.40	1042–1055	Constantine IX	Follis	0.76
1.41–2	1055–1056	Theodora	Histamenon	0.73
1.43	1057–1059	Isaac I	Histamenon	0.75
1.44	1059–1067	Constantine X	Histamenon	0.83
1.46	1068–1071	Romanus IV	Histamenon	0.71
1.47	1068–1071	Romanus IV	Miliaresion	0.68
1.48	1068–1071	Romanus IV	Follis	0.79
1.49	1068–1071	Romanus IV	Follis	0.89
1.50	1071–1078	Michael VII	Histamenon	0.82
1.51	1071–1078	Michael VII	Histamenon	0.98
1.54	1071–1078	Michael VII	Miliaresion	0.88
1.55	1071–1078	Michael VII	Follis	1.03

(*Continued*)

Table 7.3 (*Continued*)

Figure	Age	Emperor	Type	Nose/eyes ratio
1.56	1078–1081	Nicephorus III	Histamenon	0.79
1.60	1092–1118	Alaxius I	Hyperpyron	0.80
1.66	1143–1180	Manuel I	El. Trachy	0.83
1.72	1195–1203	Alexius III	El. Trachy	0.88
1.77	1295–1320	Andronicus	Basilikon	1.11
1.78	1354–1376	John V	Stavraton	0.94

The results are reported in Table 7.3 and Fig. 7.6. A mean value of 0.93 resulted with a standard deviation of 0.17, respectively. The maximum and minimum value result of 1.29 and 0.67 showing a relatively high spread. The mean value of 0.93 is lower than the reference mean values of 1.00 and 0.96, thus showing the tendency of increasing the distance of the eyes with respect to that of the nose especially around the eleventh century.

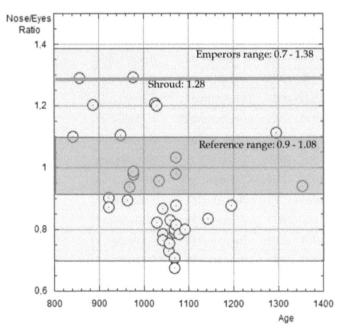

Figure 7.6 Plot of *R*-ratios of the faces of Christ on 36 coins of various Byzantine Emperors from 842 to 1376 reported in Table 7.3.

In light of the Shroud, the following considerations may be extracted.

1. Apart from the mintage of Michael III (857–886) and a coin of Basil II (976–1025) that slightly exceed the R-ratio of the Shroud face, all the other coins have lower values, while some of the first coins minted by Justinian II (692–695) are closer to the Shroud ratio of 1.28. This can also be explained by the fact that some engraver was not able to reproduce the same proportions within a few millimeters of the coin.

2. After the mintage by Michael III, the R-ratio decreases to values down to 0.87, showing that some engraver, not having had the chance to observe the Shroud directly, copied the previous mintages correcting that ratio because it did not seem suitable to a handsome human face.

3. In 944 the Mandylion-Shroud arrived in Constantinople and some years later Emperor Basil II (976–1025) again minted a face of Christ with a high R-ratio reaching 1.30 that demonstrates the possibility the engraver viewed the Shroud. This ratio remained relatively high up to the year 1028.

4. From 1028, with Emperor Romanus III, the R-ratio drastically decreases also reaching values of 0.68 leading to think that the engravers depicted the face of Christ with more freedom. Since the Shroud was still in Constantinople in this period, we can hypothesize that some engraver, perhaps belonging to *officinae* distant from the capital, did not have the possibility of observing the Shroud. Perhaps the relatively low R-ratio of this period is also influenced by the style of this period that shows many Byzantine Emperors having an R-ratio relatively low also, see Fig. 7.3.

5. A relatively high value of the R-ratio of 1.11 appears again at the end of the thirteenth century with Emperor Andronicus who perhaps had the occasion to show the engraver the Shroud or a good copy of it.

To be thorough, in addition to the R-ratio values already evaluated, the two faces of Christ not inspired by the Shroud are also taken into consideration. Those on the coins minted by Justinian II in period II (705–711), the "Syrian" Christ, see

Fig. 1.13, with an *R*-ratio of 0.90, and the coins by Manuel I–Alexius III (1143–1203), depicting a beardless Christ see Fig. 1.73, with an *R*-ratio of 0.58, are far from the 1.28 value of the Shroud image.

7.1.4 *R*-Ratios of Images of Christ Minted by Other States

We have seen in Chapter 5 that states other than the Byzantine Empire minted a face of Christ similar to the Shroud on their coins, probably because of cultural and commercial connection with it. Among them, we can see three important periods:

- the period around the eighth century of the Anglo-Saxon Sceattas;
- the period between the tenth and the fourteenth century;
- the more recent period up to now.

The analysis considers the first two periods with a brief comparison to recent coins. The results are reported in Table 7.4 and Fig. 7.7.

Table 7.4 *R*-ratios of faces of Christ on coins of various States starting from 715

Figure	Age	State	Type	Nose/eyes ratio
5.3	715–720	Anglo-Saxon	*Sceat*	1.18
5.4	715–720	Anglo-Saxon	*Sceat*	1.01
5.5	715–720	Anglo-Saxon	*Sceat*	0.85
5.15	1192–1205	Dandolo	*Grosso*	0.75
5.18	1330–1370	Chios	*Sequin*	1.09
5.20	1243–1276	Uros I	*Dinar*	0.92
5.22	1284–1372	Rep. Ragusa	*Dinar*	1.20
5.23	980–1015	Kiev	*Ruble*	1.50
5.24	1215–1246	Novgorod	*Follis*	0.97
5.26	1222–1246	Trebizond	*El. Histamenon*	0.70
5.27	1144–1174	Anatolia	*Dirham*	0.73
5.30	1218–1253	Cyprus	*Bezant*	0.65
5.36	1130–1140	Palermo	*Ducat*	0.90

(Continued)

Table 7.4 (*Continued*)

Figure	Age	State	Type	Nose/eyes ratio
5.37	1131–1166	Palermo	*Ducat*	0.80
5.38	1105–1154	Messina	*Follaro*	1.23
5.39	2000	Austria	500 *Schillings*	0.88
5.40	2015	Vatican	10 *Euro*	1.16

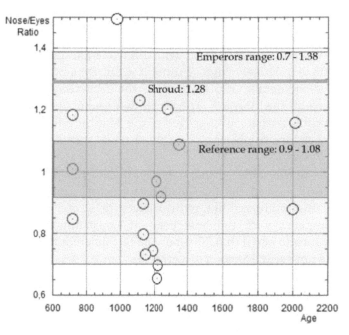

Figure 7.7 Plot of *R*-ratios of faces of Christ on coins of various States starting from 715 shown in Table 7.4.

A mean value of 0.97 resulted with a standard deviation of 0.23. Respectively, the maximum and minimum values resulted in 1.50 and 0.65 showing a wider spread than in the previous cases. The mean value of 0.97 is instead close to the reference mean values of 1.00 and 0.96.

In light of the Shroud, the following considerations may be extracted.

1. Since the Anglo-Saxon land is relatively distant from the place where the Shroud was probably conserved during that epoch, it is easy to understand why the engravers

had some difficulty in directly observing the Relic and therefore reproducing the details of its face. The variability of the face of Christ on the *sceattas* is in fact demonstrated by the R-values ranging from 0.85 to 1.18.

2. The Sicilian *Follaro* of Messina minted in 1105–1154 has an R-ratio of 1.23 with a face of Christ quite similar to that of the Shroud, which indicates that the engraver had probably the occasion to view the Shroud.

3. The Republic of Ragusa also came into contact with the Byzantines, and it is meaningful that between 1284 and 1372 *dinars* were issued with a Shroud-like face of Christ with a relatively high R-ratio of 1.20. Even with a lower level of details, the features of the face seem similar to that of the Shroud. Therefore, we should consider the possibility that an engraver of the Maritime Republic had the chance to observe the Shroud while traveling (perhaps in France).

4. During the same period, a Sicilian *ducat* of Palermo (1154–1166) showed the face of Christ which is clearly inspired by Byzantine art but with a lower level of details when compared with the best coins of Constantinople. Having an R-ratio equal to 0.80, leads one to think that the engraver did not see the Shroud directly.

5. The very high R-value of 1.50 relative to the *ruble* of Kiev is an isolated case that can be statistically considered as an outlier and therefore not commented on further.

6. The famous Venetian reproductions of the face of Christ on *grossi* and *sequins*, which lasted for several centuries, were not always very faithful to the Byzantine canons. In fact, the faces were more or less similar to the Shroud, but the R-ratio is quite variable from 0.75 to 1.09. The same can be said for the Serbian *grossi* (R-ratio = 0.92) that depict faces similar to the Venetian coins with analogous nose-to-eyes ratios.

7. A further deterioration of the features of the face of Christ can be noted with reference to some states in the neighborhood of the Byzantine empire like Trebizond (*Electrum Histamenon* having an R-ratio = 0.70), Anatolia (*Dirham* having an R-ratio = 0.73) and Cyprus (*Bezant* having an R-ratio = 0.65).

During the subsequent centuries up to now, there is a remarkable variation in the features of the faces of Christ mostly due to whether or not the engraver could make reference to the Shroud. For example, the Austrian *500 Schillings* of 2000 still reports some vague features connected to the face of Christ on the Shroud but it has a relatively low *R*-ratio = 0.88. Instead, the *10 Euro* of Vatican City minted in 2015 shows a face of Christ quite similar to the Shroud and therefore shows a relatively high *R*-ratio of 1.16.

7.1.5 Final Comments on the Evaluation of the *R*-Ratio

This numismatic quantitative analysis of the face of Christ based on the *R*-ratio seems significant in comparing the coins with the face shown on the Shroud and confirms the previous qualitative observations evidenced in the previous chapters. In this analysis, it seems evident when the engravers had seen either the Shroud or good reproductions of it to allow them to reproduce its detailed characteristics onto the coins.

For more than a millennium from the first Shroud-like coins of Christ minted by Emperor Justinian II in 692, see Fig. 6.1, till the present day, the face of Jesus Christ has been depicted in a number of coins. These have been minted by different empires and states within more than 2000 km (1200 mi) during the early centuries and all over the world in the present day.

Excluding some rare exceptions of very different faces of Christ, which probably relate back to other depictions (for example, those portrayed on the coins minted in 1500 in Lucca, Tuscany, that originates from the Holy Face of the city), all of these faces have several features in common with one prototype image, that of Christ shown on the Shroud.

Since, as observed, the face of Christ minted by Justinian II in 692 coincides in different details with the face depicted on the Shroud, we can draw the following conclusion:

1. The prototype of the face of Christ minted in 692, though being a refined production, does not depict a face with the features of a typical handsome man because it displays some details linked to the Passion that disfigure the general quality. Why did the engraver carve these features, and

why did the Byzantine canon that derived from them codify these peculiar asymmetries and swellings? Obviously, the reason is the tortured face of Christ on the Shroud.

2. The Shroud provided the prototype of the face of Christ that for more than 1000 years has been used in the coinage of several states and empires. This prototype not only developed in the numismatic field but also in painting and sculpture as other studies demonstrate [Coppini and Cavazzuti, 2000].

3. All results point to the fact that the Shroud existed in 692 and it has been a model for the first coins of Christ. The Byzantine gold *solidi* model reached the present day with its general features.

7.2 Quantitative Analysis of Metal Alloys of the Coins

This analysis summarizes a recent study [Fanti and Furlan, 2019] regarding the micro-particles vacuumed from the Shroud. In particular, some particles of *electrum* confirmed the probable presence of the Relic at Constantinople during the period in which the Byzantine coins in question were minted.

The following questions were posed. Does the composition of gold alloy micro-particles found in dust vacuumed from the Shroud show any correlation with the gold alloy of coins that could have polluted the linen fabric in the past centuries and in particular during the Byzantine Empire? Moreover, was the Shroud put in contact with *electrum* alloys of coins minted before the fall of Constantinople in 1204?

The crusader knight Robert de Clary attests to the weekly exhibition of the Shroud in Constantinople. Many historians [Antonacci, 2016; Wilson, 2010], by identifying the Shroud as the Mandylion, are convinced that the Relic was in Edessa (currently named Sanliurfa in Turkey), in the early centuries after Christ, see Section 2.4.2. The Relic was then transferred to the capital of the Byzantine Empire in 944 and it remained there until its fall in 1204.

Dust was vacuumed from the Shroud and analyzed on different occasions [Riggi di Numana, 1982, 1988; Gonella et al., 2005]. Many kinds of microscopic material have been identified including organic particles, such as fibers, mites, fungi, molds, pollen and parts of plants; inorganic particles, like clay, quartz, calcite, etc.; metal particles, like gold, silver, lead and various alloys.

The attention was focused on the gold particles and its alloys, having sizes in the range from 0.001 mm to 0.010 mm (from 0.000039 in to 0.00039 in). In trying to find an answer to the initial questions, the composition of these gold alloy micro-particles was compared with that of gold Byzantine coins minted during the seventh to thirteenth centuries.

The weight percentage of these micro-particles was determined via the following instrumentation: EDXS (Energy Dispersive X-ray Spectrometry) and XRF (X-Ray Fluorescence) analysis. The micro-particles were mounted on a bi-adhesive carbon stripe and analyzed by means of the ESEM (Environmental Scanning Electron Microscope) in order to achieve information concerning the morphology and the elemental composition of the micro-particles, see Fig. 7.8.

We have seen in Section 1.2.1 that with the crisis of the Byzantine Empire in the eleventh century, the gold coins were issued with a lower gold content than the commonly circulating metal. The so-called debasement [Hann and Metcalf, 1988] was evident especially with emperor Manuel I (1043–1080), who substituted a great percentage of gold with silver, thus obtaining an alloy named *electrum* that is an alloy of gold and silver, with trace amounts of copper.

The reduced gold content, ranging from 30% to 90%, increased the profits during the crisis of the Byzantine Empire.

Use of the *electrum* began in the third millennium BC in Egypt, but the first metal coins made of *electrum* date to the end of the seventh century BC and were minted in Lydia and East Greece. Even if the use of *electrum* for coins is relatively rare in the world, during the debasement, the coins of *electrum* were very common in the Byzantine Empire from Romanus III (1028–1034) to Alexius I (1081–1118). Therefore, finding *electrum* particles on the Shroud indicates a probable connection with the corresponding Byzantine coin having the same alloy, because the Shroud is too young to think to a possible connection with Lydian coins.

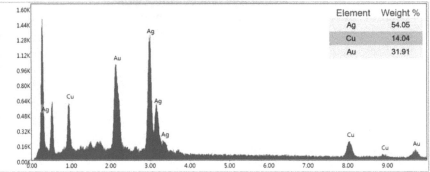

Figure 7.8 On the top, one of the 17 gold-alloy particles detected among the dust vacuumed from the Shroud (big white particle in the photo). This particle of *electrum* alloy is embedded in a fiber of the Shroud leading one to suppose a rubbing between a gold surface and the linen fabric. The metal composition of the particle, with its spectrum relative to Energy Dispersive X-ray Fluorescence analysis, is indicated on the bottom.

The micro-chemical analysis [Hann and Metcalf, 1988] considered 32 Byzantine coins minted before the fall of Constantinople in 1204 and particularly in the age of the gold debasement. The following interesting data resulted among the 17 micro-particles of gold alloy detected within the Shroud dust.

1. Five of them were 100% pure gold and could be related to the gold environment in which the Shroud was exhibited before the Byzantine debasement of the eleventh century.
2. Two of them were composed of gold (93–96%) with metallic impurities of silver and copper and could be related to Byzantine coins struck in the period 1028–1078, which have a similar composition.
3. Four of them were of the *electrum* alloy, composed of gold (70–89%). They could be related to coins struck in the period 1059–1180, which have a similar composition.
4. One of them was of *electrum* alloy also, composed of gold (32%). It could be related to a coin struck in the period 1143–1180 by Emperor Manuel I.

These results are a clear clue showing that the Shroud was probably present in the Byzantine Empire before 1204, as many other historians have indicated. The study is not able to fully demonstrate the displacement of the Shroud from the Byzantine Empire to Europe, even if the detection on the Shroud of particles of *electrum* alloy is a discriminating factor that must not be forgotten in the reconstruction of the Relic's journey.

7.3   Coins as *Third-Class Relics*?

With the collaboration of the American Shroud Encounter (in the person of Russ Breault), the author studied more in depth the results of the quantitative analysis of *electrum* alloys detected both on the Shroud vacuumed dusts and on the Byzantine coins. They presented a further development of the research at the STaTS-2019 Shroud Conference held in Lancaster, Ontario, Canada in August 2019.

This additional study was born from a comment made by a referee of the international journal that published the paper [Fanti and Furlan, 2019] who noticed that it is not easy to think that the presence of gold objects placed near the most important Relic of Christianity can deposit such a high number of gold micro-traces imbedded in the fabric.

Experimental studies have in fact shown that we need to rub a gold object like a coin on a linen fabric to obtain these micro-traces. Thus, a probable hypothesis to explain the presence of these gold and *electrum* micro-particles on the Shroud fabric is the following: the Byzantine churchgoers had rubbed their gold coins showing the face of Christ on the Relic in order to produce relics by contact[a] for personal veneration purposes.

The hypothesis of rubbing coins on the linen fabric is sustained by the micro-particle coming from the Shroud, shown in Fig. 7.8 that is contained in a long fissure of a single Shroud flax fiber. Probably the same long fissure of the fiber was produced when rubbing the *electrum* coin just minted on the Relic. It is in fact well known that coins just minted present a greater number of metal asperities.

If the proposed hypothesis will be verified in the future, we should conclude that the Byzantine churchgoers rubbed their *electrum* coins on the Shroud exposed at Constantinople to make their coins *Third-Class Relics*[b] of the Shroud and therefore of the Resurrection of Jesus Christ.

---

[a]The Catholic Church divides relics into the following classes [Mangan 2003]:

First-Class Relics are either directly associated with the events of Christ's life or the physical remains of a saint like a bone. It is prohibited to divide Relics into small, unrecognizable parts if they are used in liturgy as in an altar.

Second-Class Relics are items owned or frequently used by a saint like a rosary or a part of an item that the saint wore, like a shirt.

Third-Class Relics are any object put in contact with a *First-Class Relic* like pieces of cloth that touched the bone of a saint.

Fourth-Class Relics are any object that has come into contact with *Second-Class Relics*. They may consist of pieces of cloth that came into direct contact with some object of the saint.

To this class belong other relics that, although not directly related to a saint, and although have not come into contact with a holy body, represent an object of veneration. Examples are leaves from an olive tree of Gethsemane, a stone taken from the place of Calvary and from the soil of Jerusalem.

While nowadays it is strictly forbidden by canon 1190 of the Code of Canon Law to sell or buy "*Sacred Relics*" (meaning *First-* and *Second-Class*), the Catholic Church permits the sale of *Higher-Class Relics*.

[b]In the present case, since the Shroud is the burial cloth of Jesus Christ, which also contains His blood, it should be considered a *First-Class Relic*. Therefore, hypothetical coins rubbed on it should be considered *Third-Class Relics*.

7.4   Conclusive Remarks on Quantitative Analysis

The main purpose of chapter is to use quantitative methods for comparing the Byzantine coins depicting Christ with the body image of the Shroud.

A first method based on the relationship between the dimensional measurements of the length of the nose and the distance between the eyes has shown interesting correlations with the hypothesis that the coins' engravers had the possibility of observing the Shroud or a good copy of it.

The study on the composition of gold alloys also raised the possibility that some Byzantine coins depicting Christ had been rubbed on the Shroud to obtain *Third-Class Relics*.

These are only two quantitative methods analyzed, but future research could highlight other ones capable of providing interesting additional information. In fact, the more quantitative the details are, the more the Shroud's authenticity emerges. Faith and science on the Shroud keep on perfectly integrating with each other always adding some new pieces to the Truth.

To finish the overview on the Byzantine coinage concerning the faces of Jesus Christ, the next chapter will make some artistic considerations with the help of an expert in the sector.

Chapter 8

The Face of Christ on Coins: Aesthetic Opinion and Experiments

In the previous chapters, a quantitative analysis of the face of Christ has numerically discussed the time development of the nose-eye ratio compared with that of the Shroud. Then a probabilistic analysis applied to one gold solidus of Justinian II of the First Period (692–695) showed that almost surely the Shroud body image was the reference source for the coins of Christ. We now consider other aspects of the face of Christ on the Byzantine coins: we examine the aesthetic opinion of an artist and we show the absurdity, by means of experiments, of the hypothesis formulated by someone that the Shroud image was copied from the Christ's face of a Byzantine coin.

To fulfill this task, the author contacted Professor Veronica Piraccini[a], expert in this field asking some questions reported in

---

[a]Veronica Piraccini, Artist and Maestro in Painting, born in Bologna but Roman by adoption from childhood, at the age of 25 was entrusted with the Chair of Painting at the Academy of Fine Arts of Brera in Milan, then Palermo and Frosinone; today she is Professor in the Chair of Painting and also Phenomenology of the Sacred at the Academy of Fine Arts in Rome. Works of her invisible-visible painting called by her "*Imperceptible Painting*" have been shown at important exhibitions and placed in the Institutions of the Italian State. She participated in multiple national and international conferences and exhibitions in United States, England, Korea, China,

---

Byzantine Coins Influenced by the Shroud of Christ
Giulio Fanti
Copyright © 2022 Jenny Stanford Publishing Pte. Ltd.
ISBN 978-981-4877-88-6 (Hardcover), 978-1-003-21992-7 (eBook)
www.jennystanford.com

Section 8.1 and commissioning some experiments to be performed with her students of her Painting school of the Academy of fine Arts in Rome that will be discussed in Sections 8.2, 8.3 and 8.4. They show in a quantitative way that the Shroud was the original model for the various kinds of Christ's faces reproduced on Byzantine coins.

8.1 Expert's Aesthetic-Numismatic Analysis of the Temporal Development of Coins

To have some reliable information about the aesthetic aspects of the many faces of Christ depicted on the Byzantine coins, the author posed the following questions to Professor Piraccini:

- How is the face of Christ depicted in coins?
- Which are its somatic features?
- What morphological transformations evolved over time?
- Is it possible, as someone affirms, that the Shroud was born from the observation of the face of Christ on the Byzantine coins?

She made the following detailed answer combining all the four questions as follows, based on a series of photographs of gold/*electrum* Byzantine coins photographed by the author.

It is important to note that the author preferred to submit to expert judgment only coins of this type, neglecting those of copper, because these last were less controlled by the emperors and therefore possibly subjected to some dissimilarity from the current Byzantine canons.

8.1.1 Answer to Questions

Piraccini's [2020] answer

The idea of the author to collect the photos of Byzantine gold coins that represent Christ is a unique opportunity to deepen the

Brazil, Africa, Australia, Saudi Arabia. She has been interested in experimental studies on the Shroud from which four life-size paintings were born by contact, famous because they are exhibited all over the world; in particular, two of these works on linen were painted with the technique invented by her, of the *"Visible-Invisible Imperceptible Painting."*

Christological Iconography that for the last two millennia is part of our life immersed in art. This research allowed me to analyze the characteristics of the subject on the coins in chronological order, to find the aesthetic and morphological sense of the portrait of Christ in relation to the existence of the Shroud. The first striking thing is the extraordinary beauty of the coins under consideration. They are included in a time span that goes from Justinian II (692) to Alexius III (1203).

In studying the photos of coins provided by the author, I first grouped them in chronological order so they could be properly analyzed in an aesthetic sense. The charm of the bas-relief sculpture on the coins was created by the vitality of the movement of the light that resting on the volumes conceived by the artist, it goes to produce shadows and luminescence produced by the shapes. Artists have always been stimulated by chiaroscuro in art, with the beauty of infinite variety in the reflection of incident light on the figures. Therefore, it is clear that the shadows and the flashes of light reflected on the coin are one of the many variables desired by the artists to obtain what they saw and felt inside.

The Byzantines used the technique of *"coinage by hammer beating"* (from the Latin *cuneus*, wedge). The lower die *"Pila,"* a metal cylinder, was used fixed on an anvil of wood; an upper die *"Torsello,"* also a metal cylinder, was held by a hand and beaten with a hammer. Between the two cylinders was placed a disc of ductile and precious metal such as gold, or another alloy. Byzantine coins were the cantilevered result of the engraving by hand on the two metal cylinders surface of the upper and lower die, see Fig. 8.1.

When a coin was made, the mold after a few repetitions would wear out and should have been reproduced by cutting again the metal cylinders of both the upper and lower die. As a result, other similar, but never identical, coins were produced with the same images as the first coin, but with minimal differences made by the artist's hand.

Nowadays, instead, the coins are mounted on automatic machines, presses, or other instruments, and, even if the prototype is always made first by the artist, it is no longer engraved in the negative, but made directly in the positive, larger than the definitive, by which gives a mold *"the mother form,"* which becomes the matrix, then reduced in size with mechanical techniques.

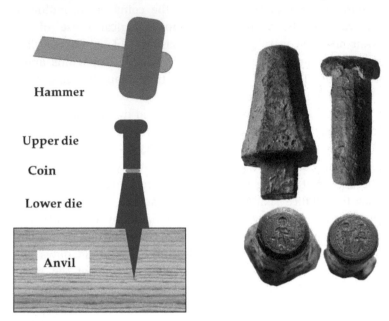

Figure 8.1 On the left, scheme (of G. Fanti) of the production of a Byzantine coin: the artisan first produced a metal disc and placed it between two carved dies. He then hit the upper die with a hammer, striking the depictions onto both sides of the disc. On the right, upper and lower dies used to produce a Byzantine *histamenon nomisma* of Romanus III (1028–1034), see Fig. 1.34. Their heights are about 9 cm and 10 cm (3.5 in and 3.9 in) and their weights respectively of 494 g and 956 g (17.4 oz and 33.7 oz); they reproduce a blessing Christ on throne on one side and the Emperor blessed by the Mother of God on the other. Photo kindly provided by Auktionshaus H.D. Rauch GmbH, Wien, Austria.

We can imagine the emotion that the Byzantine artist experienced after having minutely worked on the negative of the commissioned subject when seeing his result. After placing the disc of metal between the two metal cylinders engraved by him and hammering, the coin between the two dies was thus formed, with the negative image on the two dies forming a positive image on the coin. Since the Shroud is a photographic negative, the Byzantine engraver was the first to see the Shroud face as a positive image. We can imagine that this engraver had the same surprise that Secondo Pia had in 1898 when he photographed the Shroud and saw a positive image on his photographic plate instead of a negative image.

An aesthetic description of fifty photos of gold coins grouped according to period follows.

First Period of Justinian II (692–695)

The 20 photos of coins analyzed show a face that has important characteristics that are similar to the image on the Shroud. This includes the long prominent hair on one side, the presence of the tuft on the forehead, the long slightly asymmetrical nose, the prominent cheekbones, the bipartite[b] beard and the evident lower lip. The face appears alive with a strong-willed, proud expression and eyes that peer from the soft molded eyelids and a hint of very spherical iris.

The most imperious, but at the same time sweet example, with an expression very close to the Shroud, is that of the *solidus* shown in Fig. 6.1 among other coins of the same period, see Fig. 8.2.

Figure 8.2 Faces of Christ on various gold *solidi* of Justinian II (I Period, 692–695).

---

[b]This specific term "bipartite," referred to the peculiar kind of the beard, means being in two parts or shared by two.

We believe that the artist wanted to interpret the Man of the Shroud, by opening his eyes to engrave the model alive and present. In the other coins of the same period, see Fig. 8.3, the same characteristics appear but with an important difference. The eyelid is differently sketched as closed, sleepy, or there is not a delineation between the upper eyelid and the lower, and it is without an engraved iris, but only appears with a rounded volume without a pupil, as a "sketch." From such a tenuous result of the "rounded" sketched eye, it can be deduced that that was the sensation from which the artist was deeply inspired. Here the sensitivity of the artist identifies other emotions and therefore forms the image to reproduce the same sensation.

Figure 8.3 Faces of Christ on various gold *semisse* and *tremisse* of Justinian II (I Period, 692–695).

In addition, what could the model of the face be if not that of the Shroud? In fact, many elements fit together to make a convincing argument that the Christ depicted on the coins came from the image on the Relic. For example, the coin in Fig. 8.3 (right bottom) has a much-profiled asymmetrical nose, sketched eyes without an iris, as if closed by the eyelid, smooth hair surrounding the face and a two-part beard. All with the soft modeling of delicately sensitive volumes that obtain chiaroscuro passages, extraordinarily close to the characteristic forms impressed in a tenuous way in the face on the Sacred Cloth.

Second period of Justinian II (705–711)

The emperor Justinian II minted the coins described above with a precise Shroud-like iconography, with a courageous iconographic choice, violating the standards for what was then found in art, for example, with long hair and not like a pageboy on a triangular face according to the fashion of that era. Returning to reign after a period of exile, the Emperor changed the iconography by minting the coins shown in Fig. 8.4.

Figure 8.4 Faces of Christ on various gold *solidi* of Justinian II (II Period, 705–711).

Here, Christ has the face with large open eyes and with well-defined iris, framed by very curly short hair and beard; there is the absence of the tuft on the forehead and the face is not oval, but quite triangular and perfectly symmetrical. An aesthetic model emerges that is very distant from the image on the Shroud. This happened, in my opinion, due to the influence of the first iconoclastic signals, which shortly afterwards resulted in the proclamation of Leo III Isauricus in 726 in Constantinople.

Period of Michael III

He initially ruled with his mother Theodora (856–867), who restored the cult of sacred images with the Council of Constantinople in 843. Theodora always maintained an iconodular[c] position and in fact still today, she is venerated as Saint by the Orthodox Church. In the coins minted in this period, Christ is strongly represented Shroud-like with a well-drawn beard, a slightly asymmetrical nose, much-accentuated cheekbones with evident orbits, long hair surrounding the face and a bipartite or tripartite tuft of hair on the forehead.

This last element is found in a particular way in the coin on the left of Fig. 8.5 where there is the incredible identical shape on the forehead to the hairline in the shape of a reversed "3," typical of the Shroud face (see Fig. 2.11). It is striking that this figure is specular, that is, the "3" shaped tuft of the coin is reversed as in a mirror with respect to the "3" of the Shroud. This confirms that the artists, when possible, studied the Shroud. This shows again that the Shroud was taken as the model for the Byzantine coins.

Figure 8.5 Faces of Christ on various gold *solidi* of Michael III (856–867).

Regarding the hypothesis formulated by some scholars that the Shroud was produced in the Middle Ages by an artist who

---

[c]Term referred to one who venerates icons and defends their devotional use.

copied the face of Christ from the Byzantine coins, how could this hypothetical artist imagine blood on the forehead, looking at the coins with bipartite or tripartite tuft of hair, and interpret this hair in blood streams?

Period of Basil I (867–931)

The hair surrounds the face that is plumper, the eyes are large but sketched like "wheals," there is no iris and therefore this shape could mimic the closed eyelid of the Shroud's eyes; the eyebrow arch is also very evident as in the Relic.

Some coins have a swollen face, and among these, the one shown in Fig. 8.6 shows the swollen face, deformed with a grimace of pain to indicate the suffering of the Passion.

Figure 8.6 Face of Christ on a gold *solidus* of Basil I (867–931).

Among this group, the ones from the period 921–931, see Fig. 8.7 show the central tuft on the forehead in the shape of drops; on two of the coins of this Fig. 8.7, the hair shows (on the right side looking at the coin) evident undulations that characterize the face of the Shroud.

Other Shroud elements are the profiled nose, the highlighted lips, the evident eyebrow arch, the beard tapered at the sides with undulating lines and an accentuated chin. The eyes in some coins are wide open, but strangely the iris has faded, and this indicates the artist's willingness to make the gaze of Christ alive and present; it is precisely the Shroud that suggests this sensation.

Figure 8.7 Other faces of Christ on various gold *solidi* of Basil I (867–931).

Period of Constantine VII and Romanus I (949–959)

The similarity of the face of Christ to that of the Shroud is accentuated, see Fig. 8.8. Some of the coins, due to a mirror effect, show a swelling on the left side of the face resulting from the beatings suffered by Christ that on the Shroud show on the right cheek.

Figure 8.8 Faces of Christ on various gold *solidi* of Constantine VII with Romanus I (949–959).

In conformity with the left side of the Shroud face, the hair is longer, looking at the right side of the coin. In other coins of this period the important accentuation of the long crooked nose with a much-accentuated front arch to form a cross, typical of the Shroud, is evident. The absolute novelty of the "tears" that come down from the eyes is even more striking. These tears seem to melt as they are included without boundaries, see Fig. 8.9.

Figure 8.9 Other faces of Christ on various gold *solidi* of Constantine VII with Romanus I (949–959).

Figure 8.10 Fresco of 1100 ca. depicting Christ Pantocrator of the abbey of Sant'Angelo in Formis in Capua in Italy, which shows the lively emotion that the face of the Shroud had to inspire the painter, and in the case of coins to the engraver to get to reproduce this image.

These coins undoubtedly reveal the extraordinary and lively emotion that the face of the Shroud had to inspire the engraver, also highlighted in the fresco of Christ Pantocrator of the abbey of Sant'Angelo in Formis in Capua in Italy, see Fig. 8.10, where teary red as blood cheeks are evident. These forms also emerge on other figures that were probably born from this influence.

Period 963–1025

The coin of Nicephorus II (963-969), see Fig. 8.11, still highlights the accentuated frontal arch of the face of Christ, the sketched eyes and the longer hair on one side which are typical elements of the Shroud.

Figure 8.11 Faces of Christ on a gold *solidus* of Nicephorus II (963–969).

Also, the coins of Basil II (976 to 1025) present the face of Christ with the long, outlined nose, the beard that surrounds the chin and the eyes without iris that seem closed. The tuft of hair is very evident. The face is framed by the long hair, more evident on the right looking at the coin, see Figs. 8.11 and 8.12.

Period 1025–1203

With Constantine VIII (1025-1028) the Shroud features of the face of Christ remain, see Fig. 8.13, with eyes closed, which the artists highlight even more due to the arrival of a certain taste for realism.

Figure 8.12 Faces of Christ on various gold *histamena* of Basil II (976–1025).

Figure 8.13 Faces of Christ on various gold *histamena* respectively from the top left to the bottom right of Roman III, Constantine VIII, Constantine IX and Constantine X.

The coin of Michael IV (1034–1041) shows a severe Christ, see Fig. 8.14 (top left), with an almost angry expression.

Figure 8.14 Faces of Christ on various gold *histamena* respectively from the top left to the bottom right of Michael IV and Constantine IX.

Constantine IX (1042–1055) continues on this model. The different Emperors mint various specimens of coins with the face of Christ having eyes still sketched, as closed by the eyelid, of Shroud inspiration, flowing hair and smooth beard.

The coin of Constantine X (1059–1067) shows an extraordinarily soft model; that of Roman III (1028–1034) shows a Shroud similarity to that of Constantine VIII, while the coin of Constantine IX (1042–1055) shows a more severe expression of Christ.

In the short period of Michael VII (1071–1078), see Fig. 8.15, an interesting novelty is observed: the beard is much longer. On the Shroud, there are lines and shadows that artist might have taken for a longer beard (see Section 1.3.18). The similarity with the face of the Shroud is also accentuated mainly for the grace and ascetic sensitivity of the subtly shaded regions as well as for the barely sketched eyes, the elongated nose, the accentuation of the eyebrow arch and long hair.

Figure 8.15 Faces of Christ on various gold *histamena* of Michael VII (1071–1078).

Until 1203 with Alexius I, John II and Alexius III, coins with the image of Christ continue with peculiar Shroud-like characteristics, see Fig. 8.16 like the closed eyes, that is, without open eyelids. The face of Christ shows sketched eyes, fluid hair of the realistic inspiration that was gradually being formed in that age.

During this age, coins with the face of Christ Emmanuel minted by Emperor Manuel I (1143–1180) and of the Child Jesus, see Fig. 8.17, both with eyes like wheals sketched without iris, were produced too.

Figure 8.16 Faces of Christ on various gold coins, respectively from the top left to the bottom right, of Alexius I, John II and Alexius III.

Figure 8.17 Faces of Child Jesus with His Mother on the left and of Christ Emmanuel on the right on coins of Manuel I (1143–1180).

8.1.2 Highlights of the Piraccini's Analysis

After this detailed analysis, the author asked the expert to put in evidence the main aspects touched along this temporal development of the faces of Christ on Byzantine coins.

Piraccini's [2020] **answer**

From my analysis, some morphological-somatic-aesthetic elements are outlined which can be divided into "constant" and "divergent" elements, the latter due to the prohibition of sacred images. The constant and stable elements generate the Byzantine *"Canon of Christ"* which results from His anatomy. The divergent elements confirm His somatic veracity precisely through its absence or deformation.

I. The physical features of Christ on the Shroud were repeated for centuries on the Byzantine coins. Anatomically, we always have the same features with slight variations: a certain face with a regular tapered shape, eyes closed or slightly open or defined by only a circle as a wheal, a bipartite beard and long hair that is longer on one side. Like on the Shroud where the human body is naked, the image of Christ on Byzantine coins is simple and without ornamentation; for example, the long hair is without headdresses and precious pendants typical of the emperors. How can this simple style be explained when it is so contrary to the Byzantine culture in that era, especially for an image of Jesus who was recognized as God, if it was not copied from the image of the body on the Shroud?

II. The appearance of the eyes changed considerably over time. At the beginning, in 692 with Justinian II, they are slightly open and realistically expressive, combined with a physical interpretation in the shape of the face, hair, curl on the forehead and hieratic expression, a truly amazing correlation with the image on the Shroud. However, under the same Emperor, during his Second Period in 705–711, there appears a very different vision of Christ with very large eyes, open, wide on a triangular face with curly and short hair and beards, with distorted features. The face of Christ was not to be made resembling the Shroud so as not to bring it back to this powerful True image. With Constantine VII in the mid-900s, the eyes have eyelids and irises from which "tears" run down onto the cheeks. The eyes are surmounted by accentuated arches with a very long nose, forming a cross joining almost to the tuft of hair. At the end of the 900s, with Basil II, the coins with the same stylistic features of the Relic, with eyes like shaded buttons or wheals appear. The subsequent emperors also follow the same morphological aesthetic characteristics and even with faces having their eyes closed. In the early 1000s, with Michael IV and then following Constantine IX, we have features attributable to the Shroud, but with a more frowning expression of Christ. Towards 1060, with Constantine X, the face of Christ "softens" with very soft sensitive volumes and eyes barely hinted as closed. Even afterwards with Alexius I from 1081 onwards, the same "styleme"[d] continues. Therefore, after 1000 the eyes are increasingly sketched as rounded buttons, as if the eyelid covered the eyeball or more simply as if the eyes were closed, but expressively very highlighted and present. The oddity is that they are eyes without iris but "powerfully hypnotic." Obviously, this cannot happen by only the artist's imagination without a reference to a model, which must have been the Shroud. In works of art, the eyes are defined by the eyelids rhyme, with the iris and pupil highlighted, both engraved, sculpted, or painted or made in mosaic. Why then, at that time, would the artist distance himself from the current stylistic code that was always characterized by large incisive and well-defined eyes containing eyelids and iris if not because of a precise model such as the Shroud?

III. In the Byzantine coins, we have the continuous persistence of the tuft of hair on the forehead which is usually well highlighted. Those who suppose that the image on the Shroud was copied from the face of Christ on Byzantine coins, would have to explain why the artist interpreted the tuft of hair on the forehead as streams of blood flow on the supposed false relic. This trickle of blood clearly

---

[d]Unit corresponding to a stylistic choice in the lexical, syntactic or morphological field.

emerges on the forehead of the Shroud face, a formal motif so evident that it was an essential character for the artists to be outlined in some way, and which was thus translated into the form of a tuft of hair. It is a sign, a very characteristic styleme and it is not repeated in any of the images of Emperors, who have a triangular face with pageboys-shaped hair with a cut in the middle of the face, topped with headdresses and adorned with precious pendants.

IV. Other physical characteristics related to the Shroud are typical of the face of Christ on the coins, with variations, like long hair framing His face, which can sometimes be seen as detached. In my opinion, this can be explained by the distance between the hair and the face in the image on the Sacred Linen while it covered the dead body lying in a horizontal position.

V. Let's observe the "frontality" of the Byzantine coins with the face of Christ and the Emperor. This aspect may seem obvious, but there are heads of the Emperor in profile in various Roman and Byzantine coins minted before the seventh century. This frontal view is therefore not obvious but always present in Byzantine culture starting from the sixth century. Could the Shroud face also have influenced this? Well, this hieratic frontality, in my opinion, depended as an iconographic choice on the visual influence due to the Shroud, which had immediately inspired the arts, conditioning them for their mystery importance, so as to be transposed into a formal solution to the effigy of the Emperors. So powerful it will tend to crystallize for many centuries, and only long after in the arts will Medieval and Renaissance changes take place. One thing is certain: the "canon of the face" is present in the imperious and strong-willed frontal view of Jesus on the Byzantine coins, the Pantocrator image in art, and in the various icons of the time. The coins' images commemorate Jesus' death by crucifixion by placing a cross of light behind His head, sometimes included in the nimbus. The luminous circle indicates God.

8.2 Copies Inspired from Photos of Coins

Chapters 3–7 showed that it is practically impossible for an artist to reproduce the Shroud face on a coin with all its peculiar features. From the evident similarities between the face of Christ on the Byzantine coins and the body image on the Shroud, it is very difficult to believe that Byzantine engravers would have reproduced the faces of Christ on gold *solidi* without having seen the Relic.

This should also be evident to those who assert that the Relic is not authentic, but avoiding this conclusion, they hypothesize the face on the Shroud was copied from a Byzantine gold *solidus* in the Middle Ages!

The author tested this hypothesis by means of reproducible experiments with the help of Professor Piraccini and her students. These experiments show how debatable is this hypothesis.

The task of copying the face of Christ that is on a Byzantine gold *solidus* of Justinian II (I period, 692–695) and on a gold *histamenon* of Michael IV (1034–1041) was assigned to students of Professor Piraccini of the Academy of Fine Arts in Rome. Both the original coin and the copies are shown in Figs. 8.18 and 8.19.

Figure 8.18 Christ's face on a gold *solidus* of Justinian II (692–695) is on the top left. The other images are painted by Professor Piraccini's students.

Figure 8.19 Christ's face on a gold *histamenon nomisma*, of Michael IV (1034–1041) is on the top left. The others are copies painted by Professor Piraccini's students.

The student's artwork was analyzed by the author in terms of simplifications and dissimilarities relative to the reference image defining eight control areas, based on his studies on the Shroud for more than 20 years. These areas are whole face, shape of hair, eyebrows-forehead, eyes, nose, bipartite beard, moustaches and lower lip.

He assigned a value of two for a significant difference, a value of one for a minor difference and a value of zero for a not clearly detectable difference from the reference face on the coins. The results of this analysis are reported in Tables 8.1 and 8.2.

In each table, there are *m* columns corresponding to the drawings in question and 8 rows corresponding to the control areas. To the 8 rows, one listing a score equal to the sum of all the values of the column under analysis has been added with a last row listing the *"Normalized Score"* (NS).

Table 8.1 Analysis of dissimilarity of the student's copies in Fig. 8.18 relative to the image of Christ's face on the Byzantine coin of Justinian II (692–695)

Simplifications or dissimilarities of painting #	1	2	3	4	5	6	7
Whole face	0	2	2	2	2	0	0
Shape of hair	0	2	2	2	2	0	2
Eyebrows-forehead	2	0	2	2	2	0	0
Eyes	1	2	2	0	2	2	2
Nose	0	0	2	2	2	0	0
Bipartite beard	0	2	0	0	2	0	2
Moustaches	0	2	2	2	2	1	2
Lower lip	0	2	2	1	2	0	2
Score	3	12	14	11	16	3	10
Normalized Score	0.2	0.7	0.9	0.7	1.0	0.2	0.6

Note: The scores 2, 1 and 0, respectively, correspond to a significant, minor and negligible difference. The smaller the NS, the more similar is the copy to the image on the coin.

Table 8.2 Analysis of dissimilarity of the student's copies in Fig. 8.19 relative to the image of Christ's face on the Byzantine *histamenon nomisma*, of Michael IV (1034–1041)

Simplifications or dissimilarities of painting #	1	2	3	4	5
Whole face	0	0	0	0	2
Shape of hair	2	2	2	2	2
Eyebrows-forehead	0	2	1	0	2
Eyes	0	1	0	2	1
Nose	0	0	2	0	2
Bipartite beard	2	2	2	1	2
Moustaches	0	0	2	0	2
Lower lip	2	0	2	0	2
Score	6	7	11	5	15
Normalized Score	0.4	0.5	0.7	0.3	1.0

Note: The scores 2, 1 and 0, respectively, correspond to a significant, minor and negligible difference. The smaller the NS, the more similar is the copy to the image on the coin.

It contains a normalized value obtained by dividing the results of the values reported in the upper row of the sums by its maximum value so that all the results are equal or less than one (all results are rounded to the first decimal) and therefore they are more easy for comparison among the various tables.

For example, paintings #1 and #6 of Fig. 8.18 are the most similar to the image of Christ on the Justinian II coin, having a NS = 0.2, while painting #5, having a NS = 1.0, is the least similar to the face on the coin.

Similarly, painting #4 of Fig. 8.19 is the most similar to the image of Christ on the coin of Michael IV, having a NS = 0.3, while painting #5, having NS = 1.0, is the least similar to the image on the coin.

It is interesting to observe that while the seven copies of the Justinian II coin and the five copies of the Michael IV coin appear quite different from each other, they show some similarity to the gold coin's face, thus indicating that just the coin was copied by each painting. This aspect will be further considered in Section 8.4.

Another fact emerges from the comparison of Christ's face shown in Figs. 8.18 and 8.19: while the original image is more detailed, the copies are less detailed. Tables 8.1 and 8.2 indicate this lack of details.

This result confirms that each painter, when producing his artwork, a face in the present case, combines the image he is looking at with the image he has in his mind. In other words, the face that each painter has in his mind interferes with an accurate reproduction of the face he is looking at.

For example, let us consider the bipartite beard that is clearly visible on the Shroud face in Fig. 2.11. It is less visible on the model of the gold coin of Fig. 8.19 but it has been practically forgotten in all the copies, which reproduce a more continuous beard. Professor Piraccini underlines that this is a form of "*prejudice*" of the painter, who tends to reproduce something similar to the image stored in his mind.

8.3 Copies Inspired from the Shroud

The analysis shown in this section is similar to that presented in Section 8.2, except that the images are copied from the face of Christ on the Shroud. These copies are produced by:

- students of Professor Piraccini,
- Professor Piraccini herself,
- the artist, Maestro Benedetto Robazza[e],
- the Byzantine engravers who engraved the images on the gold coins analyzed in Section 8.1.

The task of copying the face of Christ on the Shroud was assigned to students of Professor Piraccini. Both the original Shroud's face and the various resulting copies are reported in Fig. 8.20. The analysis is performed as before and listed in Table 8.3.

Figure 8.20 The image on the Shroud is on the top left. The others are copies painted by Professor Piraccini's students.

---

[e]Benedetto Robazza was born in 1934 in Rome. He began making figures out of clay (pupazzi) for cribs and painting small landscapes. He learned to play music, to dance, and he reached the Italian championship in boxing. He worked in Belgium where he obtained a diploma in geology. He also worked in Germany and USA where in New York he has the "Benedetto Gallery." In 1984, Robazza made a bas-relief of the image on the Shroud for don Giulio Ricci of the Centro Romano di Sindonologia that has been extensively exhibited.

Table 8.3 Analysis of dissimilarity of the student's copies in Fig. 8.20 relative to the face on the Shroud

Simplifications or dissimilarities of painting #	1	2	3	4	5	6	7	8	9	10	11
Blood flows	1	1	1	2	2	2	2	1	2	2	2
Whole face	0	0	0	2	0	2	0	1	2	2	2
Shape of hair				2	2	2	1	2	2	1	1
Eyebrows-forehead	2	2	0	2	0	2	2	2	2	2	0
Eyes	1	0	0	2	0	2	2	2	2	2	2
Nose	0	2	2	2	0	2	2	2	2	2	2
Bipartite beard	1	2	0	2	0	2	2	1	2	2	0
Moustaches	2	0	0	2	2	2	2	0	2	2	0
Lower lip	0	2	0	2	1	2	2	0	1	2	2
Score	7	9	3	18	7	18	15	11	17	17	11
Normalized Score	0.4	0.5	0.2	1.0	0.4	1.0	0.8	0.6	0.9	0.9	0.6

Note: The scores 2, 1 and 0, respectively, correspond to a significant, minor and negligible difference. The smaller the NS, the more similar is the copy to the image on the coin.

Painting #3 of Fig. 8.20, having a NS = 0.2, is the most similar to the image of Christ on the Shroud, while paintings #4 and #6 having a NS = 1.0 are least similar to the original face of Christ.

This comparison leads to a conclusion similar to that reached in Section 8.2, that copies of Christ's face on the Shroud can appear uncorrelated to each other but they are more clearly correlated to the face on the Shroud.

As some may doubt the value of students copying the face of Christ on the Shroud because they are not professionals, the author considered the copies of the face of the Shroud painted by two renowned artists, Professor Piraccini and Maestro Robazza. As with the students, Piraccini and Robazza produced copies that included simplifications or dissimilarities from the original face.

Professor Piraccini, using tracing-paper on a life-size photo of the Shroud, transferred the image by hand onto a linen canvas as shown in Fig. 8.21. She accomplished this using her special *"invisible-visible painting"* technique that she calls her *"Imperceptible"* painting technique.

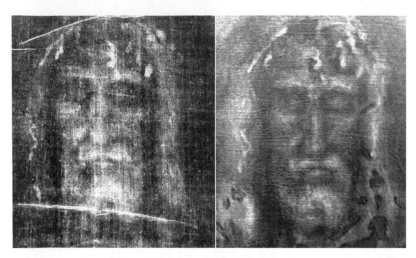

Figure 8.21 Christ's face of the Shroud on the left and a copy by Professor Piraccini on the right.

Figure 8.22 Christ's face of the Shroud on the left and a copy by Maestro Robazza on the right.

Maestro Robazza, with the help of Mons. Giulio Ricci of Centro Romano di Sindonologia, copied the face of the Shroud by adding to his handwork some observations and interpretations by Mons. Ricci, see Fig. 8.22.

Table 8.4 Analysis of dissimilarity of copies made by Prof. Piraccini and Maestro Robazza in Figs. 8.21 and 8.22 relative to the face on the Shroud

Simplifications or dissimilarities of painting #	Piraccini	Robazza
Blood flows	2	1
Whole face	0	2
Shape of hair	2	2
Eyebrows-forehead	2	2
Eyes	0	2
Nose	2	0
Bipartite beard	2	2
Moustaches	2	0
Lower lip	0	2
Score	12	13
Normalized Score	0.9	1.0

Note: The scores 2, 1 and 0, respectively, correspond to a significant, minor and negligible difference. The smaller the NS, the more similar is the copy to the image on the coin.

The result of the analysis, using the same methodology, is listed in Table 8.4. Piraccini's direct copy of the Shroud in Fig. 8.21 is the most similar to the image of Christ on the Shroud, having a NS = 0.9, while Robazza's bas-relief in Fig. 8.22 has a NS = 1.0[f].

The images on gold coins produced by the Byzantine engravers are now compared with the face on the Shroud; these are shown in Fig. 8.23. The analysis, using the same methodology, is listed in Table 8.5 indicating quantitatively how dissimilar each coin is from the face of Christ on the Shroud.

Coin #3 of Fig. 8.23 is the most similar to the image on the Shroud, having a NS = 0.2, while coins #5, #6 and #11 are least similar having a NS = 1.0.

---

[f]Perhaps a deeper analysis of differences could be necessary in the present analysis, but it appears not necessary for the aims of this study.

Figure 8.23 The image on the Shroud is on the top left. The others are images produced by engravers on Byzantine coins.

Table 8.5 Analysis of dissimilarity of images on Byzantine coins in Fig. 8.23 relative to the face on the Shroud

Simplifications or dissimilarities of image #	1	2	3	4	5	6	7	8	9	10	11
Whole face	0	1	0	1	2	2	0	1	2	1	2
Shape of hair	0	0	0	1	2	2	0		1	1	2
Eyebrows-forehead	0	1	0	2	1	2	0	0	2	2	2
Eyes	1	1	0	1	0	0	2	1	0	0	1
Nose	0	1	1	1	2	0	0	0	1	2	2
Bipartite beard	0	2	0	2	2	2	2	2	2	0	1
Moustaches	2	0	1	1	2	2	2	1	1	1	1
Lower lip	0	0	0	0	1	2	0	0	1	1	1
Score	3	6	2	9	12	12	6	5	10	8	12
Normalized Score	0.3	0.5	0.2	0.8	1.0	1.0	0.5	0.4	0.8	0.7	1.0

Note: The scores 2, 1 and 0, respectively, correspond to a significant, minor and negligible difference. The smaller the NS, the more similar is the copy to the image on the coin.

The maximum value of NS = 1.0 in Table 8.5 for coins #5, #6, and #11 indicates those coins were probably produced by Byzantine engravers that did not directly observe the Shroud, but perhaps used a copy of it as a reference model. This hypothesis is supported by the fact that some gold Byzantine coins report on the reverse a mark of the specific *"officina"* (workshop) that produced it and some of these were far from Constantinople, where the Shroud was kept and exhibited at that time.

8.4   A Cross-Correlation of Images

In the previous experiments (Tables 8.1 to 8.5), the author performed a quantitative evaluation of the degree of dissimilarity of either each painted or engraved copy from the original image.

To complete this analysis, Tables 8.6 to 8.9 show an additional evaluation where the details of all the copied images are compared each other. The target was reached by assigning the number two for a significant difference, the number one for a minor difference, and the number zero for a little difference.

In each table, there are m columns and m rows corresponding to the images in question. To the m rows, one listing a score equal to the sum of all the values of the column under analysis has been added with a last row listing the *"Normalized Score"* (NS). It contains a normalized value obtained by dividing the results of the values reported in the upper row of the sums by its maximum value so that all the results are equal or less than one (all results are rounded to the first decimal).

For example, in Table 8.6, the image #1 is similar to the image of Christ on the gold *solidus* of Justinian II (692–695) and therefore a zero value is located where column #1 intersects with row "Christ on *solidus*." Instead, the image #1 is not similar to the image #6, so the value of *2* has been assigned where column #1 intersects with row #6. Since this matrix must be symmetric, the value of *2* has been assigned in the intersection between column #6 and row #1 too.

The results of the copies obtained by the students of Professor Piraccini are shown in Tables 8.6 and 8.7.

Table 8.6 shows the cross-correlation among copies (Fig. 8.18) of Christ's face on a gold *solidus* of Justinian II (692–695). The minimum NS = 0.5 results only for the image of the copied coin, indicating that this one was most likely used as reference for making the painted copies, as it actually was.

Table 8.6 Cross-dissimilarities for the images in Fig. 8.18 of Christ's face on a gold *solidus* of Justinian II (692–695) and the painted copies

Dissimilarity between face #	Christ on *solidus*	1	2	3	4	5	6	7
Christ on *solidus*	-	0	1	1	1	2	0	1
1	0	-	1	2	2	2	2	1
2	1	1	-	1	2	2	1	2
3	1	2	1	-	1	2	1	2
4	1	2	2	1	-	1	2	2
5	2	2	2	2	1	-	2	1
6	0	2	1	1	2	2	-	2
7	1	1	2	2	2	1	2	-
Score	6	10	10	10	11	12	10	11
Normalized Score	0.5	0.8	0.8	0.8	0.9	1.0	0.8	0.9

Note: The scores 2, 1 and 0, respectively, correspond to a significant, minor and negligible difference. The smaller the NS, the more similar is the copy to the image on the coin.

Table 8.7 shows the cross-correlation among copies of Christ's face (Fig. 8.19) on a gold *histamenon nomisma* of Michael IV (1034–1041). The minimum NS = 0.2 results only for the image of the copied coin, again confirming that this one was used as reference.

Table 8.8 shows the cross-correlation among copies of the image on the Shroud (Fig. 8.20). The minimum NS = 0.6 just results for the image on the Shroud. Again, as above, this result indicates that the image on the Shroud was used as the reference to make the painted copies, as it actually was.

No cross-correlation was performed for images of Figs. 8.21 and 8.22 because there was an insignificant number of examples for an analysis.

Table 8.7 Cross-dissimilarities for the images in Fig. 8.19 of Christ's face on a gold *histamenon nomisma* of Michael IV (1034–1041) and the painted copies

Dissimilarity between face #	Christ on *histamenon*	1	2	3	4	5
Christ on *histamenon*	–	0	0	0	0	2
1	0	–	1	1	1	2
2	0	1	–	1	0	2
3	0	1	1	–	1	2
4	0	1	0	1	–	2
5	2	2	2	2	2	–
Score	2	5	4	5	4	10
Normalized Score	0.2	0.5	0.4	0.5	0.4	1.0

Note: The scores 2, 1 and 0, respectively, correspond to a significant, minor and negligible difference. The smaller the NS, the more similar is the copy to the image on the coin.

Table 8.8 Cross-dissimilarities for the images in Fig. 8.20 of Christ's face on the Shroud and the painted copies

Dissimilarity between face #	Shroud	1	2	3	4	5	6	7	8	9	10	11
Shroud	–	1	1	0	2	1	2	1	1	2	2	1
1	1	–	2	1	2	2	2	2	1	2	2	2
2	1	2	–	2	2	1	2	2	2	2	2	1
3	0	1	2	–	2	2	2	2	2	2	2	2
4	2	2	2	2	–	1	2	2	2	2	2	2
5	1	2	2	2	1	–	1	2	2	2	2	1
6	2	2	1	2	2	1	–	2	2	2	2	2
7	1	2	2	2	2	2	2	–	2	2	2	2
8	1	1	2	2	2	2	2	2	–	2	2	2
9	2	2	2	2	2	2	2	2	2	–	2	2
10	2	2	2	2	2	2	2	2	2	2	–	2
11	1	2	1	2	2	1	2	2	2	2	2	–
Score	14	19	19	19	21	17	21	21	20	22	22	19
Normalized Score	0.6	0.9	0.9	0.9	1.0	0.8	1.0	1.0	0.9	1.0	1.0	0.9

Note: The scores 2, 1 and 0, respectively, correspond to a significant, minor and negligible difference. The smaller the NS, the more similar is the copy to the image of face on the Shroud.

Table 8.9 shows the cross-correlation among images on the coins and the image on the Shroud (Fig. 8.23). The minimum NS = 0.5 just results for the image of the Shroud. Again, as above, this value confirms that the engravers used the image on the Shroud as the reference to make the images on the Byzantine coins and not vice versa as wrongly supposed by some.

Table 8.9 Cross-dissimilarities for the images in Fig. 8.23 of Christ's face on the Shroud and the engraved images on Byzantine coins

Dissimilarity between face #	Shroud	1	2	3	4	5	6	7	8	9	10	11
Shroud	–	0	1	0	1	1	2	1	1	2	1	2
1	0	–	1	0	2	1	2	2	2	2	2	2
2	1	1	–	1	2	2	2	2	2	2	2	2
3	0	0	1	–	2	1	2	2	2	2	2	2
4	1	2	2	2	–	2	2	2	2	2	2	2
5	1	1	2	1	2	–	2	2	2	2	2	2
6	2	2	2	2	2	2	–	2	2	2	2	2
7	1	2	2	2	2	2	2	–		2	2	2
8	1	2	2	2	2	2	2		–	2	2	2
9	2	2	2	2	2	2	2	2	2	–	2	1
10	1	2	2	2	2	2	2	2	2	2	–	1
11	2	2	2	2	2	2	2	2	2	1	1	–
Score	12	16	19	16	21	19	22	19	19	21	20	20
Normalized Score	0.5	0.7	0.9	0.7	1.0	0.9	1.0	0.9	0.9	1.0	0.9	0.9

Note: The scores 2, 1 and 0, respectively, correspond to a significant, minor and negligible difference. The smaller the NS, the more similar is the face on the coin to the image of face on the Shroud.

This procedure of cross-correlation confirms what should be obvious, that copies of an original image are better correlated to the original image than they are to each other. This is at least in part due to the artist's natural subjectivism when painting. In producing his product, the artist tends to combine information from his eyes and his mind. For example, if the artist sees a non-symmetric face with defects, he unconsciously tends to paint a more symmetric and less defective face, which is more similar to the reference image in his mind. This is just what results in many of the coins just analyzed.

As another example, let us consider the bipartite beard clearly visible on the Shroud face. It is less visible on the image on the gold coin in Fig. 8.19 but it has been practically forgotten in many copies of it that reproduce a more continuous beard.

This analysis confirms that you must search for the image richest in information and details when trying to detect which is the original image among many copies.

8.5   First Quantitative Demonstration of the Shroud as Acheiropoieta Image

At the end of this chapter, where a quantitative analysis is performed among the face of the Shroud and other artifacts, it is interesting to try to answer to the following question. Are there perhaps some indications, albeit preliminary in this simplified form, of the fact that the Shroud image is actually *"not made by human hands"* as some define it as of non-human origin?

To answer this question, it would be sufficient to demonstrate that the quantity of details of the artistic works performed by man is inferior to that of the Shroud image. That is why the following evaluation is carried out.

In each Table 8.6, 8.7, 8.8 and 8.9 the degree of dissimilarity between pairs of images is reported quantitatively and the Score (S) indicates the sum of the dissimilarities referred to each image compared to the other images of the same table. A high S-value indicates that the evaluated image is quite dissimilar to other images, while a low-S value indicates that the image in question is quite similar to the others.

To compare the results of the four tables, we therefore evaluate the ratios R^* between the smallest S-value and the value of S closest to this one. For example, in Table 8.9 the smallest S-value is 12 while the S-value closest to this one is 16; therefore in this case it results $R^* = 0.8$ (rounding by 0.75). The meaning of R^* is the following. When R^* approaches 1 we have that all the pairs of images considered present a similar amount of reciprocal diversity. This result may therefore indicate the presence of a considerable amount of dissimilarities found in each image; in other words, the result can be interpreted as the presence of an excessive number of details of the sample image to be copied all together by the artist.

Conversely, when $R*$ approaches 0, it turns out that there are images with varying degrees of mutual diversity and therefore some images are more similar to another. This result can therefore be interpreted as the presence of a not too high number of details of the sample image and that therefore the artist in some cases is able to copy them all together. Table 8.10 reports these results.

Table 8.10 $R*$ ratios among the scores of Tables 8.6–8.9

Table #	8.6	8.7	8.8	8.9
Face comparison	Coin-painted	Coin-painted	Shroud-painted	Shroud-coins
Smallest S	6	2	14	13
Closer S	10	4	17	16
$R*$	0.6	0.5	0.8	0.8

The highest ratios $R* = 0.8$ result from Table 8.8 and Table 8.9 which compare the Shroud image with artists results: painted images and Byzantine coins. The lower ratios $R* = 0.6$ from Table 8.6 and $R* = 0.5$ from Table 8.7 instead result from comparisons between artistic creations made by man.

These results can be interpreted in the following way. The $R*$-value is very high when the comparison is made with the Shroud image. This means that it is more difficult to be copied because the richest in anatomical details, not easy to reproduce all together by a human artist. Instead the lower $R*$-values referred to the comparisons of artist's works, less rich in details, show that is easier for an human artist to copy an artwork made by another man.

This result, preliminary for the moment because referred to a reduced number of cases, can be seen as a demonstration of a non-human but supernatural origin of the image of Jesus Christ impressed on the most important Relic of Christianity.

8.6 Final Remarks

This chapter has considered the aesthetic opinion of an artist and, by means of experiments, quantitatively the hypothesis that the Shroud image could have been copied from the face of Christ visible on Byzantine coins. About the aesthetic opinion, Professor Veronica Piraccini emphasized that on the Byzantine coins the typological somatic features of Christ, repeated for centuries with slight variations, show a stylistic figure *"impossible"* for the time, but that this result was obtained because the coin engravers referred directly to the very peculiar body image on the Shroud.

After a detailed description of the development of some somatic features like the eyes, Professor Piraccini argued in particular that the persistent presence of the tuft of hair on the forehead replacing the reversed *"3"* shape of the bloodstain on the Shroud is a clear sign that Christ's face on the coins was copied from the Shroud and not vice versa.

The results of experiments performed by the author, in which copies were made of an original image, confirm that the Shroud was the source image used to produce the face of Christ on Byzantine coins, and not vice versa, as wrongly supposed by some.

In particular, the following experiments were performed:

- Students of Professor Piraccini painted copies of Christ's face on two different Byzantine coins (Figs. 8.18 and 8.19).
- Students of Professor Piraccini painted copies of Christ's face on the Shroud (Fig. 8.20).
- Two well-known artists, Professor Piraccini and Maestro Robazza, reproduced Christ's face on the Shroud (Figs. 8.21 and 8.22).
- The same method of analysis was used to compare the images of Christ's face on Byzantine coins with that of the Shroud (Fig. 8.23).

A cross-correlation of the images posed under analysis evidenced the greater richness of details of the Shroud image of face with respect to artworks made by man.

In conclusion, the face on the Shroud, probably of non-human origin, was the original image used to produce hundreds of images of Christ's face on coins, paintings and sculptures during much of the long period of the Byzantine era.

Chapter 9

Latest Findings

While the publisher was preparing this book for publication, some interesting findings emerged that should not be overlooked; therefore, this new chapter has been included in the book.

This shows how numismatic research is constantly evolving also because it is not always easy to find information in reference to some rare medieval coins.

9.1 Coins of Christ Minted by Visigoths

We have seen in Section 1.3 that the face of Christ was probably also minted on some coins of the Visigoths around 680–710, but that it is not easy to attribute these effigies to Christ or even less to the Shroud because the face depicted is too coarse. In addition, these coins lack a written identification of the man depicted like the symbols "IC-XC," as was often used in those times to identify our Savior's face. Figures 9.1 and 9.2 show two examples of these coins (gold *tremissis*).

It is important to note that these coins were minted in the period between 680 and 687; if they actually depicted Jesus on the Cross, they would be a few years prior to the Justinian II coins,

Byzantine Coins Influenced by the Shroud of Christ
Giulio Fanti
Copyright © 2022 Jenny Stanford Publishing Pte. Ltd.
ISBN 978-981-4877-88-6 (Hardcover), 978-1-003-21992-7 (eBook)
www.jennystanford.com

which are considered to be the first official coins depicting the face of Christ, see Figs. 1.9–1.12.

Figure 9.1 Gold *tremissis* of Visigoths, Spain (680–687), Emerita (Mérida) mint showing on the obverse a coarse face probably of Christ superimposed upon a cross and on the reverse a cross potent set on three steps (courtesy of Jesus Vico Auction, Lot 427 of Auction 146, October 2016, www.jesusvico.com/es).

Figure 9.2 Gold *tremissis* of Visigoths, Spain (680–687), Emerita (Mérida) mint showing on the obverse a coarse face probably of Christ superimposed upon a cross and on the reverse a cross potent set on three steps (courtesy of Roma Numismatics, Auction, Lot 822 of Auction XVII, March 2019, www.RomaNumismatics.com).

In this case, the history of the Visigoths can help us understand that the coins in question could actually be of Christ. In fact, the

Visigoths, ancient Germanic people, derived from Gothic groups, invaded Italy of the Roman Empire in 410. Subsequently, they settled first in southern Gaul and then in Hispania, where they founded the Visigothic Kingdom. Around 589, the Visigoths converted to Nicene Christianity and in the following century, the region was dominated by the episcopate. In 711 Arabs and Berbers defeated the Visigoths and their kingdom quickly collapsed.

It is therefore easy to think that the Visigoths episcopate minted coins with the face of Christ precisely in the period in which it was debated whether it was permissible to depict the face of the Redeemer on coins or more generally in paintings and artifacts and it was confirmed by the Trullan Council in 692, see Section 1.3.1.

Two very rare coins of the Visigoths recently found, showing the face of Christ, seem to confirm the hypothesis discussed above that the Visigoths represented Jesus Christ.

Figure 9.3 Bronze *1/2 nummus* of Visigoths Emerita (Mérida) showing a face supposedly of Christ with the probable letters "XC," second part of the "IC-XC" typical of coins of Christ (evidenced on the bottom).

They are two bronze *1/2 nummus* minted in the same city Emerita (Mérida) of the gold tremisses of Figs. 9.1 and 9.2, see Figs. 9.3 and 9.4.

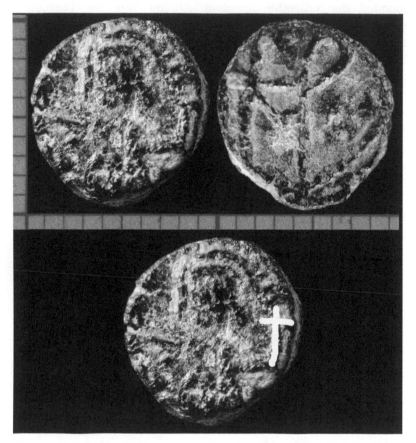

Figure 9.4 Bronze *1/2 nummus* of Visigoths Emerita (Mérida), declared as unique known in the world, probably showing blessing Christ with a cross on the left hand (evidenced on the bottom).

The *1/2 nummus* of Fig. 9.3, even if not so well conserved, shows an elongated face with long hair like that of Christ (see, for example, Figs. 5.31–5.33).

On the obverse, while it seems not possible to read any letters on the left of the coin due to lack of minting or wear, it is interesting to observe that on the right the letters "X" above "C" seem evident.

We must compare these letters with common Byzantine coins reproducing Jesus Christ (see, for example, Fig. 1.4) where to the left of Christ we read "IC" and "XC" to the right.

Given the small size of the coin in question (8–10 mm), it is therefore easy to think that the letters "IC" to the right of Christ's face have been lost, while the letters "XC" to the left of it have been written one under the other for reasons of space. If this were really the case, this coin would then self-certify as depicting the face of Christ.

The *1/2 nummus* of Fig. 9.4 (declared by the seller Aureo & Calicó, Auction 21/04/2021, lot 1252, as the only one known in the world), even if not so well conserved too, seems to show on the obverse a blessing man with a cross in his left hand who could be recognized as Christ.

Around the head also characterized by long hair similar to that depicted on the coins of Jesus (like on the Shroud, note the hair on the left longer and thicker than on the right), at least on the upper right part (because the left part of the coin is less well preserved) the typical nimbus of Christ and saints seems evident.

It would therefore seem that these two coins shown in Figs. 9.3 and 9.4 are referable to Jesus Christ. However, only future numismatic research will be able to confirm this new hypothesis.

Figure 9.5 Bronze *follis* of Crusaders in Antioch, Tancred regent (1101–1112) showing St. Peter standing facing, raising his right hand in blessing and holding a cross with his left hand on the obverse. Letters D-S-F-T (cross), Latin acronym for Domine Salvum Fac Tancredum (Lord save Tancred) on the reverse.

In fact, in-depth studies must be carried out in order not to run into possible errors; for example, at first sight the coin shown in Fig. 9.5 could be interpreted as a figure of Christ rising from the tomb too, but numismatic studies [Metcalf, 1993] have shown that instead it is an image of the apostle St. Peter.

9.2 Faces of Christ Not Similar to That of the Shroud?

In this book, it has been shown in several ways that the Shroud was known as early as 692 in the Byzantine Empire and that some engravers certainly saw it and took it as a model for the depictions of Christ in their coins.

However, someone might observe that some representations show a face of Christ not very similar to that of the Shroud even though minted in a period in which the Sacred Relic was exposed in Constantinople. This is the case, for example, of the coins minted by Emperor Manuel I (1143–1180), see, for example, Figs. 1.66–1.68.

Apart from the fact that also today many crucifixes are observed, one different from the other both in the position of the head, arms and legs and in the expression of the face of Christ, let us try to go deeper on this point.

Seeing these coins, someone could object that despite being minted during the Shroud exhibition in Constantinople, even engravers near this city preferred to reproduce models of faces not very similar to those of Christ, although these faces still depict a bearded man with mustache and long asymmetrical hair.

These people could be answered with a question: was it really necessary that the engraver always try to reproduce the maximum number of details that we observe on the Shroud, or for the Byzantine people it was sufficient that there was the name of the person depicted ("IC-XC") to recognize that Man?

Indeed, today we reason with the mentality of our century in which images are a fundamental part of our way of thinking and living, but was this also the case about a millennium ago?

The advent of photography within everyone's reach has led the image to be a fundamental expression of our thinking, but in the Byzantine era, it was probably different. The images were far rarer and people's way of observing and reasoning was based on something else; consequently, the features of an image were probably not so important to the observer.

An example of this is the fact that the faces of the emperors and co-rulers, even very young, depicted on the gold Byzantine *solidi* were for several decades not different from each other although it is not easy to think that all of them had very similar faces.

For example, Fig. 9.6 compares 11 faces of Byzantine emperors (with one of the Mother of God) showing the remarkable similarity among most of them, they are the following.

1. Basil I (867–886)
2. Constantine VII (867–886)
3. Constantine VII (920–944)
4. Christopher (920–944)
5. Romanus I (920–944)
6. Christopher (920–944), compare with image #4 of the same age
7. Constantine VII (920–944), compare with image #3 of the same age
8. Romanus II (920–944)
9. John I (969–976)
10. Mother of God (969–976)
11. Basil II (976–1025)
12. Constantine VIII (976–1025)

Therefore, we have ascertained that for more than a century the Byzantine gold *solidi* show very similar faces. However, it is unthinkable that all these emperors and co-rulers had very similar facial features, both young and old. It is therefore easy to think that the Byzantine people frequently gave not so much weight to the details of the face depicted because the culture of images was not as developed as it is today.

Figure 9.6 Various faces of Byzantine emperors (with #10 of the Mother of God) showing the remarkable similarity among most of them, in a period of more than a century from 867 to 1025.

However, some obvious exceptions appear instead for the peculiar face of Christ that is sometimes very similar to that of the Shroud. Perhaps this was the case because the engravers, who had to carry out the task of copying the face of God, were very impressed when they observed the very particular image of the face of Christ on the Shroud.

It is then explained why, although many depictions of the face of Christ reproduce numerous details of the face of Jesus on the Shroud, not all of these do.

9.3 Why Does Jesus Christ Not Always Bless with Right Hand?

Section 3.2.3 (Fig. 3.28) has already synthetically addressed this topic, but now we discuss it in more detail because this one is a focal point of the analysis of the Byzantine coinage of Christ's coins.

Starting from the first coins of Justinian II (692–695), see Fig. 1.1, until the fall of Constantinople in 1204 when the Shroud was brought to Europe and later, we find very frequently the depiction of Christ blessing with the right hand.

The earliest coins of Justinian II already show Jesus blessing not with His right hand outstretched as one might expect, but with His right arm partially wrapped in a garment, which, as we saw in Section 3.2.2, appears to be the *himation-pallium*-Shroud.

Starting with Basil I (867–886, Fig. 1.22) a new representation of Christ enthroned with His right arm outstretched and blessing appears, but already with Leo (886–916, Fig. 1.23) we find the right arm partially wrapped in a dress that looks like the *himation-pallium*-Shroud.

Figure 9.7 Copper *follis* Class C [Sear, 1987] attributed to Michael IV the Paphlagonian (1034–1041) showing a three-quarter length of the blessing Christ Antiphonetes on the obverse.

With Michael IV (1034–1041, Fig. 1.37), when the Shroud was brought triumphantly to Constantinople in 944 (see Section 2.4.3), a new representation of the Savior appears, Christ Antiphonetes, see copper *follis* of Figs. 1.37 and 9.7. The blessing right arm is still partially wrapped in a robe similar to the Shroud, but this *himation-pallium*-Shroud is also highlighted by the left arm supporting it, detached from the body.

The novelty appears with Constantine IX (1042–1055) with the bronze *follis* of Fig. 1.40 depicting Christ on the throne, who makes a small nod of blessing with His right hand holding the *himation-pallium*-Shroud. Also Theodora (1055–1056), who coined a new image of the Savior resurrected from the tomb, see Fig. 1.41, shows the right hand blessing, but at the same time holding the *himation-pallium*-Shroud.

In some coins such as the copper *follis* of Constantine X with Eudocia (1059–1067, see Fig. 1.45), the blessing right hand is less evident because it seems that the fingers prefer to support part of the dress.

While Nicephorus III (1078–1081) and Alexius I (1081–1118) preferred the figure of Christ enthroned with His right arm outstretched as a sign of blessing, see Figs. 1.56 and 1.60, John II (1118–1143) depicted both Christ enthroned with His right blessing arm outstretched on the gold *hyperpyron*, see Fig. 1.62, and Christ holding the *himation-pallium*-Shroud in His hand on the copper *tetarteron* of Fig. 1.63.

Manuel I (1143-1180), who produced a remarkable variety of numismatic representations of Christ, preferred to separate the representations of the Savior's right hand: he coined the *electrum aspron trachy* depicting both Christ enthroned with extended blessing right arm, see Fig. 1.66, and Christ rising from the sepulcher with His hand closed in a fist grasping the *himation-pallium-*Shroud, see Fig. 1.67. Successive emperors seem to have prevalently followed Manuel I's choice.

It is obvious that there must have been a very important reason for having preferred representing Christ, not with the right hand blessing but holding His garment firmly in the hand, if not one but more Byzantine emperors decided to do so.

A choice that seems obvious if instead we think that Christ, resurrecting from the Sepulcher, was clothed only in the Shroud, the most important Relic of Christianity, because in addition to being the symbol of the Resurrection, it also bears the double body image of our Savior.

The coins shown in Figs. 9.8 and 9.9 highlight this at first sight strange characteristic of Christ who, instead of blessing, holds the *himation-pallium*-Shroud tightly in the right hand. It is the case of the *Electrum* scyphate *aspron trachy* of Manuel I (1143–1180) of Fig. 9.8 and of the copper *follis* of Constantine X with Eudocia (1059–1067), see Fig. 9.9, where we see Christ resurrected holding His garment firmly in His hand.

Figure 9.8 *Electrum* scyphate *aspron trachy* of Manuel I (1143–1180) showing Christ resurrected firmly holding His garment (supposed to be the *himation-pallium*-Shroud) on the right hand not blessing.

Figure 9.9 Copper *follis* of Constantine X with Eudocia (1059–1067) showing Christ resurrected firmly holding His garment (supposed to be the *himation-pallium*-Shroud) on the right hand not blessing.

However, we must note that there are exceptions to the subdivision of the representations followed by Manuel I: Christ enthroned blessing and Christ resurrected from the Sepulcher with the *himation-pallium*-Shroud held in His hand. In fact, the copper *follis* of Constantine IX (1042–1055) shown in Fig. 9.10 depicts Christ on the throne not blessing, but again firmly holding His *himation-pallium*-Shroud on the right hand.

Figure 9.10 Copper *follis* of Constantine IX (1042–1055) showing Christ on the throne firmly holding His garment (supposed to be the *himation-pallium*-Shroud) on the right hand not blessing.

9.4 Continuation of Numismatic Iconography over Time

Section 1.3 reports the numismatic iconography of Christ in chronological order from the first coinage to the fall of Constantinople in 1204 with a brief reference to the subsequent coinage, as indicated in Table 1.3. However, we must note that the different types of depictions of Christ there presented could not be understood as being limited to the period in which they are presented. The emperors, who succeeded those who coined the first images, even in the subsequent centuries, in fact also reproduced some of these depictions.

Figure 9.11 Post-Reform silver *billon aspron trachy* of Alexius I (1092–1118), Philippolis mint, showing Christ on the throne having a beard lengthened downwards in reference of the "wet beard" of Agbar's legend.

It is the case, for example, of the image of Christ having a beard lengthened downwards in reference of the *"wet beard"* of Agbar's legend first coined by Theodora (1055–1056), see Fig. 1.40a, and more widely minted by Michael VII (1071–1078), see Fig. 1.51.

In fact, for example, more rarely we find this representation of the *"wet beard"* on the coin minted after the 1092 Reform of Alexius I (1081–1118), see Fig. 9.11. Perhaps the Emperor made this choice with the new Byzantine coinage in order not to forget the image introduced about 40 years earlier.

Also the image of the Mother of God holding before Her the Infant Christ, first coined by Michael VII (1071–1078), see Fig. 1.52, and then by Alexius I (1092–1118), see Fig. 1.61, has continued for centuries. Figure 9.12, for example, depicts the same type of image on a silver *basilikon* coined by Andronicus II and Michael IX (1295–1320).

The image of Christ blessing on the throne with the right foot smaller than the left one and tilted, first minted by Basil I (867–886), see Fig. 1.22, continued to be produced along the centuries and in various states; see, for example, the Venetian *grosso* of Fig. 5.15 and the Bulgarian *grosso* of Mihail Asen III Šišman, (1323–1330) of Fig. 9.13.

Figure 9.12 Silver *basilikon* of Andronicus II and Michael IX (1295–1320) showing the Mother of God holding before Her the Infant Christ.

These are just a few less common cases, but we must not forget the famous blessing bust of Christ, first coined by Justinian II in 692, that was also coined by John V (1354–1376), see Fig. 1.78 over six centuries later.

The inclusion of this chapter while the book was being prepared for publication testifies to the probable need for further explorations in the near future. In fact, the topics covered here are not definitive but in continuous development, depending also on possible new numismatic and non-numismatic finds that will come to light.

Even the discoveries and deductions drawn by the author in reference to the recognition of the depiction of Christ in Byzantine and more generally medieval numismatics must be subjected to scrutiny and confirmation by experts from the various sectors concerned.

Figure 9.13 Silver *grosso* of Mihail Asen III Šišman, II Empire of Bulgaria (1323–1330) showing blessing Christ enthroned.

Conclusion

This is probably the first book in the world that relates the different images of Christ on Byzantine coins with the image of Jesus Christ on the Shroud, the most important Relic of Christianity.

There are various books on Byzantine coins, but there are no specific books on the depiction of Christ on them even if the various kinds of Byzantine coins showing the effigy of Christ are the most researched and collected by numismatists. The influence of the Shroud body image on the effigy of Christ is a new argument never studied in depth. This book, which should be understandable to everyone, demonstrates the strong influence that had the Shroud in the Byzantine period up to the fall of Constantinople in AD 1204, showing that the coins minted from the seventh century onwards are a clear proof of the existence of the Shroud in the Byzantine period.

The numerous collectors of Byzantine coins depicting the face of Christ will therefore be interested, when reading this book, in not only having a numismatic analysis of these coins but also a historical-religious analysis evidencing the veiled references to the Shroud in the details shown in the coins.

This book does not claim to be a text on the history of art or numismatics, but it aims laying the foundations for joining numismatics, history of art and study of Shroud. It is *"more than ambitious project"* as it was been defined by A. Gannon and it will require various insights and comparisons with various experts in the different areas touched upon such as numismatics, history of art and Christian religion, Byzantine history, theology, scientific studies of Shroud, painting, image processing, dimensional analysis, statistics and probability calculation. In particular, the numismatic and art history analysis will have to be completed and reviewed by experts in the sector in order to discuss and confirm the innovative declarations here contained.

The main result shows the evident and indisputable very close correlation between the images on the coins and the image on the Shroud and the study highlighted the following innovations:

- The first indirect numismatic reference to the Shroud appears around 420 when the Byzantine emperors minted a mensural cross showing the dimensions of the body of Jesus Christ and such depiction continued for a century and a half. Obviously, to build a mensural cross, it was necessary to have at least the measurement of the height of Jesus Christ. And what was the way to catch this information if not to measure the length of Jesus Christ's body directly from the Shroud?

- The first official image of Jesus Christ on a coin is the one produced under Emperor Justinian II in 692. The probability that the engraver, in making the mold for the coin, was inspired by the image on the Shroud is calculated to be 99.99999999999999999%.

- An aesthetic investigation conducted with an expert in the field coupled with specific experiments shows that the hypothesis that the image on the Shroud was copied from a Byzantine coin is to be rejected. Instead, it is concluded that the Relic was the original model used to make the images of Christ on the Byzantine coins.

- The Empress Theodora in 1055–1056 produced a new important depiction of Christ which, according to numismatists, is of *"Christ standing facing out on a footstool,"* but which, from a more specific analysis, shows the image of the resurrected Christ coming from the sepulcher (referred to as a mortuary chest). This representation of the resurrected Christ was very prominent in the Byzantine Empire because various Byzantine emperors adopted it. Even some coins of the Maritime Republic of Venice copied and modified this image.

- The image of the resurrected Christ coined by the Empress Theodora in 1055–1056 confirms a very interesting detail already hinted in the previous depictions of Christ, starting from Justinian II in 692, but never so highlighted. In this image, Jesus Christ is wrapped in a robe that is so important that His right hand is no longer configured in the form of a blessing as in the previous images, but it exhibits the robe that surrounds Him. Moreover, why is this garment so important as to replace the blessing of Christ if it is not the Shroud, symbol of the Resurrection?

- The comparison between the clothes used in the Byzantine era and those reproduced on the coins either in reference to Christ or to the various emperors and co-rulers suggests that the Shroud was depicted as Christ's robe in two different ways. In the first, from the sixth to seventh century, the Shroud was wrapped around the body of Christ like a *himation-pallium*, as it also appears in many mosaics, ivories, and icons. In the second, the Shroud wrapped Christ like a simplified *loros*, as shown in several coins minted from the tenth century onwards.

- A cross-correlation among the image of the face on the Shroud, the face of Christ shown on coins and the painted copies of them gives the first quantitative demonstration of a non-human but supernatural origin of the image of Jesus Christ impressed on the most important Relic of Christianity.

- Moreover, based on the analysis of ecclesiastical vestments, it is probable that the current stole worn by Catholic priests, and in a similar form also by Orthodox priests, is directly connected to the simplified *loros* and therefore to the Shroud. It seems reasonable that the current priests wear the stole because of the resurrected Christ wrapped in the Shroud. If this is the case, the stole, a fundamental garment for priests who celebrate religious functions, would be a direct reference to the burial Shroud of Jesus Christ, a *"silent but extremely eloquent"* [S. John Paul II, April 13, 1980] witness of the Resurrection of Christ.

Many of these new results will have to be confirmed by numismatic and historical experts, but this book, based on the author's analysis, appears to be a first important step in revealing innovative aspects of the close relation between the Byzantine coins and the Shroud of Christ resurrected.

References

Abramson, T. (2012). *Sceatta List Including Stycas Simplified, Sceatta*, Charlesworth Press, Wakefield.

Adler, A. D. (1996). Updating recent studies on the Shroud of Turin, in: Orna, M. V. (ed.), *Archaeological Chemistry*, vol. 625, pp. 223–228, American Chemical Society.

Antonacci, M. (2016). *Test the Shroud: At the Atomic and Molecular Levels*, 1st ed., Forefront Publishing Company, USA.

Baima Bollone, P. (1982). Indagini identificative su fili della Sindone, *Giornale della Accademia di Medicina di Torino*, 1(12), pp. 228–239 (in Italian).

Baima Bollone, P. (1998). *La Sindone la prova*, Mondadori, Italy.

Baldacchini, G., Baldacchini, F., Casarosa, L., Falcone, G. (2020). *La Croce Mensurale di Grottaferrata*, Ed. Renzo Palozzi, Marino, Rome.

Barbet, P. (1953). *A Doctor at Calvary: The Passion of Our Lord Jesus Christ as Described by a Surgeon*, P.J. Kenedy & Sons, New York.

Barbet, P. (1963). *A Doctor at Calvary*, Doubleday Image Book, New York.

Battistini, A. (2020). http://www.legioxii.it/Testi/Abbigliamento-masc.htm.

Bellinger, A. R. (1966). *Catalogue of Byzantine Coins .... Volume One, Anastasius I to Maurice 491–602*, Dumbarton Oaks Research Library and Collection, Washington D.C. USA, https://www.doaks.org/resources/publications/books/catalogue-of-the-byzantine-coins-in-the-dumbarton-oaks-collection-and-in-the-whittemore-collection-1.

Bellinger, A. R., Grierson, P. (1973). *Catalogue of Byzantine Coins .... Volume Threee, Part One, Leo III to Michael III 767–817*, Dumbarton Oaks Research Library and Collection, Washington D.C., https://www.doaks.org/resources/publications/books/catalogue-of-the-byzantine-coins-in-the-dumbarton-oaks-collection-and-in-the-whittemore-collection-2.

Belting, H. (1994). *Likeness and Presence—A History of the Image before the Era of Art*, translated from German by Jephcott, E., University of Chicago Press, Chicago and London.

Bevilacqua, V., Ciccimarra, A., Leone, I., Mastronardi, G. (2008). Automatic facial feature points detection, in: De-Shuang, H., Wunsch, D. C., Levine, D. S., Kang-Hyun, J. (eds.), *Advanced Intelligent Computing Theories and Applications. With Aspects of Artificial Intelligence, Lecture Notes in Computer Science*, vol. 5227 (Springer, Berlin, Heidelberg), pp. 1142–1149.

Bevilacqua, M., Fanti, G., D'Arienzo, M., De Caro, R. (2014). Do we really need new medical information about the Turin Shroud? *Injury Journal* 2(45), pp. 460–464, https://www.injuryjournal.com/article/S0020-1383%2813%2900422-1/abstract.

Bogdanovic, J. (2008). *Chalke Gate/Entrance of Great Palace (Χαλκή Πύλη/ Είσοδος του Μεγάλου Παλατιού)* Academia.edu, https://www.academia.edu/2100709/Chalke_Gate_Entrance_of_Great_Palace_.

Boubakeur, S. H. (1992). Versione islamica del Santo Sudario, in: *Collegamento pro Sindone*, May–June, pp. 35–41.

Breckenridge, J. (1959). *The Numismatic Iconography of Jiustinian II*, The American Numismatic Society, New York, USA.

Brillante, C., Fanti, G., Marinelli, E. (2002). Bloodstains characteristics to be considered in laboratory reconstruction of the Turin Shroud, *IV Symposium Scientifique International sur le Linceul de Turin*, Paris.

Brubaker, L. (2016). *L'invenzione dell'iconoclasmo bizantino*, Viella Ed., Rome, 2016, pp. 123–124.

Brunati, E. (1997). A proposito di errori nel rapporto sulla datazione, *Collegamento pro Sindone*, Marinelli Ed. Rome, May/June, p. 34–39.

Bureau International des Poids et Mesures, BIPM (2008). Guide to the expression of uncertainty in measurement, Tech. Rep., BPIM474 JCGM 100, http://www.bipm.org/utils/common/documents/jcgm/JCGM 100 2008 E.pdf.

Bury, J. B. (1911). *The Imperial Administrative System of the Ninth Century—With a Revised Text of the Kletorologion of Philotheos*, Oxford University Press.

Caccese, A., Marinelli, E., Provera, L., Repice, D. (2017). The Mandylion in Constantinople: Literary and iconographic sources, in: *International Conference on the Shroud of Turin*, July 19–22, TRAC Center, Pasco, Washington D.C., https://www.academia.edu/34142677/The_Mandylion_in_Constantinople_-_Literary_and_iconographic_sources.

Cabrol, F., Leclercq, H. (1922). *Dictionaire D'archéologie Chrétienne et de liturgie*, tome V, partie I, Encaustique-Feux, Libraire Letouzey at Ané, Paris.

Cazzola, P., Fusina, M. D. (1983). Tracce sindoniche nell'arte bizantino-russa, in: *La Sindone, Scienza e Fede, Atti del II Convegno Nazionale di Sindonologia, Bologna 1981*, CLUEB, Bologna, Italy, pp. 129–135.

Cicero, M. T. (1991). *On Duties (De Officiis)*, Cambridge University Press, 1991.

Coppini, L., Cavazzuti, F. (2000). *Le Icone di CRISTO e la Sindone*, Ed. San Paolo, Cinisello Balsamo, Italy.

Damon, J. E., Donahue, D. J., Gore, B. H., Hatheway, A. L., Jull, A. J. T., Linick, T. W., Sercel, P. J., Toolin, L. J., Bronk, C. R., Hall, E. T., Hedges, R. E. M., Housley, R., Law, I. A., Perry, C., Bonani, G., Trumbore, S., Woelfli, W., Ambers, J. C., Bowman, S. G. E., Leese, M. N., Tite, M. S. (1988). Radiocarbon dating of the Turin Shroud, *Nature* 337(6208), pp. 611–615.

David, R. (1978). *Mysteries of the Mummies: The Story of the Manchester University Investigation*, Littlehampton Book Services, London, UK, pp. 119–131.

De Liso, G. (2000). Verifica sperimentale della formazione di immagini su teli di lino trattati con aloe e mirra in concomitanza di terremoti, Sindon N.S. 14, pp. 125–130.

Dufournet, J. (2004). *De Clari R., La conquête de Constantinople*, Paris, pp. 182–184.

Engberg, S. G. (2004). Romanos Lekapenos and the Mandilion of Edessa, in: Durand, J. Flusin, B. (ed.), *Byzance et les reliques du Christ*, Centre de recherche d'Histoire et Civilisation de Byzance, Monographies 17, Paris, pp. 123–142, https://www.academia.edu/8250053/Romanos_Lekapenos_and_the_Mandilion_of_Edessa.

Fanti, G., Marinelli, E. (1998). A probabilistic model to quantify the results of the research on the Turin Shroud, in: *III International Congress of Studies on the Shroud*, www.shroud.com/fanti2en.pdf.

Fanti, G., Marinelli, E. (2001). A study of the front and back body enveloping based on 3d information, in: *Dallas International Conference on the Shroud of Turin* (Dallas, USA), pp. 1–18.

Fanti, G., Maggiolo, R. (2004). The double superficiality of the frontal image of the Turin Shroud, *Journal of Optics A: Pure and Applied Optics*, 6, pp. 491–503.

Fanti, G., Schwortz, B., Accetta, A., et al. (2005). Evidences for testing hypotheses about the body image formation of the Turin Shroud, in: *Third Dallas International Conference on the Shroud of Turin* (Dallas, USA), pp. 25–28, URL www.shroud.com/pdfs/doclist.pdf.

Fanti, G., Basso, R., Bianchini, G. (2010). Turin Shroud: Compatibility between a digitized body image and a computerized anthropomorphous manikin, *Journal of Imaging Science and Technology*, 54(5), pp. 1–8.

Fanti, G., Basso, R. (2008). MTF resolution of images obtained without an acquisition system, *Proceedings of Shroud Science Group International Conference The Shroud of Turin: Perspectives on a Multifaceted Enigma*, Ohio State University, August 14–17, Libreria Progetto, Padova, Italy, 2009, ISBN 987-88-96477-03-8.

Fanti, G. (2010). Can a corona discharge explain the body image of the Turin Shroud? *Journal of Imaging Science and Technology*, 54(2), pp. 1–10.

Fanti, G. (2011). Hypotheses regarding the formation of the body image on the Turin Shroud. A critical compendium, *Journal of Imaging Science and Technology*, 55(6), pp. 1–14, https://goo.gl/lhYLkF.

Fanti, G., Baraldi, P., Basso, R., Tinti, A. (2013). Non-destructive dating of ancient flax textiles by means of vibrational spectroscopy, *Vibrational Spectroscopy*, 67, pp. 61–70.

Fanti, G., Malfi, P. (2014). Multi-parametric micro-mechanical dating of single fibers coming from ancient flax textiles, *Textile Research Journal*, 84(7), pp. 714–727.

Fanti, G., Malfi, P., Crosilla, F. (2015). Mechanical and opto-chemical dating of the Turin Shroud, in: *MATEC Web of Conferences*, vol. 36, 2015, 01001, DOI: http://dx.doi.org/10.1051/matecconf/20153601001.

Fanti, G., Zagotto, G., (2017). Blood reinforced by pigments in the reddish stains of the Turin Shroud, *Journal of Cultural Heritage*, 25, pp. 113–120, DOI: 10.1016/j.culher.2016.12.012, http://www.sciencedirect.com/science/article/pii/S1296207417300092.

Fanti, G. (2018). Why is the Turin Shroud authentic?. *Global Journal of Archaeology and Anthropology*, 7(2), 555707, https://juniperpublishers.com/gjaa/pdf/GJAA.MS.ID.555707.pdf.

Fanti, G., Furlan, C. (2019). Do gold particles from the Turin Shroud indicate its presence in theMiddle East during the Byzantine Empire?, *Journal of Cultural Heritage*, 42, pp. 36–44, https://www.sciencedirect.com/science/article/pii/S1296207419304534.

Fanti, G. (2019). Is the "Holy Fire" related to the Turin Shroud?, *Global Journal of Archaeology and Anthropology*, 10(2), 555782, https://juniperpublishers.com/gjaa/pdf/GJAA.MS.ID.555782.pdf.

Fanti, G., Malfi, P. (2020). *The Shroud of Turin—First Century After Christ!*, 2nd ed., Jenny Stanford Publishing, Singapore.

Fashion Era, https://www.fashion-era.com/coronation_dress.htm#The%20White%20Colobium%20Sindonis%20Dress%C2%A0.

Gannon, A., (2011). Coins, images and tales from the Holy Land: Questions of theology and orthodoxy, new perspectives, in: Abramson, T. (ed.), *Studies in Early Medieval Coinage*, 2nd ed., Woodbridge, Boydell & Brewer, 2011. pp. 88–103, https://www.academia.edu/490921/Coins_images_and_tales_from_the_Holy_Land_Questions_of_Theology_and_Orthodoxy.

Gannon, A. (2013). *Sylloge of Coins of the British Isles*, 63 British Museum Anglo-Saxon-Coins I, British museum Press, London.

Gannon, A. (2013a). Lies, damned lies and iconography, in: Hawkes, J. (ed.), *MakingHistories, Proc. Sixth Int. Insular Art Conference—York 2011*, Donnington, 2013, pp. 291–302.

Gannon, A. (2015). Series X and its international framework: An art historical contribution to the study of early-medieval coinage, in: *Golden Middle Age in Europe, Proceedings of the II Dorestad Congress*, Lieden, The Netherlands.

Gannon, A. (2020). Private communication.

Garello, E. (1984). *La Sindone e i Papi*, Ed. Corsi, Turin, Italy.

Garlaschelli, L. (2010). Lifesize reproduction of the Shroud of Turin and its image, *Journal of Imaging Science and Technology*, 54(4), pp. 1–14.

Ghiberti, G. (2002). *Sindone le immagini 2002*, ODPF, Turin, Italy.

Gonella, L., Riggi di Numana, G., Pinna Berchet, G., Berbenni, G. (2005). *Il giorno più lungo della Sindone. Cronache e documenti sulle operazioni di prelievo dei campioni per la radiodatazione del telo sindonico, 1986–1988*, editore 3M, Milano 2005.

Goodacre, H. (1967). *A Handbook of the Coinage of the Byzantine Empire*, Spink & Son Ltd, London.

Goodwin, T. (2006). *An Introduction to Arab-Byzantine Coinage*, https://www.academia.edu/30857954/AN_INTRODUCTION_TO_ARAB_BYZANTINE_COINAGE.

Grierson, P., (1973). *Catalogue of Byzantine Coins in the Dumbarton Oaks Collection and in the Whittermore Collection*, Dumbarton Oaks

Research Library and Collection, Washington D.C., https://www.doaks. org/resources/publications/books/catalogue-of-the-byzantine-coins-in-the-dumbarton-oaks-collection-and-in-the-whittemore-collection-3.

Grierson, P. (1982). *Byzantine Coins*, Methuen & Co. Ltd, London.

Grierson, P., Mays, M. (1992). *Catalogue of Late Roman Coins in the Dumbarton Oaks Collection and in the Whittermore Collection*, Dumbarton Oaks Research Library and Collection, Washington D.C., https://www.doaks.org/resources/publications/books/catalogue-of-late-roman-coins-in-the-dumbarton.

Grierson, P., Hendy, M.F. (1993–99), *Catalogue of Byzantine Coins in the Dumbarton Oaks Collection and in the Whittermore Collection*, Dumbarton Oaks Research Library and Collection, Vol. II-V Washington D.C., https://www.doaks.org/resources/publications/books/catalogue-of-the-byzantine-coins-in-the-dumbarton.

Grierson, P. (1999). *Byzantine Coinage*, Dumbarton Oaks Research Library and Collection, Washington D.C., https://www.doaks.org/resources/publications/books/byzantine-coinage.

Guerreschi, A., Salcito, M. (2002). Ricerche fotografiche e informatiche sulle bruciature e sugli aloni visibili sulla sindone e conseguenze sul piano storico, in: *IV Symposium Scientifique International du CIELT* (CIELT, Paris), pp. 31–65.

Guerreschi, A., Salcito, M. (2005). Further studies on the scorches and the watermarks, in: *Third Dallas International Conference on the Shroud of Turin*, Dallas, USA, pp. 1–10, http://www.shroud.com/pdfs/aldo4.pdf.

Guscin, M. (2009). *The Image of Edessa*, Leiden-Boston, pp. 7–69.

Hann, W., Metcalf, W. (1988). *Studies in Early Byzantine Gold Coinage*, The American Numismatic Society, Numismatic Studies No. 17, New York, printed in Belgium at Cultura, Wetteren.

Hetherington, P. (1981). *The Painter's Manual of Dionysius of Fourna*, Sagittarius Press, London.

Jackson, J. P., Jackson, R. S., Propp, K. E. (2000). On the late Byzantine history of the Turin Shroud, in: Walsh, B. J. (ed.), *Proceedings of the 1999 Shroud of Turin International Research Conference, Richmond, Virginia*, Glen Allen, Richmond, Virginia, pp. 185–195.

Judica Cordiglia, G. B. (1986). La sindone immagine elettrostatica?, in: *La Sindone, nuovi studi e ricerche, Atti del III Congresso Nazionale di Studi sulla Sindone*, Trani, Italy, pp. 313–327.

Jumper, E. J., Adler, A. D., Jackson, J. P., Pellicori, S. F., Heller, J. H., Druzik, J. R. (1984). A comprehensive examination of the various stains and images on the Shroud of Turin, in: *Archaeological Chemistry III*, American Chemical Society, pp. 447–479.

Lattarulo, F. (1998). L'immagine sindonica spiegata attraverso un processo sismoelettrico, in: *III Congresso Internazionale di Studi sulla Sindone*, Turin, Italy, pp. 334–346.

Lavoie, G. (2000). *Resurrected*, Thomas More, Texas, USA.

Lindner, E. (2002). The Shroud of Jesus Christ: The scientific gospel to renew the faith in Resurrection, in: *Atti del Congresso Mondiale Sindone 2000*, Gerni Editori, Orvieto, Italy, pp. 165–170.

Loconsole, M. (1999). *Sulle tracce della Sacra Sindone di Torino, un itinerario storico-esegetico*, Ladisa Editori, Bari, Italy.

Malantrucco, L. (1992). *L'equivoco Sindone*, LDC Leumann, Turin, Italy.

Mangan, C. (2003). *Church Teaching on Relics*, www.catholiceducation.org.

Marinelli, E. (2014). *The Shroud and the iconography of Christ*, St. Louis Conference, https://www.shroud.com/pdfs/stlemarinellipaper.pdf.

Metcalf, D. M. (1993). *Thrymsas and Sceattas in the Ashmolean Museum, Oxford*, Ed. Ashmolean Museum, Oxford.

Moon, P., Bywater, J. (2020). *The Loros the Epitaphios and the Shroud of Turin*, https://www.academia.edu/43687969/The_Loros_the_Epitaphios_and_the_Shroud_of_Turin.

Moroni, M. (1983). L'ipotesi della Sindone quale modello delle raffigurazioni artistiche del Cristo Pantocrator. Conferma numismatica, in: *La Sindone scienza e fede*, CLEUB, Bologna, Italy, pp. 175–180.

Moroni, M. (1986). Teoria numismatica dell'itinerario sindonico, in: *La Sindone, nuovi studi e ricerche*, Ed. Paoline, Cinisello Balsamo, Italy, pp. 103–122.

Moroni, M. (2000). L'iconografia di Cristo nelle monete bizantine, in: *Le icone di Cristo e la Sindone*, Ed. San Paolo, Cinisello Balsamo, Italy, pp. 122–144.

Nicoletti, A. (2011). *Dal Mandylion di Edessa alla Sindone di Torino*, Ed. dell'Orso, Alessandria, Italy.

Paci, S. (2008). *Storia delle vesti liturgiche–Forma, Immagine e funzione*, Ed. Ancora, Milano, Italy.

Parani, M. G. (2003). *Reconstructing the Reality of Images—Byzantine Material Culture Iconography (11th–15th Centuries)*, The Medieval Mediterranean Peoples, Economies and Cultures, 400–1453, Brill Leiden, Boston, USA.

Parani, M.G. (2019). Private communication, October 23.

Pfeiffer, H., (1986). *L'immagine di Cristo nell'arte*, Città Nuova, Rome, Italy.

Picciocchi, P., Picciocchi, P. (1979). L'impronta a epsilon sulla fronte dell'Uomo della Sindone: Nuova ipotesi sulla modalit`a di produzione, *Arch. di medicina legale, sociale e criminologia*, 24(3), pp. 261–274.

Piraccini, V. (2020). *La Sindone e l'Arte. Nuove rivelazioni dalle monete Bizantine*, About Art Online, www.aboutartonline.com/la-sindone-e-larte-nuove-rivelazioni-dalle-monete-bizantine/.

Psellus, M. (1018-after 1078), *Chronographia*, Fordham University, New York, https://sourcebooks.fordham.edu/basis/psellus-chronographia.asp.

Raes, G. (1976). Rapport d'analyse, in: *La S. Sindone, ricerche e studi della commissione di esperti nominata dall'Arcivescovo di Torino, Card. Michele Pellegrino, nel 1969*, Rivista diocesana Torinese, Turin, pp. 79–83.

Raes, G. (1995). Historique de l'échantillon, in: *Le prélévement du 21/4/ 1988 – É tudes du Tissu, Actes du Symposium Scientifique International (Paris 1989)*, OEIL, Paris, pp. 71–74.

Reiske, J. J. (1829). *Constantini Porphyrogeniti Imperatoris De Ceremoniis Aulae Byzantinae libri duo graece et latini e recensione Io. Iac. Reiskii cum eiusdem commentariis integris*. Corpus Scriptorum Historiae, Ed. Leich, Johannes Heinrich, Ed. Weber Bonn, Germany, https://archive.org/details/corpusscriptorum07niebuoft.

Rezza, D. (2013). *La Crux Vaticana o Croce di Giustino II*, Museo Storico Artistico del Tesoro di San Pietro, ATS Italia Editrice, Edizioni Capitolo Vaticano, Rome.

Riani, M., Atkinson, A. C., Fanti, G., Crosilla, F. (2013). Regression analysis with partially labelled regressors: Carbon dating of the Turin Shroud, *Statistics and Computing*, 23(4), pp. 551–561.

Riggi di Numana, G. (1982). *Rapporto Sindone 1978–1982*, 3M Edition, Milano, Italy.

Riggi di Numana, G. (1988). *Rapporto Sindone 1978–1987*, 3M Edition, Milano, Italy.

Righetti, M. U. J. D. (1950). *Manuale di Storia Liturgica*, Vol. 1, II ed., Ancora Editrice, Milano, Italy.

Rinaudo, J. B. (1998). Image formation on the Shroud of Turin explained by a protonic model affecting radiocarbon dating, in: *III Congresso internazionale di studi sulla Sindone*, Turin, Italy, pp. 474–483.

Rodante, S. (1994). *La Scienza convalida la Sindone*, Massimo, Milan, Italy.

Rogers, R. N., Arnoldi, A. (2002). Scientific method applied to the Shroud of Turin, a review, https://www.shroud.com/pdfs/rogers2.pdf.

Rucker, R. (2020). *Understanding the 1988 Carbon Dating of the Shroud*, www.shroudresearch.net, https://independent.academia. edu/RuckerR.

Salatino, L., Dubini, S. (2005). *Il giorno più lungo della Sindone. Cronache e documenti sulle operazioni di prelievo dei campioni per la radiodatazione del telo sindonico, 1986–1988*, Fondazione 3M Edizioni, Turin, Italy.

Savio, P. (1957). *Ricerche storiche sulla Santa Sindone*, Torino, pp. 190–191;

Savio, P. (1965). Le impronte di Gesù nella Santa Sindone, in: *Sindon, Quaderno n. 9, May*, pp. 12–23.

Scheuermann, O. (2003). *Hypothesis: Electron Emission or Absorption as the Mechanism That Created the Image on the Shroud of Turin: Proof by Experiment*, 1st ed., Fondazione 3M, Segrate, Italy.

Schwalbe, L. A., Rogers, R. N. (1982). Physics and chemistry of the Shroud of Turin: A summary of the 1978 investigation, *Analytica Chimica Acta*, 135(1), pp. 3–49.

Sear, D. R., Bendall, S., O'Hara, M. D. (1987). *Byzantine Coins and Their Values*, 2nd ed., Seaby, Imprint of Spink & Son, London, UK.

Sommer, U.S. (2010). *Die Muenzen des Byzantinichen Reiches 491-1453*, Battenberg Gietl Verlag, Germany.

Soyel, H., Demirel, H. (2007). Facial expression recognition using 3D facial feature distances, in: Kamel, M., Campilho, A. (eds.), *Image Analysis and Recognition, Lecture Notes in Computer Science*, vol. 4633, Springer, Berlin, Heidelberg, pp. 831–838.

Suarez, R. (2010). *Eric II–The Encyclopedia of Roman Imperial Coins*, Dirty Old Books™, Tumwater, WA, USA.

Travaini, L. (2003). La zecca merovingia di Avenches e le prime monete col volto di Cristo, *Quaderni ticinesi di numismatica e antichità classiche*, XXXII, pp. 291–301.

Van Haelst, R. (2000). The Shroud of Turin and the reliability of the 95% error confidence interval, in: *Proceedings of the 1999 Shroud of Turin International Research Conference*, Richmond, Virginia, Magisterium Press, Glen Allen, Virginia, pp. 321–325. Battenberg Verlag, Germany.

Vasilita, S. (2020). Coins auctioned, https://www.coins-auctioned.com/it/learn/coin-articles/ancient-byzantine-coinage.

Vial, G. (1995). Le linceul de turin, étude technique, in: *Le prélévement du 21/4/1988: Études du Tissu*, Actes du Symposium Scientifique International (Paris 1989), OEIL, Paris, pp. 75–106.

Vignon, P. (1938). *Le Saint-Suaire de Turin devant la Science, l'Archeologie, l'Histoire, l'Iconographie, la Logique*, Masson et C. Editeurs, Paris.

Volckringer, J. (1991). *The Holy Shroud: Science Confronts the Imprints*, The Runciman Press, Manly, Australia.

Whanger, A. D., Whanger, M. (1985). Polarized image overlay technique: A new image comparison method and its applications, *Applied Optics*, 24(6), pp. 766–772.

Whanger, A. D., Whanger, M. (1998). *The Shroud of Turin, an Adventure of Discovery Technique: A New Image Comparison Method and Its Applications*, Providence House, Franklin, USA.

Whanger, A. D. (2000). Icone e Sindone, in *Le icone di Cristo e la Sindone* (Ed. San Paolo, Cinisello Balsamo, Italy), pp. 122–144.

Whanger, A. D., Whanger, M. V. (2007). *The Impact of the Face Image of the Shroud on Art, Coins and Religions in the Early Centuries*, part 3, Council of Study of the Shroud of Turin, July 2007, 2, 11.

Williams, J. W. (1999). *Imaging the Early Medieval Bible*, Pennsylvania State University Press.

Wilson, J., Schwortz, B. (2000). *The Turin Shroud: Unshrouding the Mystery*, Michael O'Mara Books Ltd.

Wilson, I. (2010). *The Shroud: Fresh light on the 2000-Year-old Mystery...*, Bantam Books, London, UK, pp. 239–240, 412.

World4, https://world4.eu/byzantine-fashion/.

Wroth, W. (1908). *Catalogue of the Imperial Byzantine Coins in the British Museum*, Vols. 1 and 2, British Museum. Department of Coins and Medals, London.

Zachariae, R. (1924). *Historia ecclesiastica vulgo adscripta*. Brooks, E. W. (ed.). Louvain, https://archive.org/details/BrooksHistoriaEcclesiasti caZachariaeRhetoriVulgoAdscriptaText1/page/n13/mode/2up.

Zaninotto, G. (1988). Orazione di Gregorio il Referendario in occasione della traslazione a Costantinopoli dell'immagine edessena nell'anno 944, in: *La Sindone, indagini scientifiche, Atti del IV Congresso Nazionaledi Studi sulla Sindone*, Siracusa, 1987, Ed. Paoline, Cinisello Balsamo, Italy, pp. 344–352.

Zaninotto, G. (1995). L'immagine Edessena: impronta dell'intera persona di Cristo. Nuove conferme dal codex Vossianus Latinus Q 69 del sec.

X, in: Upinsky, A. A. (ed.), *L'identification scientifique de l'Homme du Linceul: Jésus de Nazareth*, Actes du Symposium Scientifique International, Rome-Paris, pp. 60–61.

Zaninotto, G. (2002). La Sindone/Mandylion nel silenzio di Costantinopoli (944–1242), in: *Sindone 2000, Atti del Congresso Mondiale, Orvieto*, August 27–29, 2000, San Severo, Foggia, Vol. II pp. 463–482 and Vol. III pp.131–133, p. 468.

Zugibe, F. (2005). *The Crucifixion of Jesus, a Forensic Inquiry*, M. Evans & Co., New York.

Appendices

Appendix 1: Probability Calculation

A1.1   Generalities

Before proceeding with the probabilistic analysis of the face of Christ on the gold *solidus* of Justinian II (692–695) considered in Section 6.1, it is necessary to recall some probabilistic concepts [Fanti and Marinelli, 1998].

The inferential or inductive statistic, concerns the control of hypotheses that must have a statistic nature. The evaluation of the unknown quantity is realized applying the Bayes formula where three kinds of probabilities appear: the a priori or initial probability P^I, the a posteriori (or final) probability P^{II}, and the likelihood (or conditional) probability P^{III}.

In the present case, we have to combine the probabilities of 12 mutually compatible events in which the engraver decided to reproduce some peculiar features of the face of Christ on the gold coin. The probability resulting from the combination of these events may appear, at first, to correspond to the product of the probabilities. For example, the probability that number 6 will occur two times in a roll of two dice is the product of the probabilities $(1/6 \times 1/6) = 1/36 = 0.02778$.

In reality, things are a bit more complex in the present case because we must eliminate the probabilities of the mixed results relative to the 12 mutually compatible events. For example, the alternative #1 named "False" could be combined with alternative #2 named "True."

In the example of the dice, it is the same in determining the probability that number 6 will occur two times in a roll of two dice, when only the possibilities that the couples of equal values 1-1, 2-2, 3-3, 4-4, 5-5 or 6-6 are considered. In this way, all the other possible mixed combinations are excluded. With this constraint, the probability is not *1/36* as determined above, but it increases to *1/6*.

An event *E* is defined as a set of outcomes of an experiment to which a probability is assigned. For example, when tossing a coin, the outcome is the coin landing "head" or "tails." These two are the events connected with the experiment. In other words, it is the measure of the degree of confidence attributed to the happening of a certain alternative. It is necessary to first define the alternatives of the event and subsequently, through the analysis of the results, to define a degree of a posteriori probabilities and the likelihood for each alternative.

The following two statistical principles of probabilities must be recalled. The principle of total probabilities states that the probability $P(E)$ occurring to at least one of several mutually incompatible events $P(E_i)$ with $i = 1,..., n$, is equal to the sum of the probabilities of the individual events:

$$P(E) = \sum_{i=1}^{n} P(E_i) \tag{A1}$$

For example, the probability that either *1* or *3* or *6* will come out in a roll of a dice is $(1/6 + 1/6 + 1/6) = 0.50$.

The principle of compound probabilities or multiplication, states that the probability of the occurrence of several mutually compatible events $P(E)$ is equal to the product of the probabilities $P(E_i)$ of the single events:

$$P(E) = \prod_{i=1}^{n} P_i (E_i) \tag{A2}$$

For example, as mentioned above, the probability that *1* will come out two times in two rolls of a dice is $(1/6 \times 1/6) = 1/36 = 0.02778$.

The probabilistic model follows three steps: definition of the alternatives, assignment of the probabilistic values and result evaluation based on the adopted model.

A1.2   Definition of the Alternatives

In the present case, we have two alternatives: that either the engraver, who molded the face of Christ in question, referred to the Shroud face for the details or he did not observe this reference image. The events in question, therefore, are the following:

- Alternative F (false): the engraver reproduced the face of the coin in Fig. 6.1 by pure chance without knowing anything about the Shroud.

- Alternative T (true): the engraver copied the face from a reference image, which was the Shroud or a good copy of it.

A1.3   Assignment of the Probabilistic Values

The statements subjected to probabilistic analysis must be mutually independent. If a possible dependence is noticed, the corresponding probabilistic coefficient must be consequentially corrected.

According to the principle of the total probabilities, the probabilities assigned for a certain statement should be in total 1 or 100%, for each statement. Once assigned the probability $P^I_n(F)$ of the statement n for the alternative F, the probability $P^I_n(T)$ of the statement n for the alternative T results:

$$P^I_n(T) = 1 - P^I_n(F) \tag{A3}$$

The two events T and F are mutually exclusive. To the alternative F, we assign a priori probability $P^I(F) = 0.5$ and to the alternative T a priori probability $P^I(T) = 0.5$.

For each of the 12 features described in Section 6.2, the a posteriori probabilities P^{II}, of the alternative F, are reported in Table A1 in terms of 1 chance in k possibilities.

The a posteriori probabilities are arbitrarily assigned in a subjective way. It seems therefore better to suppose that the assigned probabilities can vary within a predefined range to reduce the degree of uncertainty of the result due to the subjectivity. The two columns following that of the assigned chance of Table A1 indicate the uncertain limits which have been respectively obtained by halving and doubling the assigned probabilities.

The a posteriori probabilities $P_n^{II}(F)$ and $P_n^{II}(T)$ of all the 12 features are reported on Table A2 where $P_n^{II}(F)$, $P_n^{II'}(F)$ and $P_n^{II''}(F)$ have respectively been obtained by calculating the reciprocal values of Table A1 in correspondence to the columns relative to the assigned chance, their lower limits and upper limits. $P_n^{II}(T)$, $P_n^{II'}(T)$ and $P_n^{II''}(T)$ instead result from the application of Eq. A3.

Table A1 A posteriori probabilities P^{II} of the alternative F assigned to the 12 features under consideration

N.	Feature	Assigned: 1 chance in $k =$	Lower limit: 1 chance in $k =$	Upper limit: 1 chance in $k =$
1	Unattractive face	500	1000	250
2	Asymmetry of the face	20*	40*	10*
3	No crown or decorations	200	400	100
4	Long wavy hair	30	60	15
5	Tuft of hair	200	400	100
6	T-shaped nose-eyebrow	10	20	5
7	Long nose	10	20	5
8	Closed and big eyes	10	20	5
9	Swollen right cheek	100	200	50
10	Beard sparse on the right	50	100	25
11	No beard under lower lip	4	8	2
12	Bipartite beard	300	600	150

*This value was reduced for a possible correlation with Feature #1.

As an example, consider Feature #1 of Table A1. The author supposes that the engraver had only 1 chance over 500 to reproduce the face we see on the coin without having observed the Shroud. This is because the face of Christ in question is similar to the face of the Relic with many signs of torture produced there. It is not in agreement with the commonly accepted idea that Jesus Christ was the most beautiful among all the men.

The corresponding a posteriori probability of Feature #1, assigned as 1 chance over 500, corresponds on Table A2 as $P_1^{II}(F) = 1/500 = 0.002$. Due to the uncertainty of the evaluation, the lower limit assigned to this feature #1 is 1 chance over 1000 corresponding to $P_1^{II'}(F) = 0.001$ and the upper limit is 1 chance over 250 corresponding to $P_1^{II''}(F) = 0.004$. By applying Eq. A3 to $P_n^{II}(F)$, $P_n^{II'}(F)$ and $P_n^{II''}(F)$, respectively results in $P_n^{II}(T) = 0.998$, $P_n^{II'}(T) = 0.999$ and $P_n^{II''}(T) = 0.996$.

Table A2 A posteriori probabilities for each of the 12 features under consideration

n	$P_n^{II}(F)$	$P_n^{II'}(F)$	$P_n^{II''}(F)$	$P_n^{II}(T)$	$P_n^{II'}(T)$	$P_n^{II''}(T)$
1	0.002	0.001	0.004	0.998	0.999	0.996
2	0.05	0.025	0.1	0.95	0.975	0.9
3	0.005	0.0025	0.01	0.995	0.98	0.99
4	0.033	0.017	0.066	0.967	0.983	0.934
5	0.005	0.0025	0.01	0.995	0.9975	0.99
6	0.1	0.05	0.2	0.9	0.95	0.8
7	0.1	0.05	0.2	0.9	0.95	0.8
8	0.1	0.05	0.2	0.9	0.95	0.8
9	0.01	0.005	0.02	0.99	0.995	0.98
10	0.02	0.01	0.04	0.98	0.99	0.96
11	0.25	0.125	0.5	0.75	0.875	0.5
12	0.0033	0.0017	0.0066	0.997	0.9983	0.9934
P^{II}	5.44×10^{-20}	3.52×10^{-24}	5.58×10^{-17}	0.48	0.691	0.196

A1.4 Result Evaluation

The probabilistic model based on Bayes formula allows defining the combined probabilities of alternatives F or T (composed of all the 12 assigned features) excluding the probabilities of mixed cases (consisting of some features having alternative F alongside some other features having alternative T).

Phase I. The a priori probabilities $P^l(F) = 0.5$ and $P^l(T) = 0.5$ have been assigned ignoring the result of the research.

Phase II. The a posteriori single probabilities $P_n^{ll}(F)$ and $P_n^{ll}(T)$ of the 12 features are reported on Table A2. The a posteriori combined probabilities $P^{ll}(T)$ and $P^{ll}(F)$ result from the composition of the single probabilities according to the principle of the composed probabilities, see Eq. A2:

$$P^{ll}(T) = \prod_{i=1}^{12} P_i^{ll}(T) = 0.48$$

$$P^{ll'}(T) = 0.691;$$

$$P^{ll''}(T) = 0.196$$

$$P^{ll}(F) = \prod_{i=1}^{12} P_i^{ll}(F) = 5.44 \times 10^{-20};$$

$$P^{ll'}(F) = 3.52 \times 10^{-24};$$

$$P^{ll''}(F) = 5.58 \times 10^{-17}$$

The final probabilities $P^*(T)$ and $P^*(F)$ without accounting for the Bayes constant $P(E)$ are:

$$P^*(T) = P^l(T)\, P^{ll}(T) = 0.50 \times 0.48 = 0.24$$

$$P^{*'}(T) = P^{l'}(T)\, P^{ll'}(T) = 0.50 \times 0.691 = 0.345$$

$$P^{*''}(T) = P^{l''}(T)\, P^{ll''}(T) = 0.50 \times 0.196 = 0.098$$

$$P^*(F) = P^l(F)\, P^{ll}(F) = 0.50 \times 5.44 \times 10^{-20} = 2.72 \times 10^{-20}$$

$$P^{*'}(F) = P^{l'}(F)\, P^{ll'}(F) = 0.50 \cdot \times 3.52 \times 10^{-24} = 1.76 \times 10^{-24}$$

$$P^{*''}(F) = P^{l''}(F)\, P^{ll''}(F) = 0.50 \times 5.58 \times 10^{-17} = 2.79 \times 10^{-17}$$

According to the principle of the total probabilities, see Eq. A1, the probability $P(E)$ of the event E, also called Bayes constant results in:

$$P(E) = P^{l}(T)\, P^{ll}(T) + P^{l}(F)\, P^{ll}(F) \tag{A4}$$

$P(E) = 0.24;$

$P'(E) = 0.345;$

$P''(E) = 0.098.$

Phase III. Being possible the alternatives F and T of the considered event, but among them excluding, the mixed possibilities have to be rejected. Therefore the final probabilities $P^{lll}(T)$ and $P^{lll}(F)$ are evaluated based on the Bayes formula:

$$P^{lll}(T) = \frac{P^{l}(T) \cdot P^{ll}(T)}{P(E)} = \frac{P^{*}(T)}{P(E)} \tag{A5}$$

$$P^{lll}(F) = \frac{P^{l}(F) \cdot P^{ll}(F)}{P(E)} = \frac{P^{*}(F)}{P(E)} \tag{A6}$$

The probabilities $P^{lll}(F)$ that the engraver reproduced the face of the coin by chance, from Eq. A6, result in the following:

$P^{lll}(F) = 1.13 \times 10^{-19}$ *or about 1 chance over 10 billion billion*
$P^{lll'}(F) = 5.1 \times 10^{-24}$ *or about 5 chances over 1 million billion billion*
$P^{lll''}(F) = 2.45 \times 10^{-16}$ *or about 2 chances over 10 million billion*

Therefore the probability $P^{lll}(F)$ that the engraver reproduced the coin in question, without knowing anything about the Shroud body image, is about 1 chance in over 10 billion billion. Considering the uncertainty of the assigned probabilistic values, it is in the range between 5 chances over 1 million billion billion and 2 chances over 10 million billion.

We can make an example in reference to the roulette game to clarify the meaning of this result. We have *37* numbers (from 0 to *36*). As the chance of hitting a foreseen number is *1/37*, there are $1/37^2 = 1/(37 \times 37) = 1/1369$ chances to hit for two consecutive times the same number.

The chances of hitting for *12* consecutive times the same number are $1/37^{12} = 1.52 \times 10^{-19}$, a number very close to $P^{lll}(F) = 1.13 \times 10^{-19}$. Therefore, we can state that the probability

$P^{III}(F)$ for the engraver to obtain the face of Christ without having seen the Shroud corresponds to hitting for *12* consecutive times (or in the range from 10 to 15 considering the uncertainty) the same number at the roulette game.

Considering the example of the dice with six faces, a number close to $P^{III}(F) = 1.13 \times 10^{-19}$ corresponds to the chance of having the number 6, 24 consecutive times in this game, that is $1/6^{24} = 2.11 \times 10^{-19}$. Therefore we can state that the probability $P^{III}(F)$ of obtaining the face of Christ without having seen the Shroud is equivalent to rolling a 6 on dice *24* consecutive times (or in the range from 20 to 30 considering the uncertainty).

Obviously, the hypothesis that an engraver was able to depict that face of Christ on the coin in question without having seen the Shroud or a good copy of it is extremely improbable.

Appendix 2: The Face of Christ on a Medal

Following the interesting results reported in Chapter 6, where it is proved from a probabilistic point of view that the face of Christ on the Shroud was taken as reference to the image of Christ on the gold solidus of Justinian II minted in 692 of Fig. 6.1, the author recently produced some bronze medals, see Fig. A1. There it is possible to directly compare the face of Christ on the Shroud, on the obverse, with that coined by Justinian II, on the reverse.

Figure A1 Medal produced by the author comparing the face of Christ on the Shroud, with that of Fig. 6.1 minted by Justinian II; on the obversethe writings "*Resurrexit sicut dixit*" ("He has risen as He said") and "*S. Sindon—33 A.D.*" (Holy Shroud 33 A.D.) are evident.

Name Index

Subject Index